UNVEILING OUR TRUE REALITY

UNVEILING OUR TRUE REALITY

WITH THE WISDOM OF THE AWAKENED MASTERS

STELIAN ACONI

The following is a research work into the teachings of the spiritual masters with many quotations from their teachings coming together harmoniously into a teaching of truth which penetrates the complexity of life.

Unveiling Our True Reality
with the Wisdom of the Awakened Masters
Copyright © 2024 Stelian Aconi

ISBN: 978-1-7636357-0-8 (Paperback)
ISBN: 978-1-7636357-2-2 (eBook)

A catalogue record for this book is available from the National Library of Australia

Edited By: Ursula Acton
Cover design by: Helen Christie, Blue Wren Books
Typesetting by: Shaun Stevens, Rosa Type

Published by Stelian Aconi
onemodernyogi@gmail.com

*This book I dedicate to all spiritual Masters of
past, present and future, and to all beings.*

But especially

*To the Lord of Love who lives in
all beings,
and who by his love gives life to all,
and awaits patiently, our
return into the Love supreme.*

Love is Life & Life is Love.

CONTENTS

CHAPTER 1

INTRODUCTION

I have chosen the title for this book because in many scriptures it is written that we are all part of the same reality and in unveiling this reality, each one of us in our own time gain our true freedom. I have been prompted to write this book firstly for myself, so that I can understand and may be helpful to others who seek to grasp the energy behind the words like Love, Life, Truth, Reality and God. Before getting into what the book would like to convey, we should establish something important. Any language that is spoken in the world is just a tool of communicating the seen and unseen and is limited in its ability to truly describe what the real thing is. As one of the great spiritual teachers, Jiddu Krishnamurti, has stated numerous times, *"The word is not the thing."*

Words by themselves have limited meaning but once they are put in phrases and sentences, they become concepts and ideas pointing to something. Before we can have deep insight into what is real, we might be inclined to see and relate to words in their literal meaning and thus not have deep insight into the energy the word, idea or concept is pointing to. The real language is silence.

Silence is the language of the heart, which is the true language of communion: the rest is but a poor translation.

For example, we look at a mountain, but the word *mountain* is not the mountain itself. Words hardly define the object they point to. The word is just a pointer to something. It is the same with the word *God*, a word which is a pointer to an energy that cannot be grasped only by hearing the word. This is the reason why the teachings of our greatest prophets give rise to endless contradictions when we try to understand them by following their words and not by realizing them in our own lives. The problem we have is that we are too lost in words and miss the energy behind the words. We become like a fisherman caught up with the mending of the nets and thereby neglecting the fishing. The words we say drive our reality and we are just following along instead of it being the other way around. I hope when someone reads this book, they will try to pay attention to the energy behind the words in order to really connect and grasp the meaning of what the idea, concept or thing represented is in its own fullness. It takes people a long time to gain insight that penetrates through everything without being conditioned by any idea, concept or thing, and very few are endowed with that insight from birth.

This book is trying to convey ideas in simple language and will try to avoid the pitfalls of being too concerned with the nets at the expense of fishing. Chinese master Lao Tzu in his marvelous book *Tao Tee Ching* stated that simplicity, compassion and patience are the three true treasures. Hopefully this book will help you to connect to the root of all wisdom and see how the wisdom realized by the masters of all religious and non-religious traditions can help us penetrate and grasp the true reality of who we are. Once that wisdom is achieved, there will be no question left unanswered. Nothing written in this book is new; everything was spoken and written before, and it is the same truth written in a new form to correspond to the present time.

INTRODUCTION

The truth conveyed by this book will affect everyone differently and will connect to the knowledge that is already naturally in us. Each of you will recognize it, more or less, but if you read with an open heart, then the connection between inner life and outer life merges into oneness, leaving duality behind. During the course of anyone's life, I am pretty sure at some point in time, young or old, we have asked the question, "What is the real purpose of our lives?" We have been given different answers depending on the level of insight of the person answering the question. We may have received the answer from a teacher, parent or religious figure, or from our own wisdom. Wherever the answer came from, it would not have been too satisfactory, because the answer would have come from words. Even if the answer depicted the truth in its essence, we would not have had the capability to connect fully with the energy behind the words, so the answer would have only been left as an idea or a concept and not had much impact as it was just an intellectual understanding.

When I was a small child, I was conditioned to the idea of God by my family, the church and so on. At the time, I found church boring and sad, and everyone there was serious and afraid. In that atmosphere of sobriety, I thought of God as an old man with a white beard sitting on the throne looking at us from above. In contrast, when I used to pray in my room alone, I always felt warmth, a peaceful energy, surrounding me. I somehow felt that God – wherever he was – could not just be that boring old man sitting on the throne and giving judgements and punishing people for their mistakes. That did not make sense to me, and I am pretty sure to most of you who read this book.

After a long search for reality, I can say that if anyone has the intention to find out the truth for themselves and to answer for themselves the big questions that most of our past prophets and masters of all traditions have already answered, then that intention will take you there, there is no doubt. That intention grows when there is loneliness in us and when we have come to a point of dissatisfaction with life and the endless quest for happiness through the pursuit of pleasures. Jesus Christ has stated:

> *Whoever has come to know the world has found the (dead) body.*
> *But whoever has found the (dead) body, of him the world is not worthy.*

-Gospel of Thomas: 80

Here, Christ is showing that whatever you do in the world, whatever you possess, nothing can bring you everlasting joy. He is saying clearly that the happiness of this world can never fully satisfy us. When we realize this, we start to be dissatisfied with the world and our intention to find everlasting joy will start to manifest, for that intention or desire is inherent in us all.

Jesus Christ's highest teaching incorporates all teachings of all traditions and is the very reason this book is written: to take us into that energy by which all existence and non-existence emerges from pure Love.

Jesus says:

> *Love your brother like your life!*
> *Protect him like the apple of your eye!*

-Gospel of Thomas: 25

Here, by *brother*, Christ means a fellow human being (male or female) and in order to get to pure love, one has to love and protect all human beings regardless. This is the teaching of all traditions, they try to get us to unveil our inner essence, which is Love in its purest form untouched by thought. In the books of Kabballah, it is written also that the highest commandment is "Love your friend as yourself," *friend* here meaning all beings.

Buddha also preached this Love when he told his disciples how to reach the state of Brahma-Vihara, the joy of living in Brahman.

> *He who wants to reach this stage, according to Buddha, "shall deceive none, entertain no hatred for anybody, and never wish to injure through anger. He shall have measureless love for all creatures, even as a mother has for her only child, whom she protects with her own life. Up above, below, and all around him he shall extend his love, which is without bounds and obstacles, and which is free from all cruelty and antagonism. While standing, sitting, walking, lying down, till he falls asleep, he shall keep his mind active in this exercise of universal goodwill."*

-Rabindranath Tagore

Here we see that Buddha, Christ and all other traditions are insisting that without grasping the energy of Love as an inherent energy in us all and without realizing the fulness of Love in ourselves and all around there can never be peace and harmony in the World.

The Upanishads, the Indian scriptures, state:

> *From joy does spring all this creation, by joy is it maintained, towards joy does it progress, and into joy does it enter. It means that God's creation has not its source in any necessity; it comes from his fullness of joy.*

-Rabindranath Tagore

Before we go on, I would ask you to continue reading with faith, but we must make the distinction between faith and belief, and here we quote Alan Watts from his book *The Wisdom of Insecurity: A Message for an Age of Anxiety*:

We must here make a clear distinction between belief and faith, because, in general practice, belief has come to mean a state of mind which is the opposite of faith. Belief, as I use the word here, is the insistence that the truth is what one would believe or wish it to be. The believer will open his mind to the truth on the condition that it fits in with his preconceived ideas and wishes. Faith, on the other hand, is an unreserved opening of the mind to the truth, whatever it may turn out to be. Faith has no preconceptions; it is a plunge into the unknown. Belief clings, but faith lets go. In this sense of the word, faith is the essential virtue of science, and likewise of any religion that is not self-deception.

-Alan Watts

Jesus talks about this faith:

"Because of your unbelief; for assuredly, I say to you, if you have faith as a mustard seed, you will say to this mountain, 'Move from here to there,' and it will move; and nothing will be impossible for you."

-Matthew 17:20

The Buddha expresses faith thus:

Faith and prayer are both invisible, but they make impossible things possible.

-Buddha

Like Christ, Buddha explains that faith is the foundation and the drive of everything and if one has it all is possible. Kabir, one of great Sufi mystics, stated that faith comes from the heart.

You will never enter paradise until you have faith, and you will not complete your faith until you Love one another.

-Muhammad

Krishna telling Arjuna how faith forms who we are:

*Every man's faith conforms with his inborn nature, Arjuna.
Faith is a person's core; whatever his faith is, he is.*

-Lord Krishna

Guru Nanak-Japji Sahib says:

*The faithful have intuitive awareness and intelligence. The
faithful know about all worlds and realms. The faithful
shall never be struck across the face. The faithful do not
have to go with the Messenger of Death. Such is the Name
of the Immaculate True One. Only one who has faith comes
to know such a state of mind.*

-Guru Nanak

Guru Nanak states that in faith lies intuitive alertness and intelligence and also all knowledge, and by that knowledge one comes to know a state of mind that is free from death.

*Faith is a relational power or a relationship which brings
about the immediate perfect and supranatural union of the
believer with the God in whom he believes.*

-St Maximos the Confessor

Saint Maximos the Confessor also describes faith as a direct union of the one who believes with the one in which one believes, as faith here throws out belief. From all awakened beings' messages, we can understand that without faith one cannot move into the spiritual realms and have the means of finding one's own reality. Wherever one's tradition or path is, without faith one will be like a ship at sea without a mast. All spiritual masters have reverberated the same truth, and in this book, we have quoted some of the masters for one cannot incorporate all traditions and masters in one book, but if you have read teachings that have not been included in this book, you are welcome to observe and see how they relate to each other.

In the chapters that follow, we will explore creation, God, the five senses, the Mind, the ego-self, the world of duality, suffering, attachment and identification, fears and desires, death and reincarnation, the five poisons (ignorance, attachment, aversion, pride, envy), yoga, society, happiness, and many more. At the end, you will have an insight into how all traditions and masters point to the same door and that door does not have a lock or a key to open it. Likewise, it cannot be opened by another; it can only be opened by one whose heart is open as the sky, and in it is the supreme love that includes everything and everyone without exclusion. When we can come to fully understand that we are all beings of light, then we are at home and heaven is here and now.

As Christ stated:

> *Now having been questioned by the Pharisees as to when the kingdom of God was coming, He answered them and said, "The kingdom of God is not coming with signs to be observed; nor will they say, 'Look, here it is!' or 'There it is!' For behold, the kingdom of God is in your midst."*

> -Luke 17:20–21

So, forgive the writer if not all masters were quoted here for that will have been a tremendous task and would have taken lifetimes to complete. I am certain they all teach the same truth and play the same song of love. Let's try now to look at how creation occurred and try to comprehend true creation, which is beyond any description, as descriptions are only pointers to it. Of course, there are many ways of interpreting it and here we have chosen only a few.

CHAPTER 2

CREATION

We could look with the perspective that all created things have a creator – whether God, Brahman, Allah, Emptiness or the big bang – given that some energy has created and is sustaining all of existence. Today, the science in quantum physics has proven that all existence is energy, and the consciousness of man has evolved to enable us to understand the truth that all is energy and revolves around the atom. Swami Sri Yukteswar Giri, a renowned astrologer and realized Yogi, describes in one of his books, *The Holy Science*, how creation was made from the Hindu and Christian perspective, referring to the Vedic scriptures and the Holy Bible, and he demonstrates how the two traditions clearly point to the same process but, of course, each with different language relating to the culture and times of the writings.

We therefore must understand and observe that creation, as we call it, and all that is seen and unseen, is just energy in movement; even a solid state has fluidity in it. The ancients, Hindus and masters from all traditions understood that to be the case thousands of years ago.

Life itself, it should be observed, is energy, yea, the primal energy of the living creature and so is the whole economy of the living creature, its functions of nutrition and growth, that is, the vegetative side of its nature, and the movement stirred By impulse, that is, the sentient side, and its activity of intellect and free-will. Energy, moreover, is the perfect realization of power. If then, we contemplate all these in Christ, surely, we must also hold that He possesses human energy.

-St John of Damascus

Saint John, in the statement above, relates that all is energy and this energy we also find in humans, as he relates that even Christ possessed the human energy.

Here we need a general understanding of how creation unfolded. Sri Yukteswar explains that all creatures, from the highest to the lowest in the link of creation, are found eager to realize three things: existence, consciousness and bliss. In the first chapter of his book, Yukteswar explains – from the astronomical point – how the planets evolved around the Sun, as in our present stage, but he goes further saying,

The Sun also has another motion by which it revolves around a grand center called Vishnunabhi that is the seat of the creative power, Brahma (God), the universal magnetism. Brahma regulates dharma, the mental virtue of the internal world.

-Swami Sri Yukteswar

He also describes how, in this movement, there are four yugas (ages). The Sun makes a descending and ascending movement through these ages. Swami shows how we just entered Dvapara Yuga, the second yuga of ascending, which is an age when humanity will understand all the electric energies and magnetism, where the human consciousness will start to awaken to more subtle energies. This age, according to Swami Sri Yukteswar, will take us from 1899 to 4099. If one would like to know more, I recommend reading his book, *The Holy Science*. One further point to make is that Swami was a realized being with very deep spiritual knowledge and the next quote from this book gives light to that.

> *In this book certain truths such as those about the properties of magnetism, its auras, different sorts of electricities, etc., have been mentioned, although modern science has not yet fully discovered them. The five sorts of electricity can be easily understood if one will direct his attention to the nerve properties, which are purely electrical in nature. Each of the five sensory nerves has its characteristic and unique function to perform. The optic nerve carries light and does not perform the functions of the auditory and other nerves; the auditory nerve in its turn carries sound only, without performing the functions of any other nerves, and so on. Thus, it is clear that there are five sorts of electricity, corresponding to the five properties of cosmic electricity. So far as magnetic properties are concerned, the grasping power of the human intellect is at present so limited that it would be quite useless to attempt to make the matter understood by the general public. The intellect of man in Treta Yuga will comprehend the attributes of divine magnetism (the next Treta Yuga will start in 4099). There are indeed exceptional personages now living who, having overcome the influence of Time, can grasp today what ordinary people cannot grasp; but this book is not for those exalted ones, who require nothing of it.*

-Swami Sri Yukteswar

God is described in all traditions and religions as omnipotent, omnipresent, omniscient and the creator of all. Only Buddha made an exception, as he did not want to make God a personal being or an object, so he called it *emptiness* and he indicated that all of us must find out for ourselves what that emptiness is. As we have stated earlier, the Bible refers to God the Father from whom all creation comes:

> *So, God created man in his own image, in the image of God created he him; male and female created he them.*

> -Genesis 1:27

Sutra 3

> *Parambrahma emanates creation, inert Nature (Prakriti), to emerge. From Om (Pranava, the Word, the manifestation of the Omnipotent Force), come Kala, Time; Desa, Space; and Anu, the Atom (the vibratory structure of creation).*

> -Swami Sri Yukteswar

The image of God is not the idea that he is like us, which is the ignorant perception, but the truth that we are like him in our inner being as Sutra 3 explains. Swami Sri Yukteswar goes further in the explanation.

> *The Word, Amen (Om), is the beginning of Creation. The manifestation of Omnipotent Force (the Repulsion and its complementary expression, Omniscient Feeling or Love, the Attraction) is vibration, which appears as a peculiar sound: The Word, Amen, Aurn. In its different aspects Om presents the idea of change, which is Time, Kala, in the Ever-Unchangeable; and the idea of division, which is Space, Desa, in the Ever-Indivisible.*

> -Sami Sri Yukteswar

The Bible speaks to this as well.

These things saith the Amen, the faithful and true witness,
the beginning of the creation of God.

-Revelation 3:14

In the beginning was the Word, and the Word was with
God, and the Word was God. ... All things were made by
him; and without him was not anything made that was
made And the Word was made flesh and dwelt among us.

-John 1:1,3,14

The Bible also says that all creation come from one word Amen (Om); the energy of the word Om gave birth to all manifestation. This is why Yogis in the past have meditated on the Om, for they knew that by understanding it and merging in it, they become one with all existence. Swami Sri Yukteswar explains how everything revolves around the atom and our being as Purusha, son of God, as he states:

Twenty-four Elders. These five gross matters and the afore-
said fifteen attributes together with Manas, the Mind;
Buddhi, the Intelligence; Chitta, the Heart; and Ahamkara,
the Ego, constitute the twenty-four principles or Elders, as
mentioned in the Bible.

The five elements (earth, water, fire, wind, space) together with fifteen attributes, the five senses (smell, taste, sight, touch, hearing) + the five organs of action (excretion, generation, motion (feet), manual skill (hands), and speech) + the five organs of sense (nose, tongue, eyes, skin, ears), plus the mind, intelligence, heart and ego constitute the twenty-four principles as the twenty-four elders described in the Bible.

See Revelation 4:4:

> *And round about the throne were four and twenty seats;*
> *and upon the seats I saw four and twenty elders.*

Further, Swami Sri Yukteswar explains how the Vedas and the Bible both describe how God created man in his own image:

> *The aforesaid twenty-four principles, which completed the creation of Dark ness, Maya, are nothing more than the development of Ignorance, Avidya; and as this Ignorance is composed only of ideas as mentioned above, creation has in reality no substantial existence but is a mere play of ideas on the Eternal Substance, God the Father.*

> -Swami Sri Yukteswar

Sutra 13

> *This universe is differentiated into fourteen spheres, seven Swargas and seven Patalas.*

> -Swami Sri Yukteswar

Here this sutra explains how the creation consists of having fourteen stages known as Swargas (Spheres) and Patalas (Points). The Vedic scriptures explain the seven Swargas as Chakras and they start from perineum up to the crown of the head while the Patalas start from perineum down to the feet. In the Bible, the same concept is mentioned thus:

And being turned, I saw seven golden candlesticks, and in the midst of the seven candlesticks one like unto the son of man.
And he had in his right hand seven stars…
The seven stars are the angels of the seven churches.
… and the seven candlesticks which thou sawest are the seven churches.

-Revelation 1:12,13,16,20

The Bible also describes the four stages of creation, but many interpretations are given, all of them different, due to the level of consciousness of the individual making the interpretation. Here we need to go further in our understanding of how we were created. The Vedic scriptures and the Bible help us further in the understanding our own being.

Sutra 14

Purusha is covered by five koshas or sheaths.

-Swami Sri Yukteswar

Jesus says:

Blessed is he who was, before he came into being.
If you become disciples of mine (and) listen to my words, these stones will serve you.
For you have five trees in Paradise that do not change during summer (and) winter, and their leaves do not fall.
Whoever comes to know them will not taste death.

-Gospel of Thomas: 19

The **five trees** are the same as the five Koshas, referring to the Five Worlds of the mystical Jewish Kabbalah: Asiyah, Yetzirah, Beriah, Atzilut and Adam Kadmon – descriptive of dimensional levels related to the soul's progress towards unity with or return to the Creator.

Five Koshas or Sheaths. This Purusha, the Son of God, is screened by five coverings called the koshas or sheaths. They are:

- Annamaya-**kosha** (food sheath, Earth element)
- Pranamaya-**kosha** (vital sheath, Water element)
- Manomaya-**kosha** (mental sheath, Fire element)
- Vijnanamaya-**kosha** (intellect/intuitive sheath, Air element)
- Anandamaya-**kosha** (bliss sheath, Ether/Space element)

Swami Sri Yukteswar goes on to explain further how the five Trees (koshas) work and relate to the world.

> *Attraction, the Atoms, being attracted toward one another, come nearer and nearer, taking ethereal, gaseous, fiery, liquid, and solid forms. Inanimate kingdom. Thus, this visible world becomes adorned with suns, planets, and moons, which we call the "inanimate" kingdom of creation. Vegetable kingdom. In this manner, when the action of Divine Love becomes well developed, the evolution of Avidya, Ignorance (the particle of Darkness, Maya, the Omnipotent Energy manifested), begins to be withdrawn. Annamaya Kosha, the Atom's outer coating of gross matter being thus withdrawn, Pranamaya Kosha (the sheath composed of Karmendriyas, the organs of action) begins to operate. In this organic state the Atoms, embracing each other more closely to their heart, appear as the vegetable kingdom in the creation.*
>
> *Animal kingdom. When the Pranamaya Kosha becomes withdrawn, the Manomaya Kosha (the sheath composed of Jnanendriyas, the organs of sense) comes to light. The Atoms then perceive the nature of the external world and, attracting other Atoms of different nature, form bodies as necessary for enjoyment, and thus the animal kingdom appears in the creation.*
>
> *Mankind. When Manomaya Kosha becomes withdrawn, Jnanamaya Kosha (the body of Intelligence composed of*

electricities) becomes perceptible. The Atom, acquiring the power of determining right and wrong, becomes man, the rational being in the creation.

Devata or Angel. When man, cultivating the Divine Spirit or Omniscient Love within his heart, is able to withdraw this Jnanamaya Kosha, then the innermost sheath, Chitta, the Heart (composed of four ideas), becomes manifest. Man is then called Devata or Angel in the creation.

-Swami Sri Yukteswar

This is why Christ stated that the one who will get to know the five trees is free of all troubles and therefore will never taste death. Here we see how two traditions refer to the same truth. This process is also indicated in Buddhist Tantras and similar descriptions are given but we will not go into it for the Buddhism cosmology has its roots in Hindu cosmology anyhow and both depict the same process. Awakened people like Sri Yukteswar had deep insight into the nature of things and their insight penetrated the truth. All tradition refers to the one God, one energy of pure consciousness, pure intelligence untarnished by thought. They all point to the unity in diversity.

The whole of the cosmos is one living being rising from God, pure consciousness. Adi Shankara stated that (1) Brahman (God) is real, (2) the cosmos is unreal and (3) the cosmos is Brahman (God). Here one may think that the first and second contradict each other but the third statement explains that the world is real if perceived as the self and unreal if perceived apart from the self.

This is why we will misunderstand creation if we look with the view that we are apart from creation and not a part of it. Jiddu Krishnamurti stated, *"You are the world, and the world is you,"* and as long as we think we are apart from it and think of the world like an object to be manipulated as we please, we are often caught in illusion and therefore creating mischief and suffering for ourselves and the world.

One may ask why, if we are a part of the creation, do we produce so much suffering and seem to never be at peace with ourselves and others. Could it be that maybe a mistake occurred when we were created or that we wanted to experience the freedom of knowing reality and not just sit in a garden of Eden, so to speak, and be in that forever state of mind of joy and love? We can also take the view that in the big bang, God himself expanded from emptiness into an infinite number of forms in order to turn himself from the formless into a multitude of forms and then to bring all forms back into the emptiness where all come from. We could see the possibility that life is a way for all beings to enjoy the play, as is said in the Upanishads:

> *From joy came all this creation, by joy is it maintained, toward joy is it directed, and into joy it enters.*

The Upanishads also explain creation in a simple statement:

> *"Now may I ask you, where is that Self? The sage replied: 'Within this body dwells The Self with his sixteen forms, gentle friend.' The Self asked himself, 'What is it that makes Me go if it goes and stay if it stays?' So he created prana, and from it desire; and from desire he made space, air, fire, water, the earth, the senses, the mind, and food; from food came strength, austerity, the scriptures, sacrifice, and all the worlds; And everything was given name and form. As rivers lose their private name and form when they reach the sea, so that people speak of the sea alone, so all these sixteen Forms disappear when the Self is realized. Then there is no more name and form for us, and we attain immortality. The Self is the hub of the wheel of life, And the sixteen forms are only the spokes. The Self is the paramount goal of life. Attain this goal and go beyond death!"*

-The Upanishads

We can look at creation from many perspectives and traditions. Whichever angle and through whichever traditional lenses one may look, no one will depict the reality of how creation really occurred. Hopefully, we have now a general understanding of the creation and next we could look at the creative force by which all creation moves. When one merges back into oneness, one then will understand how love moves, creates and destroys till then one cannot grasp it fully.

Because the different traditions have called it many names, let's assume that all traditions, regardless of the name given to this creative force, are pointing to the same source, and for simplicity's sake, we will call it God.

CHAPTER 3

GOD

God cannot be described by thought, for thought can never touch reality, love or truth. God has been described by all masters and prophets as the undeniable energy that is all existence and non-existence. The God that can be described is not the true God; it is only an idea or a concept. The words can only somehow point to the truth but not describe it, they are limited and incapable of describing reality, it can only be lived and never can be pinned to a board, as an object.

In *Tao The Ching*, Lao-Tzu describes God thus:

> *The universe is eternal, and earth is lasting.*
> *The reason they are eternal and lasting*
> *is that they do not exist for themselves.*
> *That is why they endure.*
> *The wise humble themselves —*

and because of their humility, they are worthy of praise.
They put others first, and so become great.
They are not focused on outcomes or achievements;
therefore, they always succeed.

-Lao Tzu

Christ says:

The images are visible to humanity, but the light within them is hidden in the image.
The light of the Father will reveal itself, but his image is hidden by his light.

-Gospel of Thomas: 83

Here, Christ shows how we work with images, ideas, and concepts and all that arises in the mind comes from the light and that light is hidden in the image itself. The light will be revealed to people who have reached the awakened state, but the image of the Father will be hidden in the light. Moses on Mount Sinai has seen the burning bush as the light of God which spoke to him, but he has not seen God in any particular form. God cannot be seen as an object and his image cannot be seen; he cannot be reflected into a mirror for he is also the mirror.

From here we can see that God cannot be contained in an image of our own thinking. We can imagine him as we like, but whatever we see is not the real God.

In the *Bhagavad Gita*, Krishna describes himself.

All right, Arjuna:
I will tell you a few of my manifestations,
the most glorious ones;
for infinite are the forms in which I appear.
I am the Self, Arjuna, seated in the heart of all beings;
I am the beginning and the life span of beings, and their end

as well.
Of the sky gods, I am Vishnu;
of the heavenly lights, the sun;
Marichi, chief of the wind gods;
among stars, I am the moon;
Of the Vedas, I am the hymns;
Indra among the gods;
the mind among the six senses;
the consciousness of all beings;
of the storm gods, I am Shiva;
of the demigods, Kubera;
Agni among the bright gods;
and Meru, highest of mountains.
Know, Arjuna, that among priests I am Brihaspati;
of generals, the war god Skanda; of waters, I am the ocean;
of the great seers, I am Bhrigu;
of words, the syllable Ôm;
of worship, I am the mantra;
of mountain chains, Himalaya;
of trees, the sacred fig tree;
of divine sages, Narada;
of the high celestial musicians, Chitraratha;
of saints, the wise Kapila;
of horses, Ucchaishravas, Indra's favorite, born of the sea
foam;
of elephants, Indra's winged Airavata;
of men, I am the king;
of weapons, Indra's thunderbolt;
of cows, Kamadhuk, the wish-granter;
Kandarpa, the god of love;
the king of reptiles, Vasuki;
of divine snakes, I am Ananta, the cosmic serpent;
Varuna among the gods of the ocean;
of the blessed forefathers, I am Aryaman;
of the controllers, Yama, the god of death;
of demons, the devout Prahlada;

of things that compel, I am time;
the king of animals, the lion;
Garuda among the birds;
of purifiers, the wind;
of warriors, I am Rama;
of sea monsters, Makara;
of rivers, the holy Ganges;
of creations, the beginning and end and the middle as well,
Arjuna;
of knowledge, knowledge of the Self;
of orators, I am the speech;
of letters, the first one, A;
I am imperishable time;
the Creator whose face is
everywhere; death that
devours all things;
the source of all things to come;
of feminine powers, I am fame, wealth, speech, and memory,
intelligence,
loyalty, forgiveness;
of chants, I am the great Brihat;
of poetic meters, the gayatri;
of months, Margashirsha, the first month;
of seasons, flower-lush spring;
of swindles, I am the dice game;
the splendor of the high and mighty;
determination and victory;
the courage of all brave men;
of the Vrishi clan, I am Krishna;
of Pandavas, I am Arjuna;
of the sages, I am Vyasa;
of poets, the sublime Ushanas;
of punishers, I am the scepter;
the astuteness of the great leaders;
the silence of secret things;
and I am the wisdom of the wise.

*I am the divine seed within all beings, Arjuna;
nothing, inanimate or animate, could exist for a moment
without me. These are just a small number of my infinite
manifestations; were I to tell you more, there would be no
end to the telling.*

-Lord Krishna

In these verses, Krishna points out the infinite the supreme (God) as the essence of all existence and non-existence. Christ points to the same essence in three verses.

Jesus says:

*I am the light that is overall. I am the All. The All came
forth out of me. And to me the All has come. Split a piece
of wood – I am there. Lift the stone, and you will find me
there.*

-Gospel of Thomas: 77

We have met with these verses in the Creation chapter, but it is worth mentioning them again to show how all traditions depict the same Supreme God. Nothing exists without him; everything is in him and he is in everything. He is the essence and the manifestation all in One. We may call him by any name, he answers them all: God, Allah, Brahman, etc.

The Kena Upanishad says that the Supreme Reality is beyond the perception of the senses and the mind, because the senses and the mind can visualize and conceive only objects, while Reality is the Supreme Subject, the very precondition of all sensation, thinking, understanding, etc. No one can behold God because He is the beholder of all things.

We have to came to the understanding that God cannot be confined by any image or concept: he can only be known when we know our own reality and have done away with all illusions and ignorance which ego invents. We can give more examples and explanations, but it is up to each individual to find the reality of God and each will find it in their own time and way.

God is described as the Lord of Love in the beginning prayer of the Katha Upanishad:

May the Lord of Love protect us.
May the Lord of Love nourish us.
May the Lord of Love strengthen us.
May we realize the Lord of Love.
May we live with love for all;
May we live in peace with all.

Muhammad in the *Quran* said:

Your God is but one God. There is no god other than Him, Compassionate and Merciful. In the creation of the heavens and the earth, in the alternation of night and day, in the ships that ply the seas to the benefit of man, in the water sent down from the heavens to revive the earth after its death, in the different species of animals scattered across the earth, in the rotation of the winds, in the clouds that are subordinate to God's command between heaven and earth, in all of this, there are signs for men who use their intellects"

-Quran 2:163–164

Like Krishna, Christ and all the masters, Muhammad describes God as being the only real existence and one God who is omnipotent, omnipresent and omniscient.

Buddha was often asked if there was a God, and he answered, he did not know. When asked about right conduct, he would reply, "Do good and be good." There came five Brâhmins, who asked him to settle their discussion. One said, "Sir, my book says that God is such and such, and that this is the way to come to God." Another said, "That is wrong, for my book says such and such, and this is the way to come to God"; and so the others. He listened calmly to all of them, and then asked them one by one, "Does any one of your books say that God becomes angry, that He ever injures anyone, that He is impure?" "No, Sir, they all teach that God is pure and good." "Then, my friends, why do you not become pure and good first, that you may know what God is?"

-Swami Vivekananda

All realized beings have stated that God is in everything and is everywhere, but we have to realize that for ourselves; the other way is merely a statement. This is why Christ told us, "The kingdom of heaven is within you." By intellectual understanding alone, one can't comprehend what cannot be comprehended.

A master of non-dualism from a lineage of teachers from the Navnath Sampradaya, Shri Siddharameshwar Maharaj was the guru of Shri Nisargadatta Maharaj, a well-known contemporary master. He describes God thus:

This God is the same as the "King of Knowledge" who, while swallowing a mouthful of food, tastes and enjoys it. It is He who discriminates between fragrance and stench. It is He who understands which sound is pleasant to the ear and which sound is harsh. It is He who observes the difference between a beautiful, or a fierce and ugly form. It is He who understands the soft or hard touch. He is always present, reigning supreme in every being's heart. How utterly misguided is the idea that we worship any other God than this One. Just think of which God is worshipped when the Christians worship Christ, the Hindus worship Vishnu or Shiva, the Parsees worship their Zoroaster, or the Buddhists their Buddha? Are they not merely worshipping the corpses of these mentioned Gods? However, what is the feeling of the devotee who is worshipping? Ask anyone from any religion "Describe your God," and they will answer "My God is Conscious, Luminous, Solid, Omniscient, Omnipresent, and Omnipotent. He animates all and owns all. He is without birth, and without death."

-Shri Siddharameshwar Maharaj

The Christian saints declare God thus:

We, therefore, both know and confess that God is without beginning, without end, eternal and everlasting, uncreate, unchangeable, invariable, simple, uncompounded, incorporeal, invisible, impalpable, uncircumscribed, infinite, incognizable, indefinable, incomprehensible, good, just, maker of all things created, almighty, all-ruling, all-surveying, of all overseer, sovereign, judge; and that God is One, that is to say, one essence.

-St John of Damascus

Here we see that all traditions describe God as omnipresent, omnipotent, and omniscient. This is the simple and more ample description that all use, and God cannot be seen, but only lived and realized in his essence.

Then we can also look at what Ramana Maharshi has said regarding God:

All creeds are but preliminaries for the masses, leading up to the real truth of the Self. The religions are not necessarily the highest expression or the highest wisdom of their founders, who had to consider the times in which they lived and the mental capacities of the people. The highest wisdom is too subtle for most minds, and so a whole scheme of worlds, gods, bodies, evolution, etc. had to be given out because people seem to find it easier to believe all these things rather than believe the simple Truth of the one reality – Self. Thus, reincarnation, astral planes, survival after death, etc. are true but only from a lower standpoint. It is all a matter of standpoint. From the highest, that of the real Self, all else disappears as illusory and only the Reality remains. It is true that subtle astral bodies exist, because in order to function in the dream-world a body is necessary for that world, but it too is real only on its own plane whereas the Oneself is always real, always and eternally existent, whether we are aware of it or not. Hence it is better to seek that because the other self-bodies are only conditionally real. An ordinary Christian is only satisfied when told God is in some far-off heaven, not to be reached by us unaided, that Christ alone has known Him, and he alone can save us. Hence when told the simple truth that the kingdom of heaven is within you, he is not satisfied and will read far-fetched meanings in the statement. Mature minds alone can grasp the simple truth in all its nakedness.

-Sri Ramana Maharshi

Many questions have to be answered, but one important one is: why is so much suffering in the world and what is the cause of it? Is God responsible or is it just our own ignorance that produces all the mischief and suffering for ourselves and others? We can see that God is everything and that he is not an exclusionist; in him all existence and non-existence exist, and we can know that reality only by allowing our own being to merge into being. We should now look at how one interacts with the world.

CHAPTER 4

THE FIVE SENSES

Our five organs of sense – eyes, ears, skin, nose, and tongue – are our gateway to the world around us. They allow us to interact with our environment, perceive the world, and gather information. Whether it is through sight, hearing, touch, smell, or taste, we constantly receive stimuli that help us navigate through life. The brain then processes this information and helps us make sense of the world we live in. However, the mind is another complex topic altogether, and we will dive into that later.

Throughout our lives, we experience three fundamental sensations that shape our perception of the world: pleasure, pain, and neutrality, the latter being a state of pause between the former two. While the nature of pain and pleasure may be similar for most people, the degree of attraction or aversion to them may differ. It is through our sense faculties that we experience these sensations, and since time immemorial, humans have been drawn to pleasure and repelled by pain. Every being in the world, whether a human, an ant, or an eagle, perceives the environment through their senses. However, each being has a unique view or perception of the world, and it is challenging to determine who has the most accurate perception of reality. We humans tend to think that we are the only ones who can see the world as it is, but the reality we perceive is limited to what our senses are presenting us with.

The five senses – sight, hearing, touch, smell, and taste – are limited and cannot offer us a complete sense of reality, but only a limited one. We can observe this limitation through various instruments, such as telescopes, stethoscopes, and microscopes, which enable us to perceive the world in ways that our naked senses cannot. Therefore, we must accept and understand the limitations of our senses.

While the senses play a crucial role in helping us interact with the world and survive as a species, they also help us fulfill our deepest desires, including the pursuit of everlasting happiness. However, it is important to recognize that our senses are merely tools that aid us in our quest for happiness; they are not the sole determinant of it.

In short, our senses are limited and therefore what we see is not a full reality but a limited one. The Vedic tradition of India gives an ample explanation of how the senses and sense organs operate and function. Through the senses we experience pleasure and pain, and every individual would like to experience more pleasure, because that pleasure gives a sense of happiness and fulfillment. Few creatures desire pain, though there may be some exceptions. Whatever we may choose – pain or pleasure – it is the desire of any being to be happy by whatever means, to fulfill themselves through the objects of desire. The senses gather information which then gives rise to sensations; the sensations are interpreted by thought, giving rise to desire or sensations based on previous experience or based on the level of pleasure it gives. Here, we are caught in all sorts of desires – physical or mental – from this process the *five poisons* are born. These five poisons give rise to our illusions and the self becomes egoistic, covering our true reality with the veil of illusion. This is why the masters of all religious and non-religious traditions point out that without restraint of the senses, we can never be at peace because we will always be busy running after the pleasures of the senses. The pursuit of pleasure in any form automatically brings pain because pleasure expresses itself through experience which is, of necessity, limited. This means pleasure must have an end and on the other hand is pain or disappointment, depending on the circumstances and conditions in which the pleasure arises or how it is manifested.

In the *Bhagavad Gita*, Krishna describes how the senses keep us under illusion.

> *If a man keeps dwelling on sense-objects, attachment to them arises; from attachment, desire flares up; from desire, anger is born; from anger, confusion follows; from confusion, weakness of memory; weak memory – weak understanding;*
> *But the man who is self-controlled, who meets the objects of the senses with neither craving nor aversion, will attain serenity at last. In serenity, all his sorrows disappear at once, forever; when his heart has become serene, his understanding is steadfast. The undisciplined have no wisdom, no one-pointed concentration, with no concentration, no peace; with no peace, where can joy be?*
>
> -Lord Krishna

Krishna beautifully points out how we are tempted by the senses, and therefore, by pursuing them at all costs, we lose our discipline of mind and are thrown into confusion. Unless we truly understand this fact and observe this in our daily life, we can never come to a state of mind which is free, desireless and full of joy. One should not pursue anything by effort, but rather accept whatever comes and goes – that is, enjoy whatever is presented and allow whatever is taken to go without resistance or clinging; then joy and peace are there in that acceptance.

In the next statement a Christian Saint give the same description:

> *When the mind is guided by the senses, it feeds with them upon the food of the beasts but when the senses are guided by the mind, they feed with it upon the sustenance of the angels. Vain glory is a servant to fornication. If it is concerned with behavior, to haughtiness. To humility, brevity is proper. Love of glory is connected with prolixity. The former through constant concentration, attains contemplation and arms the soul unto chastity. The latter through the continual wandering of the mind, gathers provisions through contact with (outward) things, and defiles the heart.*

-St. Isaac the Syrian

We see the above two traditions pointing to the same truth, and in observing that in our own lives we can discover for ourselves that we are always pulled into the world by the senses and therefore the mind is always occupied running after objects of the senses and is never at peace. Krishna, similarly to Saint Isaac, shows that when self-knowledge allows the mind to control the senses, wisdom is acquired and then we act the right way with love and peace for all.

Control of the senses and understanding their proper role in life slowly guides the mind and soul into chastity, into the natural purity of mind and heart. Our natural self, free from ego, is pure joy and we do not need a reason to be joyful. We are like a baby who always smiles, unless some disturbances occur like sickness or hunger. In the course of anyone's life we may have woken up from a deep sleep with no dreams and before we are fully awake, where thinking has not yet arisen and there is a moment or two when one feels joyful without any reason. Unfortunately, only a few moments of joy in a life burdened by so many troubles.

In the Katha Upanishads, Lord Yama teaches Nachiketa the secret to life eternal:

> *Ignorant of their ignorance, yet wise in their own esteem, those deluded men Proud of their vain learning go round and round Like the blind led by the blind. Far beyond their eyes, hypnotized by the world of sense, opens the way to immortality. "I am my body; when my body dies, I die." Living in this superstition, they fall life after life under my sway.*

-Katha Upanishad

In the above statement, Lord Yama teaches Nachiketa that as long as we are caught in the world of the senses and identify with the body, we do not recognize our own divinity, therefore we will be lost in the pleasures of the world, where we create suffering for ourselves and others. The suffering is created by desire and attachment to the pleasures they bring and in doing so keep us in the cycle of birth and death.

Saint Isaac the Syrian gives another pointer as to how the senses have imprisoned us:

> *No one is able to come near to God save only he who is far from the world. For I do not call separation the departure from the body, but from the bodily things. Excellence consists therein that a man in his mind be a void as regards the world. As long as the senses are occupied with (outward) things, it is not possible for the heart to rest from imagining them. Nor do the afflictions cease, nor evil thoughts end except in the desert and the wilderness.*

-St Isaac

Saint Isaac points out how the senses are drowning us in mischief, and we need to have self-control over them. He states that one way is to be alone in a secluded place where there is not too much distraction for the senses. The senses are the platform where the ego takes flight; they are the support the ego needs. If the support is cut off, the ego is slowly dissolved by self-knowledge, which leads to wisdom.

If we carefully observe our lives and the endless pursuits of creating or maintaining pleasures we are inclined to enjoy, we can observe how we are caught in the world of duality and the mind is never at rest, never free. Though we might be free physically – that is, have the money and the means to pursue anything we desire – yet we always feel shallow, empty, and lonely. Just observe the wealthy who have the means to fulfill their desires but are never really happy and cannot escape suffering, some even committing suicide. Money can only give us comfort but never true happiness, as this cannot be purchased at the altar of demand. Whatever we experience in our lives, we do it through the mind. Buddha has stated that the mind has the power to liberate us or keep us in bondage. He means that if we really understand the working of the mind, we will be free from all troubles. Next, we should look at the mind.

CHAPTER 5

THE MIND

Before we begin talking about the mind, we have to understand the brain. Even the creation was created from a simple pattern that developed into bigger patterns reflecting the simple one. These patterns are called fractals, and science has proven that all that exist are just patterns of energy in movement. That is why we always start with the simple in order to understand the complex. The brain is just an apparatus, like a computer, which performs internal functions automatically and external functions by reacting to stimuli like the environment and making the body respond accordingly. The mind, on the other hand, is much more. It is like space, where all the brains – regardless of who has the brain, an ant, or a human – operate within the space which we call the mind. We also see that every action happens in space for without space nothing can move. The same happens with the mind. One may be physically in one place, but one can go to another place by thought, which operates through the mind. The brain cannot be there because it is just physical matter, but the mind is everywhere and is used by all brains within their capacity to operate. This is nothing out of the ordinary; what we exposed here is just a fact.

Science still has many unanswered questions about the human mind as such. Let's look at another example: in a dream state the mind can take us to many places and we can experience lots of things (existent and non-existent), but the brain is still operative in the dream and cannot take us where the mind can go.

In one of his books, *Vivekacudamani*, Adi Shankara, an Indian saint, explains:

> *In dreams, when there is no actual contact with the external world, the mind alone creates the whole universe consisting of the experiencer and the like.*
> *Similarly, in the waking state also, there is no difference. Therefore, all this phenomenal universe is just a projection of the mind.*
> *In a dreamless sleep when the mind is reduced to its natural state, there exists nothing (for the person asleep), as is evident from universal experience. Hence a man relative existence is simply the creation of his mind and has no objective reality.*
> *Clouds are brought in by the wind and again driven by the same agency. Similarly, man bondage is caused by the mind, and liberation too is caused by that alone.*
>
> -Adi Shankara

Here, Adi Shankara shows that what we think of as reality does not have any foundation. Likewise, Buddha has also said that nothing in the phenomenal existence exists independent of other things, but all are interdependent, so everything exists in relation to other things or beings. Life itself is just a matrix of relationships; it is a unity of beings in a diversity of forms.

Milarepa, one of the great Yogis of Tibet, sent one of his disciples to meditate and find out what the mind is, and after a few days the disciple could not, but described it as- it does not have color or form, it cannot be seen, and it cannot be grasped. It is there one moment and nowhere the next. Many masters from all traditions have looked into the mind with the mind in order to go beyond it.

The Amritabindu Upanishad says:

> *The mind may be said to be of two kinds, Pure and impure. Driven by the senses It becomes impure; but with the senses Under control, the mind becomes pure. It is the mind that frees us or enslaves. Driven by the senses we become bound; Master of the senses we become free. Those who seek freedom must master their senses. When the mind is detached from the senses One reaches the summit of consciousness. Mastery of the mind leads to wisdom. Practice meditation. Stop all vain talk. The highest state is beyond reach of thought, for it lies beyond all dualities.*

> -Amritabindu Upanishad

The Upanishads, like Buddha, point out that where thought is, the mind is also; where there is no thought, the mind is not, or the mind is in its pure state. We can observe for ourselves the validity of that statement and therefore we can say that thought is an important thing (I call it a "thing" because science has proven that thought is matter; a subtle form of energy but still matter). Mind can keep us in bondage or liberate us, as Buddha mentions in the following statement:

> *We are Shaped by our thoughts; we become what we think. When the mind is pure, joy follows like a shadow that never leaves.*

> -Buddha

In the Gospel of Mary, Jesus points out that where the mind is there is the treasure also, and in a pure mind one will find that treasure; when the heart is pure, love, joy and peace are there in a natural state.

> *And she began to speak to them these words: she said, I saw the Lord in a vision, and I said to Him, Lord I saw you today in a vision. He answered and said to me,*
> *Blessed are you that you did not waver at the sight of Me.*
> *For where the mind is there is the treasure also.*
> *I said to Him, Lord, how does he who sees the vision see it, through the soul or through the spirit?*
> *The Lord answered and said, He does not see through the soul nor through the spirit, but the mind that is between the two that is what sees the vision and it is [...]*

-The Gospel of Mary

In the Upanishads it states:

> *Beyond the reach of the senses is he, but not beyond the reach of a mind stilled Through the practice of deep meditation. Beyond the reach of words and works is he, But not beyond the reach of a pure heart Freed from the sway of the senses.*

-The Upanishads

Here, the Upanishads declared that God is beyond the reach of the senses but not beyond a pure mind and pure heart. In order to find reality, we have to clean the mind by prayer, meditation, contemplation and so on until the mind and heart are purified, allowing love and bliss supreme to flow endlessly. In the next statement Saint Isaac points to this same truth.

The true sight of the angels is emotion by spiritual under-standing concerning their domain. But it is impossible for us to see the nature of spiritual forces without the mind. When man is deemed worthy of seeing them in their nature and in their place and as they are in their spiritual creation, grace moves his mind by the revelation of spiritual insight concerning them. When the soul has been purified and is worthy of seeing its fellows, their sight is perceived with these eyes. They are not objects and they cannot be seen as they are, without alteration, but by psychic sight which is true contemplation. This means without deterioration of their nature by sight. This sight cannot be acquired by any man without the second purification of the mind.

-St Isaac the Syrian

Saint Isaac backs up the statement of Christ in the fact that the mind holds the secret in connecting the soul with the spirit and love supreme.

From all these statements made by – Buddha and Christ, Upanishads and saints – we see that thought can create, for whatever we see in the world today we can attribute to thought and thinking. Also, if we look from a religious perspective, we know that the Bible, the Vedas and the Torah agree that all creation started with the word and the word was with God. Each tradition refers to different word, but they all agree that everything was created by an energy some of us call God. Likewise, each one of us is a creator for we create things and also create our own lives, don't we? Buddha in his teachings has never denied the existence of God or soul, but he did not want to make it personal, and he directed his disciples to find out the truth for themselves and not just copy others' wisdom without really grasping the reality for themselves.

Here it is worth mentioning that the first word – Amen or Om – is the first thought and is the primordial thought (I) from which all other thoughts arise, and it is the birth of the mind, which is just a tool of creating. Nevertheless, real creativity comes when thought is not there; anything that comes from thought is relative and illusory. This is not to say that it is not existent but does not have any substance and is always dependent on other things. We could conclude that all created things have a creator even if we may not understand the creator or the process of creation. To understand how the brain and the senses work, is explained very beautifully in the Katho Upanishad with the help of the model of a chariot.

In this analogy, the chariot is the body, the horses are the five senses, the reins in the mouth of the horses are the mind, the charioteer is the intellect, and the passenger seated behind is the soul residing in the body. The senses (horses) desire pleasurable things. The mind (reins) is not exercising restraint on the senses (horses). The intellect (charioteer) submits to the pull of the reins (mind). So, in the materially bound state, the bewildered soul does not properly direct the intellect, thus the senses decide where the chariot will go. The soul experiences the pleasures of the senses through the mind. Seated on this chariot, the soul (passenger) is moving around in this material world for eternity.

Here we introduce the soul into our model because most religious traditions of the world have found that something must be behind the mind; that conscience that makes us feel guilty after we have done something without being told if it is bad or good; that conscience always tells us what is right or wrong. Some pay attention to it, some not. From this we can see that the mind is the space where everything happens. Intellect – or intelligence – can operate as directed by the senses or as directed by the soul, or we can say pure intelligence just operates. The intellect directed by the soul is pure intelligence in operation, or selfless creation, but when directed by the senses, intelligence is corrupted and therefore operates in a selfish way.

Most of us are caught in the senses, and this is why we are in the never-ending cycle of rebirth and death or pain and suffering. Some do not believe in rebirth but that is not of the essence. What is of the essence is whether we can ever be free of suffering and reach a state beyond it. All the prophets and spiritual masters have said that it is very much possible if one has the intention to find out for themselves.

Mind is not something personal; it is an energy shared by all sentient beings. Thoughts can be personal for a particular being but realized masters, who have understood the working of the mind and got in touch with the core of all existence, can see all thoughts because for them there is not separation; they are whole beings, *whole* meaning one with all existence.

We have talked about the mind a little and the senses so far; next we should look to see how these operate together and what makes the individual an individual.

CHAPTER 6

THE EGO-SELF

We need to point out that when we call it *ego-self,* the ego is there, and when only *self,* the ego is not present; therefore the self is alone, which is our natural state. The ego alone cannot exist where the self has its own existence. The ego only attaches to the self, thereby giving the impression that it is self-existent where in fact it is just an illusion.

The individual is the ego-self, by definition, as long as one works with the ego. In English, *individual* refers to a unique entity with its own characteristics, tendencies and so on. We all are individuals living in the world according to our conditioning, that is, our developed personality with its tendencies and desires, together with our experiences and memories, the organism (the body) and a name on top, this is what makes up the totality of an individual or ego-self. This is what we consider to be an individual, and for most people this is it and nothing more.

We need to make a distinction here that the ego and the self are not two identities but one, and when the self acts in a selfish way, we claim that the individual is acting for personal gain, unlike when the self acts for the benefit of the self and others in oneness. To annihilate the ego is to always act with wisdom, love and intelligence which operates without the filter of conditioning and therefore is always acting for the benefit of all. In acting free from ego there is only the self, which is just awareness of being.

In the Upanishads it is stated:

> *Like two golden birds perched on the selfsame tree, Intimate friends, the ego and the Self Dwell in the same body. The former eats the sweet and sour fruits of the tree of life While the latter looks on in detachment.*

> -Upanishads

Above, the Upanishads describes how the ego and the self dwell in the same body, and we can see therefore that there is only one self not two, though it can appear to be two when the acting is done selfishly and becomes one when it is done unselfishly. As long as the ego is, duality will always exist.

> *This māyā, that is to say, the ego, is like a cloud. The sun cannot be seen on account of a thin patch of cloud; when that disappears, one sees the sun. If by the grace of the guru one's ego vanishes, then one sees God.*

> -Sri Ramakrishna

There are people who believe in God and the soul and others who do not believe in such. Even the latter still believe in the non-existence of it and are therefore still caught in belief. Early in the book, we discussed the distinction between belief and fate. Fate is an opening of the mind to truth without any restrictions whereas belief is still an opening of the mind but restricted by a preconceived idea, therefore limiting the individual's ability to be open to truth. We are all conditioned from birth; we have been conditioned by family, school, institutions, culture and through our learning and experiences. Unless all human beings are ready to overcome their conditioning, we can never ever meet heart to heart and therefore never can have a true relationship based on pure Love.

The physical condition is like the culture we live in; as the way we prepare meals or do any physical activity and so on. Each of us has lived in different physical environments and therefore have adapted accordingly, but psychological conditions – I am smarter, I am richer, my country is better, I am a Catholic and so on – are the seed of all conflicts and evil in the world. If this conditioning (which is much more rooted than physical conditioning) is not uprooted, there will never be peace and love in the individual and therefore we will never have Love and Peace in the world. If we are willing to look, we can observe that all evil comes from that feeling of separateness, of selfishness, which is fed by our own egoistical upbringing. Physical conditions, like how we prepare a meal or do any physical activities, can be shared; with the advent of the internet, it is very easy to learn from different cultures but the psychological conditioning is more difficult to share because each person is attached to and identifies with his own.

Ego, which covers the self, functions more or less for the happiness of the ego in order to fulfill numerous desires. This is where we are not only running after all sorts of sensations that the senses produce, but also we find that our conditioning is affected by negative energies like greed, power, jealousy, anger, pride, envy and hatred. These energies affect each individual in different ways but in the end they all produce suffering for the individual and society at large. One has to observe how the self not only has the desires to fulfill himself through the ego but also has the tendency to do good for the family or society as a whole, when acting without ego. It is fair to say then that the self has an inherent desire to be healthy and for that healthiness to be shared with all; this intrinsic desire has been rooted in us since the beginning of time.

Our real desire is everlasting happiness; everyone is searching, through different means, for this elusive everlasting happiness. It may appear that there are exceptions but in fact there are not; even a criminal who has inflicted suffering on others is searching for his own happiness, though his means are negative and destructive. The self therefore can work in a selfish way for its own gratification or in the other direction for the benefit of others. If we observe our own lives, each of us encounter a feeling of happiness when we have made another person happy. This happens when the ego is not at the fore, and we call it selfless action. If the self only does the action for a reward – even if one does it for the happiness of others – it is still a selfish action because one waits for a reward and ego is involved. The right action is the one that does not have the intention of a reward; it is called real charity and comes from a mind that is free and works in unison with the heart.

The thought of our individual selves gives rise to the ego with all the memories and habits of the past changing in the present and projecting into the future. This ego is needed on the physical level of existence to drive a car, to learn in school, to relate to others; it is an essential tool to help us to function in this world but on the psychological level it should not interfere at all. All the realized masters have taught that the self must be known, and this is why all traditions have pointed out that the path of self-knowledge is the highest path. When the self is known then the ego takes its proper place, that is, only to perform the functions it needs to perform and nothing more. We can also state that it has been dissolved or merged into the real self which can function with no ego. Either way, ego needs to surrender all control to the self.

Christ says:

> *When you come to know yourselves, then you will be*
> *known, and you will realize that you are the children of the*
> *living Father.*
> *But if you do not come to know yourselves, then you exist*
> *in poverty, and you are poverty.*

-Gospel of Thomas: 3

Christ here is very clearly showing that when we find out who we really are, then the real will manifest in us and we will become one with all, which he refers to as God the Father. The Vedas and the Kabbalist and all other traditions point out that self-knowledge is essential in finding reality.

> *As long as we think we are the ego, we feel attached and fall*
> *into sorrow. But realize that you are the Self, the Lord Of*
> *life, and you will be freed from sorrow.*
> *Those who dwell on and long for sense-pleasure are born*
> *in a world of separateness. But let them realize they are the*
> *Self And all separateness will fall away.*

-The Upanishads

> *One should understand "Who am I?" Giving up the false*
> *sense of "I" (ego) one should be "Oneness" alone. Then,*
> *naturally contentment will be acquired within oneself.*

-St Shri Samartha Ramdas

Prophet Muhammad in Hilyat al-Awliya' stated:

> *Whoever knows himself, knows his Lord.*

-Muhammad

Same as Christ, all Enlighted beings have stated that without self-knowledge one cannot touch reality (God).

Krishna says, in the *Bhagavad Gita*,

> *A lamp sheltered from the wind*
> *will not flicker, so*
> *to this is compared the true man of yoga,*
> *whose mind has vanished in the self.*
> *When his mind has become serene*
> *by the practice of meditation, he*
> *sees the self through the self And*
> *rest in the self, rejoicing*
> *He knows the infinite joy*
> *that is reached by the understanding*
> *beyond the senses: steadfast,*
> *he does not fall back from the truth.*

-Lord Krishna

Here Lord Krishna tells Arjuna how a yogi should meditate in order to find the true self. Ramana Maharshi, an Indian self-realized master, has pointed out the path of self-enquiry in order to come to understand our true reality. He has pointed out that we should try to find the source from where the *I* arises and where it finds its rest.

Another statement from the Upanishads upholds the above statements:

> *There is only one way to know the Self, and that is to realize*
> *him yourself. The ignorant think the Self can be known*
> *by the intellect, but the illumined Know he is beyond the*
> *duality of the knower and the known. The Self is realized*
> *in a higher state of consciousness when you have broken*
> *through the wrong identification that you are the body,*

subject to birth and death. To be the Self is to go beyond death. Realize the Self, the shining goal of life! If you do not, there is only darkness. See the Self in all and go beyond death.

-Upanishads

Above, as in numerous statements given to us from the awakened beings of light, we see that reality is beyond the dual mind and can only be found in a mind that has transcended beyond being conditioned by likes and dislikes; as long as we are still caught in an intellectual web of reasons and where we identify with the body and its numerous desires, we will find it hard to drop this identification. This identification disappears when we reach a state of equanimity of mind where the likes and dislikes do not affect the body and the mind. Without the realization of oneness, we are caught in duality and therefore in conflict and darkness and subject to suffering.

The battle of Kurukshetra in the *Bhagavad Gita*, the battle of Rama with Ravana in Ramayana, the battle of David in the Bible and the battle of Jihad in Quran were but battles with our own ego; if we pay attention to them and are willing to learn and look with no prejudice, we will recognize this truth. We may ask why there is so much suffering and sorrow in the world and in our own being. We can observe that in us there is always a battle, an inner war going on in our own mind between good and evil and, of course, this war extends also in our outer world. It is the war between good and bad, right and wrong, etc. Here we come to see how we are living in the world of duality, and we are like a tennis ball caught between two racquets always hitting the two sides of the same coin, so to speak.

This duality plays an important role in our everyday life, for without it the world would not really exist as it is. This duality is a dance between two forces, which even at first glance, seem to fight with one another but in fact are the same energy dancing and showing the two faces of the same coin. This is why most traditions and masters have shown that this duality needs to be understood and one needs to go beyond it in order to find what is real. Hope that you have grasped, even if only intellectually at this stage, the role the self plays in everyday life and what the self is. The self is real; the ego should be just a tool. When we need to dig a hole in the yard, we take a shovel and use it to do the job and after we are finished, we place the shovel back in the shed. The ego is just a tool; if used correctly it will not hinder us in any way. It is there to be used and to function in practical ways, but it is never to be used in a psychological aspect because there it will take control of the self and create chaos. Tagore explains how the self seems to have two aspects.

> *We can look at our self in its two different aspects. The self which displays itself, and the self which transcends itself and thereby reveals its own meaning. To display itself it tries to be big, to stand upon the pedestal of its accumulations, and to retain everything to itself. To reveal itself it gives up everything it has; thus, becoming perfect like a flower that has blossomed out from the bud, pouring from its chalice of beauty all its sweetness.*

-Rabindranath Tagore

Here, Tagore expresses beautifully how the self can keep us in bondage or give us freedom. Teachings of the early saints of the Christian tradition have pointed out how one has to be watchful all the time; this watchfulness was also taught by Buddha as mindfulness. It is really a fight with the passions, with the senses that produce the passions through all sorts of desires. Christ has warned us to guard ourselves against the passions, for through them we decline and lose ourselves to immorality and we will be in this world of desires and sorrow.

Christ says:

> *That is why I say: When the master of the house learns that the thief is about to come, he will be on guard before he comes (and) will not let him break into his house, his domain, to carry away his possessions.*
> *(But) you, be on guard against the world!*
> *Gird your loins with great strength, so that the robbers will not find a way to get to you.*

-Gospel of Thomas: 21

Christ points out that the robbers are the passions, the desires that fulfill themselves through the ego thereby robbing us of all our goodness and love.

In The Path to the Kingdom, Arsenie Boca, a saint of the Orthodox church, writes:

> *So long as man uses his instincts for the purpose intended by God, they will not give him trouble because they will find approval and satisfaction in fulfilling their original, legitimate purpose. Instead, the vast majority of people distort the original purpose of those blind forces of nature, looking only for the pleasure they can offer, but in ignoring their purpose they become slaves to the passions. In the case of slavery, the mind censorship has weakened so much that the passions begin leading the mind, at which point man will soon lose his freedom. The conscience of a man who becomes enslaved to the passions loses its ability to confess his misdeeds. His conscience as if asleep has reached a standby mode although he is still alive. Now, man conscience is in a state of unbelief and dismissive of God, and he will start living in a state of sin. Because sin means: the moral defeat of the conscience by Satan through the passions of the body.*

-St Arsenie Boca

Here we see that Satan, the ego that is infiltrated by negative energy, works through the passions in order to keep us in ignorance or Maya, as the Hindu called it. Therefore, the self has no room to expand through the mind for the mind is taken over by the ego. Another important factor Father Arsenie Boca points out is that sin is in fact the immoral state of mind wherein one has fallen prey to the senses and is in a state of only satisfying the senses, thereby making the mind powerless to regain its natural state.

Below Saint Isaac the Syrian points to the same fact:

> *I have learned by experience that the principles of all good things and the regaining of the soul from the captivity of the enemies, and the way towards life and light, consist in two things: abiding in one and the same place, and constant fasting. This means: that a man, being wise, shall lay down a fair law for his belly, by untroubled, constant sitting [alone]. Proceeding from here he will reach the subduing of the senses; further: watchfulness of mind; further: tranquillizing of brutish passions stirring in the body. Further: quiet thoughts. Further: enlightened impulses of the spirit. Further: application to excellent works. Further: high and subtle insights. Further: immeasurable tears at all times. Further: watchful chastity, without any connection with the experience of the image in the spirit.*
>
> -St Issac the Syrian

We can also consider the Buddhist point of view that there is no ego and that the mind is just a tool that we use in order to function in this world and therefore is conditioned and taken over by the passions and afflicted to such extent that we can never find peace only in the things of pleasure or convenience. Whichever way we may look, it is in the mind where we must find peace in order for the soul or conscience to unite with all existence and express pure Love.

It does not matter what religion or spiritual practice we follow; the goal of all religions and yoga is the extinction of all energies but Love. One may call it God, Intelligence, Emptiness, Truth: the names point to the same energy. It is clear that all religions point to this unconditional Love and when one is grounded in it, everything else is second best. Love is the one universal energy that is not consumed by anything and cannot be extinguished or divided. It is eternal.

Then Jesus said to His disciples:

> *If anyone desires to come after Me, let him deny himself, and take up his cross, and follow Me. For whoever desires to save his life will lose it, but whoever loses his life for My sake will find it. For what profit is it to a man if he gains the whole world, and loses his own soul? Or what will a man give in exchange for his soul?*

> *-Matthew 16:24–26*

We see clearly in Christ's statement that if our mind is dominated by ego-centric ideas and we only worry about ourselves, thus lost in the pleasures the world offers, we cannot enter the Christ consciousness or awaken to our true reality, for the passions will keep us in bondage and we cannot escape the wheel of Samsara (birth and rebirth), as Buddha states.

> *And our Lord, seeing that among those who wish to renunciate completely, there are some in such a state of mind, that their will is ready but their thoughts are drawn backwards by fear of troubles, on account of their love of the body which they have not yet thrown away – He will take from them this lassitude of mind saying to them briefly: If any man will come after me, let him first deny himself (Matt 16:24). What is the denial that is spoken of here? It is the denial of the flesh. And one who is destined to suffer crucifixion, he accepts the thought of death, and goes forth,*

as one who does not think that he has any further share in this life. This is [what is meant by] taking up the cross and following me. The cross denotes the will prepared for any trouble. And declaring why this is so, Me says: Whoever will save his soul in this world, will lose it in the true life (Matt 10:39). And whoever will lose his individuality here for my sake, will find it there.

-St Isaac the Syrian

Here, Saint Isaac clearly explains the saying of Christ, as other masters have; that for as long as we are identified with the body, the ego will keep us in prison and tied to the pleasures the world has to offer through the body. "Let him deny himself" means to deny the ego and use it only for its intended purpose in a practical manner – for functioning in the world like a true human being. This is almost impossible - for most of us are identified with it completely - and in giving it up we feel annihilated. This is terrifying and it is why most of us cannot follow in the way of the awakened masters, by putting our egos in the right place, therefore entering pure consciousness, and in doing so becoming like them pure Love, pure Joy and Peace eternal.

Buddha taught elimination of the non-self and did not speak about true self. He wanted us to find out on our own if the soul of the true self really exists. In the end, the whole charade is happening in our minds. This is why the monks and yogis of all traditions retired to caves, forests, and mountains – secluded but pleasant places – in order to overcome the ego, or the afflictions of the mind, and free themselves from the suffering they produce, therefore allowing that pure energy to emerge. Buddha called the state of liberation of Christ consciousness *Nirvana*. He chose this word, though it is a negative word, because this is not something to aspire to – like liberation (Moksha) or other things we can imagine and hope to achieve – and therefore does not allow the ego-mind to be identified with it. Nirvana means to blow out, to expand or extinguish the flame which is the ego. It is like the light of the candle in the afternoon sun that becomes one with the light of the Sun. This is why Buddha asked us to surrender the ego and in doing so we will find out for ourselves if there is anything remaining after we have fully extinguished the light of the ego and find the self to be the only reality.

In early Christianity, the passions were called demons; Buddhists call them afflictions of the mind. The root of these afflictions are the five poisons (ignorance, attachment, aversion, pride, envy). They all arise through personal ego-centric desire.

Shantideva states in his book, *A Guide to the Bodhisattva's Way of Life*:

> *Should even all the gods and demi-gods*
> *Rise up against me as my enemies, They could not lead*
> *nor place me in The roaring fires of hell.*
> *But the mighty foe, the mind afflictions,*
> *In a moment can cast me amidst (those flames) Which*
> *when met will cause not even the ashes Of the king of*
> *mountains to remain.*

-Shantideva

Here, Shantideva shows how afflictions arise from desires and attachment to objects or ideas and therefore are a product of our own minds which can keep us in our own hell (state of mind). The Upanishads in Hindu tradition describe the battle of the soul or self with the ego in the same way, as does the *Bhagavad Gita* where Krishna is the Pure Spirit and Arjuna is the afflicted mind.

> *When a man has become unattached to sense-objects or to*
> *actions, renouncing his own selfish will, then he is mature*
> *in yoga.*

-Lord Krishna

Here, Krishna tells us that in order for us to grow spiritually, we need to renounce the selfish will, the selfish desires, and in doing so we come closer to the union with the absolute God.

Ramana Maharshi also said:

> *As all living beings desire to be happy always, without misery, as in the case of everyone there is observed supreme love for oneself, and as happiness alone is the cause for love, in order to gain that happiness which is one's nature and which is experienced in the state of deep sleep where there is no mind, one should know oneself. For that, the path of knowledge, the enquiry of the form "Who am I?" is the principal means.*

He states that in order to find the everlasting happiness all of us are searching for, is imperative to find out who we really are and as he and many other saints and teachers have pointed out, the most direct path is self-knowledge. Here the most well-known scientist in the world, Albert Einstein, also agrees with the ancient masters that we need to shed the blinkers of illusion that we have put on as an optical delusion and in doing so we can then extend our love to all beings:

> *A human being is a part of the whole, called by us "Universe," a part limited in time and space. He experiences himself, his thoughts and feelings as something separated from the rest – a kind of optical delusion of his consciousness. This delusion is a kind of prison for us, restricting us to our personal desires and to affection for a few persons nearest to us. Our task must be to free ourselves from this prison by widening our circle of compassion to embrace*

*all living creatures and the whole of nature in its beauty.
Nobody is able to achieve this completely, but the striving
for such achievement is in itself a part of the liberation and
a foundation for inner security.*

-Albert Einstein

Below, Rabindranath Tagore explains how our own ego is stopping us from realizing the self:

*This is why the Upanishads describe those who have
attained the goal of human life as "peaceful" and as "at-one-
with-God," meaning that they are in perfect harmony with
man and nature, and therefore in undisturbed union with
God. We have a glimpse of the same truth in the teachings of
Jesus when he says, "It is easier for a camel to pass through
the eye of a needle than for a rich man to enter the kingdom
of Heaven," which implies that whatever we treasure for
ourselves separates us from others; our possessions are our
limitations. He who is bent upon accumulating riches is
unable, with his ego continually bulging, to pass through
the gates of comprehension of the spiritual world, which
is the world of perfect harmony; he is shut up within the
narrow walls of his limited acquisitions. Hence the spirit
of the teachings of Upanishad is: In order to find him you
must embrace all. In the pursuit of wealth you really give
up everything to gain a few things, and that is not the way
to attain him who is completeness.*

-Rabindranath Tagore

So far, we are hopefully beginning to understand that the suffering humanity undergoes is created by us through identification with our own ego-self. How this identification comes about is another question to understand before we start to talk about how to put ego into its own natural place. We have to observe for ourselves how the ego functions and in that pure observation the ego will slowly surrender control to the self, allowing the individual heart to expand through the mind and aligning the body, heart and mind into one unitary being full of love and in full unison with all existence, life. This is the only way towards realizing Love, Peace and Harmony in the world.

It is same as when we watch a magic trick being performed. We see its magic and think it is real until we observe how it works and when we find out by our own knowledge then it is no longer magic. Likewise, with the ego: when we find out for ourselves how it works and how it keeps us in bondage then we no longer trust it by allowing the tricks to go on.

All traditions point out that if the senses are not controlled, then we run into the trouble of enjoying too much the pleasures they have to offer and therefore being attached to the pleasures of the world. Here we get a paradox of how we are to overcome our senses: do we need to suppress them, control them, or just run with them? Most monks and yogis are suppressing them, though some are enjoying them and run with them. In the Katha Upanishads, Lord Yama explains who is the ruler of the senses:

That through which one enjoys form, taste, smell, sound, Touch, and sexual union is the Self. Can there be anything not known to That Who is the One in all? Know One, know all. That through which one enjoys the waking and sleeping states is the Self. To know That As consciousness is to go beyond sorrow. Those who know the Self as enjoyer of the honey from the flowers of the senses, ever present within, ruler of time, Go beyond fear. For this Self is supreme!

-Katha Upanishad

Once we have realized the self then the senses will not give us any trouble and can be used to enjoy life, then whatever life presents to us would be joy and if we are enjoying the senses through the true self then we have made sorrow a thing of the past. Also, it is up to us which avenue we take in order to realize the self and be free of the hold of the senses. Once the ego surrenders, the self, which is never selfish, remains the ruler of our life and in doing so acts for the benefit of all beings. This is why Christ stated that to deny yourself is the death of the ego and one can then follow him and in doing so one will never taste death. The senses need to be restrained for some, some need to stay away from them and some can run with them. It is up to the individual and to the guru who can advise, for a true guru will know the best avenue for each person.

Very few are blessed with the required energy to overcome the senses for that is hard task indeed. If we are able to overcome them, the ego surrenders for it does not have any support and without support cannot feed itself, so it gives up. We are then free to act with the supreme will, always acting for the benefit of all, including ourselves. We then have attained the state of absolute freedom.

This state of being free is called *Turiya* and is explained by Ramana Maharshi:

> *Q. What is turiya?*
> *A. Turiya is the mind in quiescence and aware of Self. There is the awareness that the mind has merged in its source. Whether the senses are active or inactive is immaterial. In nirvikalpa samadhi the senses are inactive. To know implies the subject and object. To be aware means to be thought-free.*
>
> -Sri Ramana Maharshi

It is important to understand how the senses work and how they can actually keep us in a prison of our own doing, enforcing the dualistic view of mind. Next, we should have a look into the world of duality, for because of this duality, the self divides itself into two and therefore keeps us in conflict and misery.

CHAPTER 7

THE WORLD OF DUALITY

Good & bad, right & wrong, positive & negative, inner & outer, etc. are energies that oppose each other. The movement between these energies is the dance of life. Life is a movement; it is a dance, but it is also a cessation of movement in stillness. In this world, all beings apart from humans all flow with life with the natural flow of existence. Human beings think they know better and by thinking that they try to control nature and flow against the natural flow of life. Here we can observe that humans have introduced an element of destruction by flowing against life. To flow with life is to surrender to life, to what is, to the present moment. This surrender is very difficult to achieve, for in order to do so, the ego must surrender all control to the real self. To surrender to what is, to the present moment, to life or God is the most difficult thing to do. As long as we identify in any form with the ego, we will be afraid to surrender, anticipating annihilation, not knowing – due to ignorance – that total surrender is liberation, is union with existence, love, God, whatever you call it. It cannot really be named because as soon as you name it you reduce it to the level of the ego and make it personal. God, Life, Love, intelligence can only be known by being one with it.

Jesus says:

> *If they ask you: "What is the sign of your Father among you?" (then) say to them: "It is movement and repose."*
>
> -Gospel of Thomas: 50

Here, Christ is saying that we are the essence of the Father, which is in the repose, and we are also the manifestation, which is the movement that also is the Father. This movement is not something apart from God, but because we are in the world of duality, we see it as separate. Again, here we bring a couple of sayings of Jesus regarding this duality.

Jesus says:

> *If two make peace with one another in one and the same house, (then) they will say to the mountain: "Move away," and it will move away.*
>
> -Gospel of Thomas: 48

Here he refers to when the duality has ceased in us and when the ego melts into the true self and surrenders control fully. At this point, we will be able to move the mountain he refers to as the ego, when ego is gone, we will be free of all troubles and become one with the father, with all existence. The ego will not die a physical death, only a psychological one, and can then fulfill its own purpose, to help the self to manifest through the body, mind, and spirit in this world, the three working in total unison. If the ego dies, we will not be able to sustain the union of body, mind and spirit and will die a physical death.

Jesus said to them:

> *"When you make the two into one, and when you make the inside like the outside and the outside like the inside and the above like the below – that is, to make the male and the female into a single one, so that the male will not be male and the female will not be female – and when you make eyes instead of an eye and a hand instead of a hand and a foot instead of a foot, an image instead of an image, then you will enter [the kingdom]."*
>
> -Gospel of Thomas: 22

Here, Christ clearly indicates again that the world of duality has to be transcended in order for us to enter the kingdom and become one with all existence and nonexistence. We can see that unless we melt the ego into the self and the two become one working as a single unit, we cannot enter the kingdom, which means we will not recognize our own divinity and therefore never can feel the unity with the All. The ego is the devil in disguise and our hearts can only reveal God when the ego has given up all control, all power and surrender to God.

> *In the multiplicity of beings there is diversity, dissimilarity and difference. But in God, who is in an absolute sense one and alone, there is only identity, simplicity and similarity. It is therefore not safe to devote oneself to the contemplation of God before one has advanced beyond the multiplicity of beings. Moses showed this when he pitched the tent of his mind outside the camp (cf. Exod. 33:7) and then conversed with God. For it is dangerous to attempt to utter the inexpressible by means of the spoken word, for the spoken word*

*involves duality or more than duality. The surest way is to
contemplate pure being silently in the soul alone, because
pure being is established in undivided unity and not among
the multiplicity of things.*

-St Maximos the Confessor

Saint Maximos the Confessor here points out beautifully how we
have to overcome the world of duality and only after this is done
can we establish ourselves in the awareness of being free from
the intellect and words, which are always in duality and always
separate, while God is undivided unity among the multiplicity of
things.

In Tibetan Buddhism, Tantra/Vajrayana, the 'male' and 'female'
terms, symbolize the bliss/bodhicitta (male) and emptiness/
wisdom (female). They are thus symbolic of the union of the ultimate nature of reality and mind. Visualizations of deities in union
embody the actual nature of ultimate reality and mind, and so
they are continually present in all beings inseparably. The practice of tantra is to transcend the world of duality of the two into
one.

In the Buddhist tradition, it is clearly stated in all the teachings that before one gets to the state of Buddhahood, one has to
transcendent the dualistic mind. Here Longchenpa, a realized
Buddhist master, writes:

*This is the primordial state, The one and single nature: The
dharmakaya (The body of the absolute reality, God) where
the apprehending subject And the apprehended object is not
found. And where an unstained luminosity Arises like the
essence of the sun. No center does it have, no limit: Blissful,
clear, and free from thought.*

-Longchenpa

There is physical duality per se, but also psychological duality. Psychological duality needs to be understood and overcome and that is not an easy task as long as we work from a center – the *me* – with all its mischief. That center is the core of all troubles and the root of all ignorance.

Adi Shankara explains also in *Atmabodha*:

> *"It is only because of ignorance that the Self appears to be finite and brought down to 'name and form'. When ignorance is destroyed, the non-dual Self, which does not admit any multiplicity whatsoever, truly reveals Itself by Itself, its true nature being non-dual, just as the sun when clouds are removed".*

> -Adi Shankara

Shankara stated that when the true self is known, not merely subjected to *me* and *mine*, then the true reality reveals itself and the world of duality disappears. Now the person is free of the prison the ego created and God can reveal his glory and manifest through that person.

Here another explanation from *Dasbodh*:

> *Without proper investigation, many people say that the soul of man and the soul of woman are different. However, the Self of all is only one. This subtle secret must be experientially understood. The distinction appears because of the gross forms, but in subtle experience, everything is understood to be one. This definitely must be experienced to be understood. It has never happened that procreation can take place from one woman enjoying sex with another woman. Thus, a woman inwardly has the longing for a man. Outwardly the nature of a relationship is of a man with a woman, but the subtle relationship is only of the Self with itself.*

The desire in a man is itself the female principle. Like this Prakriti is present in Purusha. However, it is in the female principle (Prakriti) that the male principle (Purusha) becomes manifest. Thus, it is correctly said that the male and female principles are one. By looking to the gross body as a reference, see the universe and gain an experiential understanding of the universe. If you do not understand, then gain understanding through repeated explanation and investigation. The original desire for duality is the Primal Illusion itself. From there the entire world becomes manifest. Therefore, see how both the Primal Illusion and the world have appeared. Here the large task of clarification has been completed. The doubts of the listeners have been removed, and the nature of the male (Purusha) and female (Prakriti) principles have been explained."

-St Shri Samartha Ramdas

We have to understand that this world of duality exists because we identified ourselves as the ego, and this ego is the most cunning person in existence and will do everything in its power to keep us in its control, therefore forever keeping us in ignorance. But without duality we also could not realize our true nature. It is evident then, that the desire for duality is the primal illusion, but whose desire is it? We can say it is the self, desiring to experience itself in a multitude of forms and this is how creation may have started.

Jiddu Krishnamurti in *Reflection of the Self*, is asking each of us to discover for ourselves how thought and time are sustaining the ego. Here is a script from one of his talks.

Thought and time are always together.
So, one of the factors of the why human beings are fragmented, is thought. Please, give your attention to this. And also, one of the factors is time. So, time. Time is the past, the present and the future. Right? Time, that is the past:

all my memories, all the memories, experiences, knowledge, all that human beings have achieved which remains in the brain as memory, which is the past. Right? That is simple. That past is operating now in the present. Right? Is that simple, clear? The past – all the memories, all the knowledge, all the experience, the tendencies and so on – the background.

And that background is operating now. So, you are the past. And the future is what you are now, perhaps modified, but the future is the past, modified. Right? See this, please understand this. And so, the past modified in the present is the future. Your tradition as a cultural country for the last three to five thousand years, this vast accumulation of knowledge, culture, all the things human beings have been struggling, enquiring, having a dialogue, all that is splashed in the present, because the economic conditions demand, and past is broken up, modified and is going to be the future. Right? This is a fact. So, the past modifying itself in the present is the future. Right? So, in the present if there is no radical change, tomorrow will be the same as you are today. So, the future is now. I wonder if you understand this. You understand this? The future, not the future of acquiring knowledge, but the psychological future, that the psyche, 'the me', the self, is the past, memory, and that memory modifies itself now and goes on. So, the future and the past are in the present. So, all time – the past, present – is contained in the now. Right, sir? It's not complicated, please. It is logical.

-Jiddu Krishnamurti

Krishnamurti's talks explain, in a simple way, that thought and time go hand in hand, and they are always limited. The sacred, the divine, is beyond time and space. Whatever is infinite, limitless, is beyond thought and time, therefore never bound by anything and can never be understood by that which is limited.

Albert Einstein sustains Krishnamurti's statement:

Time does not exist – we invented it. Time is what the clock says. The distinction between the past, present and future is only a stubbornly persistent illusion.

-Albert Einstein

All sages from all traditions have exposed this truth. Krishnamurti, as Buddha, has invited us to find out for ourselves and deeply enquire into the nature of the mind. Even Christ, as stated earlier, indicated that one has to have knowledge of the self in order to come to the Father. Ignorance veils and Love unveils. Everyone has to find their own way to reality. The way to truth is a pathless land. There is no specific method or idea to get you there because there is nowhere to get to and nothing to be achieved.

Also, Christ says that time is a deterrent into seeing the truth:

The disciples said to Jesus: "Tell us how our end will be."
Jesus said: "Have you already discovered the beginning that you are now asking about the end? For where the beginning is, there the end will be too.
Blessed is he who will stand at the beginning. And he will know the end, and he will not taste death."

-Gospel of Thomas: 22

Christ is saying here that we must stay with the present moment for life, truth, intelligence is to be found only in the present moment: where the beginning is so is the end, which means that time is not. So as long as we cannot live in the moment, we will create duality. Also, he goes on in saying that one who can stay in the present moment and surrender fully to it will not taste death for death is in time and space, but God is beyond. If we really surrender fully, worries, pettiness; if we let go of identification with the body, we become one with God where there is no death for what is then prone to death? If identification with the body and ego is gone, there is nothing left to die. The surrender itself is the death, and therefore we have to die every moment when we realize we are working from ego, and that is the denying of oneself as all masters have pointed out.

Ramana Maharshi, an Indian realized master, points out that the first thought to arise is the *I* thought and from the *I* all other thoughts arise. When we understand and find the source from where the *I* arises, then we understand that the nature of thought is limited, divisible and finite, and this thought can never comprehend the Infinite which is beyond space and time. One who has understood stops all searching, all seeking, for they realize that the mind and thought can never touch truth, the one sacred reality. Thought can create space in the mind, but that space is still limited. It is not real freedom because it is limited by thought, which is in time and comes with its own boundaries.

The Amritabindu Upanishad states:

> *The highest state is beyond reach of thought, For it lies beyond all duality.*
>
> -Amritabindu Upanishad

The above Upanishad says that the highest state of consciousness is beyond duality, beyond thought, beyond everything that is finite. Ramakrishna also points out how we are caught in the dualistic view of the world and how we also create our own states of heaven and hell. He states that the goal of all religions is to dehypnotize the soul that is under a veil of illusion created by our own ignorance.

The Immortal becomes a victim of birth and death. The Changeless undergoes change. The sinless Pure Soul, hypnotized by Its own māyā (illusion), experiences the joys of heaven and the pains of hell. But these experiences based on the duality of the subject-object relationship are unreal. Even the vision of a Personal God is, ultimately speaking, as illusory as the experience of any other object. Man attains his liberation, therefore, by piercing the veil of māyā and rediscovering his total identity with Brahman. Knowing himself to be one with the Universal Spirit, he realizes ineffable Peace. Only then does he go beyond the fiction of birth and death; only then does he become immortal. And this is the ultimate goal of all religions – to dehypnotize the soul now hypnotized by its own ignorance.

-Sri Ramakrishna

Many humans have searched and wanted to comprehend the truth but have stumbled and remain within the field of thought and very few have gone beyond. Everyone looking for truth wants to have spiritual experience, not knowing that experience, no matter how beautiful and uplifting it may be, is still in the field of thought and time, and therefore limited.

The reason is that the ego is cunning and smart and always sustains itself by thought. Most of us are compulsive thinkers and can never keep for a moment without thinking, without being bored to bits. Today, if you notice, every human being is craving information, which is easily accessed with the advent of the internet.

Yes, technologies are useful but how one uses the technologies is another question. They can be used for good or evil, the same as a knife can cut bread or someone's throat. If used in selfish ways, one will be more attached to the world and immersed in duality, always rising to pleasure and pain, therefore never at peace and always suffering.

Thought can only exist in duality because it is divisible and always creates conflict and suffering. Thought comes from the past, changes somehow in the present and then projects itself into the future, thus always being sustained by time. This is why we can never comprehend reality as it is by thought but can only see reality as projected, depending on our memories and the conditions we are attached to. True understanding can never occur in time. It is instant and deals only with what it is, with the facts. It is pure intelligence not touched by thought. Jesus expresses this nicely in the next teaching.

> *Know what is in front of you, and what is hidden from you will be disclosed to you.*
>
> -Gospel of Thomas: 5

Here, Christ indicates we should look without any judgement, staying in the moment, observing and listening. In that way, we will recognize the truth. In that moment duality does not exist, therefore the self as reality remains without the ego, the me, the knower, the analyzer, the observer, interfering. In the space of true insight, the me does not arise anymore.

In the *Bhagavad Gita*, Krishna also tells Arjuna that the world of duality has to vanish psychologically in order for one to be free.

> *Just as, in this body, the Self passes through childhood, youth, and old age, so after death it passes to another body. Physical sensations – cold and heat, pleasure and pain – are transient: they come and go; so, bear them patiently, Arjuna. Only the man who is unmoved by any sensations, the wise man indifferent to pleasure, to pain, is fit for becoming deathless. Nonbeing can never be, being can never not be. Both these statements are obvious to those who have seen the truth.*
>
> -Lord Krishna

So, the psychological world of duality exists because of our identification with the ego, which, as we have seen, is sustained by thought. The question then arises how we can live without thinking. Thinking in everyday life is a necessity but that thinking has to come naturally and spontaneously without the ego, which is the observer, the analyzer with all its intricacies and judgements. We then will be able to act in the right way, in an unselfish way, then seeing and acting becomes one. We have talked about the world of duality because here we suffer when we pursue pleasure, which is always accompanied by pain.

In the Tejobindu Upanishad, it is said:

> *Brahman cannot be realized by those who are subject to greed, fear, and anger. Brahman cannot be realized by those who are subject to the pride of name and fame or to the vanity of scholarship. Brahman cannot be realized by those who are enmeshed in life's duality. But to all those who pierce this duality, whose hearts are given to the Lord of Love, He gives himself through his infinite grace.*

-Tejobindu Upanishad

The above states that unless we are free from the five poisons and free of the ego that covers the self, we cannot win the grace of the Lord of Love that reveals itself through the self. Only when we pierce the dualistic life can we be free. Then the benediction of love will come upon the one who has pierced through the dualistic view.

The next statement uses the story of a thorn: to get a thorn out one uses another and when the job is done both are disposed of. Saint Sri Ramdas uses the correct imagination of duality to get rid of incorrect imagination and once the job is done, correct imagination is dissolved along with duality.

Through continuous contemplation on one's identity as one's Self Nature, the thought of duality dissolves, and one gains the conviction of the knowledge of non-duality, which is what is called correct imagination. That which imagines non-duality is considered correct imagination, and that which imagines duality is considered incorrect imagination.

The incorrect imagination is what is commonly called tainted or polluted imagination. The meaning of saying that there is something that is considered correct imagination is that it leads to the firm conviction of non-duality, while that which is called incorrect imagination is said to be polluted in the sense that it imagines duality. When the imagination of non-duality is utilized, it shines, and at that moment, duality is eliminated. When duality disappears, the incorrect imagination vanishes along with it. The wise understand that imagination is removed with imagination like this. When the incorrect imagination is gone, afterwards only the correct type of imagination remains. With the correct type of imagination, one imagines one's Self Form. When imagining one's Self Form, one becomes one with it, and the correct imagination falls off too.

-St Shri Samartha Ramdas

In duality we always are subject to suffering, always in the cycle of birth and death and therefore the saints and sages have given many teachings on the subject. Next, we should look at suffering that is caused by a view of duality in the first place.

CHAPTER 8

SUFFERING

We all have suffered – one way or another – in our lifetimes. Some have managed to come out stronger because of it; some have fallen into deeper suffering and never got out. Only a few have gone beyond all suffering like the great masters, rishis, and yogis from all traditions: Buddha, Christ and so on. The masters are not restricted to only religion traditions or yogis; they can be from all walks of life, like Nisagarada Maharaj and many others. Wherever you look in our daily life, you can see suffering in different forms like physical pain, chronic pain, anxiety, depression, boredom, problems in relationships, work, etc.

One important question arises, is suffering restricted to an individual or is it common to all? If we look carefully and observe, we discover that we all encounter suffering in one form or another almost daily – some more, some less – but the fact is that suffering is part of our daily life and sometimes we are affected indirectly by other people's suffering. We can say it is common to all. Suffering is of two kinds – physical and psychological; one is to do with our bodies and one with our minds. Either one can influence the other.

For example, if we have physical pain, the mind is also disturbed and if we have mental anguish that also will affect the body even if we are not aware of it; any kind of mental suffering will affect the body in some way. We can then see that suffering is really of one kind, is it not? It can manifest through the body or the mind, depending on the conditions and circumstances that arise. These conditions are sometime obvious and sometime are hidden in our psyche. Many people go to psychologists or psychiatrists to help cure their minds of different problems. We can see that all suffering is generated by our own minds, regardless of what the cause is. An accident, for example, can be caused by us through inattention or by somebody else's inattention but it is still caused by the mind of one individual not being attentive. If someone wanted to hurt us, it still is the mind that will cause the suffering.

Suffering therefore, regardless of the avenue by which it comes to us, is still caused by the mind and lives in the mind also. In order to understand suffering and to overcome all suffering, we must investigate how suffering comes about and how it is produced by the mind. In any way we look at suffering we can see clearly that it is caused by our mind and how the mind perceives reality depending on the level of our conditioning and our reactions to what we encounter. Suffering therefore is not mine or yours; it is an energy in movement touching all people who cannot grasp true reality and are thus maintaining that movement of suffering.

When one suffers, everyone in connection with that person will be affected more or less. The suffering is then an energy like all matter. As we know from physics, all matter is energy; light and sound vibrating at different frequencies giving rise to matter. If we observe and pay attention to suffering and enquire, where does it arises from, we will find that it arises in the mind.

Let us look at an accident that resulted in a broken hand. Of course, physical pain will be there but that physical pain should not be transformed into mental suffering by the mind, by thinking about the incident, and bringing all sorts of blame to others or to oneself, like I will lose my job, I will not have money, oh this idiot did this or that, nobody is there to help me and so on; the usual chatter that goes on in our minds. This kind of suffering produced by the ego is not healthy for the body or the mind. An awakened person in touch with reality is not affected by anything. Even if pain is there, he can endure it easily because there is no chatter in the mind and the energies are not dissipated therefore healing can take place. Someone unmoved by the ups and downs of life can absolutely stay with what is in the present moment. Our brains consume 20% of our energy daily – some more, some less, depending on how much thinking occurs – but that is the average. Obsessive thinkers would go maybe up to 40%, meaning other processes and functions in the body will lack energy. Why is there so much cancer in the world? It is because of mental stress and our lifestyle.

When we sleep poorly, the body does not have time to mend properly and if we continue to lose energy we will be affected in the long run. This is why in this yuga (era), the life of a human is only around 72 years, where in the past yugas (era), human life, as mentioned in the Bible and Vedas was much longer. In the future, human life will get longer and longer because of advancements in medicine and technologies and also because of our opening of consciousness into reality.

What stops our bodies from healing is the ego. Our minds chatter for hours every day – inner and outer chatter being the same – not allowing healing to take effect through the mind, for the mind is taken by the ego which then is creating all the chattering and conflicts. We are all related in this field of consciousness for what one does affects others and vice versa. If we are observant, we can recognize that the ego is the most destructive element on earth when we are under its control in any shape or form. We can see that all suffering is attributed to it. Also, we have to realize that as long as we pursue our desires, we will always suffer because plea-sure is always accompanied by pain. We mention here our desires for it is the selfish desires that create all conflict and misery. In order for us to have so much, another has to have so little.

Imagine a world where we do not pursue any selfish desires, and everyone pursues only the common desire for everyone to be happy. It will only happen when the ego takes its designated place, being just a tool to help us function on the practical level and be totally at rest on the psychological level. We can see that suffering comes, as Buddha has stated, because we desire and therefore get attached to the pleasures the desires have to offer. Through desire we pursue pleasure and as we have seen before, we are then thrown into the world of duality where we bounce endlessly like a ball between pleasure and pain. There is nothing wrong with desire, but to be attached to any desire is a problem because the stronger the attachment is, the more we will be trying to hold on to the particular desire, trying to maintain and sustain that desire, thereby doing all kinds of mischief.

Everyone wants to be happy and as a result, in our ignorance, we pursue happiness through the avenues of pleasure. These will always bring pain, for the two can never be separated yet continuing trying to separate them causes us much grief. Fear arises also, and the greatest for most of us is the fear of death – of becoming nothing or perishing into the unknown. This is mostly deeply rooted fear and if this fear is understood and overcome, we are liberated in an instant from all suffering and pain. This fear will exist as long as we are slaves to the ego and identify with the body and all the ideas and concepts fabricated around it. All fears are illusions; they are our inability to comprehend reality. In the state of pure bliss, all fears vanish just as the clouds disappear on a clear day with blue sky. All sages and other awakened beings have told us that the cause of suffering is desire.

Christ states:

> *When you know yourselves, then you will be known, and you will understand that you are children of the living Father. But if you do not know yourselves, then you live in poverty, and you are the poverty."*

-Gospel of Thomas: 3

Here, Christ tells us that unless we find our own reality and are only looking to fulfill our desires we will always live with suffering and become one with that energy of suffering, never free of it. The main cause of desire is the identification of our body with ideas, concepts and the many attachments we have to objects, people, places and ideas. This identification has been deeply rooted in the mind for millennia. This means it is very difficult to uproot it, thus only a few people in a generation can do it. The road to truth is narrow; it is like walking on a razor edge and only few will have the courage to travel on it.

> *Enter through the narrow gate. For wide is the gate and broad is the road that leads to destruction, and many enter through it. But small is the gate and narrow the road that leads to life, and only a few find it.*

-Matthew 7:13–14

We humans create all the havoc in the world through our own ignorance and our inability to realize that the cause of all destruction and suffering is us trying to change the world and control everything for our own selfish ends. Patriotism, cultures, ideas, and concepts about life mean that politics and greed in the society which we ourselves create, contribute every day to the suffering of all human beings. Western societies – even those that may look to be in a working order, clean and organized – are rotten from the inside, controlled by ignorance and avarice, and this is not hard to see if we have the eyes to see it.

One does not change society from outside for that is little more than a sugar coating. Unless every individual realizes his own divinity the world – even though it may appear to be changing for the better – will not change; it will always be a pattern of thought, of destruction and suffering at the individual level and also at the world level. The change has to come from within, for that is where the kingdom of heaven is and when a greater number of people realize this truth fully, then a true revolution will happen. The purpose of every individual is to realize his or her divinity for we all have the Buddha's nature in ourselves; we are all the children of the living Father. Everything and everyone have to return to the root of all existence which is God, Love, Life, Intelligence and Truth (whatever you want to label it for it cannot be labelled). In that realization, change is the true revolution that comes from us with its own laws and order directed by Love. How can one live fully in Love with all beings in the middle of the wolves and sharks of the world? This is where the inner teachings of our awakened masters come to give us guidance on how to live with love for all. The ego interferes with all our efforts to find our own reality and will do all in its power to keep us away from it.

Here, Jesus Christ stated:

But seek ye first the kingdom of God, and his righteousness; and all these things shall be added unto you.

-Matthew 6:33

Here, Christ is inviting us to find our true reality and he has pointed out to us that the kingdom of heaven is within us. We have to find this reality and when we find it, all desires are fulfilled and whatever we need will be provided. When we live in that reality, we become one with everything and in that reality we will not have any desires for we will have everything within.

This is not easy for us to understand, even at the intellectual level, and it is a mighty task to grasp it with all our being. It can only be lived when the mind gives up all seeking and we have understood its limits. At that point, we surrender with full faith to the unknown and the unknown will become the known revealed in its fullness of love.

All wars from time immemorial have as their cause greed for power or control over others. They may be based on religion, greed for land in order to have a better position or an interest in world resources, but whatever the cause, someone always wants to be better, to have more or dominate through any means and be in control. Wars – however noble or moral they may seem – always breathe destruction for the invaders and for the ones who are invaded. There are no winners, only losers. Everyone is in a state of conflict – a physical conflict and a psychological one. Conflicts between individuals, families or nations are still conflicts created by our ignorance. It does not matter about the complexity of it, it is still a conflict. Conflicts exist because of our inability to comprehend our true reality. How conflicts arise in us and how we struggle with them in our lives are questions we need to answer. Circumstances and conditions in life cannot be fully controlled but we do control how we react to what appears and disappears. That control is dictated by our state of mind, by our conditioning, and when there is no conditioning at all, the right reaction will arise and intelligence operates with the help of the self in total awareness.

All conflicts arise in the mind because of our inability to see what is in front of us without judging, comparing or analyzing according to what we know. As soon as judgements come into being, we stop seeing things in their reality for we want to transform the situation or things according to our expectations and what we expect is only what we know, what we are familiar with or conditioned to by the past. All memories are a dead thing. If situations or things do not suit our conditioning, we are in a state of conflict between what it is and what we would like to be. But if we accept fully and stay with what it is, seeing only what is, there is a possibility for a solution to present itself that can free us of conflict and therefore make way for peace.

My son is in school, I expect him to do well and excel, and if he does not live up to that expectation, conflict arises between what I expect and what is. We all function like this, whether as individuals, institutions, or nations.

We project with our mind our dreams in life and work towards what we have projected, and if what we project comes to fruition, we are happy; if not, we are sad and suffer. There is nothing wrong with projecting our lives, for that is creation, but it is totally wrong to get attached to the result of our actions and this is why we undergo suffering: our attachment to what we have projected is the problem.

We work with images, bring them from memory and try to change or shape them according to our desires in the present and then project them into the future. We have been conditioned to think and act in this way and this conditioning is what prevents us from seeing the real as it is. We meet a woman or man, and the attraction is there. We become close and form a relationship, in this relationship we project images about one another and these images prevent us from seeing each other for who we truly are. When these images do not fit reality, there is conflict and suffering when we cannot let go of them and accept reality as it is.

Attachment and identification are the main factors of our suffering. As children, we get attached to our toys. As we grow, we get attached to people, things and family. We get attached to all that gives us satisfaction and try to detach from everything that does not. This is, more or less, how we operate. We are always in a state of attachment and aversion and very rarely at peace. If things do not go our way, we become angry, anxious, or upset. Some of us identify very strongly with family, with a political party, with the nation, with a football club and so on. There is nothing wrong with supporting a team but it is very wrong to put down another. Why not enjoy a game and let the best team win and accept the result as it is, not as one wishes it to be? There can never be a winner unless there is also a loser. When both give their best, both should be equally respected, and both should be praised for their efforts.

We live today in a society that is corrupted by violence, greed, prejudice, and envy and few are not affected by these negative energies that we all sustain and create. When we are angry, is the anger a part of us or does it come as a gift we can discard if we do not like it? Anger cannot be discarded easily for the person who is angry is the anger itself. Anger does not come from outside; it comes from inside, from our inability to clearly see the truth.

For example, if someone at work calls us stupid for whatever reason, in that moment we can find adrenalin rising up to defend the image we have created about our self and the stronger the image, the stronger the response will be. If we cannot respond, we will form an image regarding the person who insulted us, then anger or hatred are born in our minds of that person because our ego was bruised. In this case, we are not different from hate or anger; we are one with it. All feelings and emotions are created in similar fashion.

This is why Buddha said,

What you think, you become.
What you feel, you attract.
What you imagine, you create.

-Buddha

An awakened person will see why the person is being insulting. Perhaps the other person really is stupid, or maybe the capacity and character of the individual making the statement is problematic. Whatever the reason, the awakened individual will not respond or will respond with wisdom which is part of love for only love can create peace. Nothing else can – no gun, no atomic bomb, no powerful armies, nothing apart from love. When every individual on this beautiful earth becomes aware of this fact, then and only then may suffering come to an end.

Suffering comes mostly when we have expectations, and these expectations are not met. We develop expectations according to our conditioning and how we work through images we created about our spouse, friends and so on. When the images we create do not match reality, we become disturbed. If a girlfriend or wife or a friend ends our relationship – whether by death or for any other reason – we may feel grief or a shock of loneliness if we very much depended on that person. This loneliness is a feeling that is an outcome of our inability to stay unattached. Most of us try to escape or avoid this loneliness in any way possible; few are the ones who can stay with it and understand its workings. Boredom is another face of loneliness.

Here we have touched on attachment and identification; let us go further into the subjects and see how they affect our lives.

CHAPTER 9

ATTACHMENT & IDENTIFICATION

Attachment is born from identification, and any form of identification – whether with country, religion, spouse, etc. – can be a cause of fear. Because of fear, we pursue security in identification, and fear is mostly the cause of our identification.

Attachment also is a feeling born out of fear, of being alone or lonely, especially for adults. In childhood or in nature, there is a natural process of needing to be cared for until we are able to function alone, and as this process unfolds, attachment naturally becomes detachment. Only humans have developed and distorted the process by using it in a selfish way, so to speak. Attachment to anything will bring pain and suffering when life (circumstances and conditions) forces us to detach from the object of attachment. The stronger the attachment, the stronger the pain. Attachment will lead to dependence on spouse, kids, house and so on. This dependence is then ingrained in our psyche and becomes our deep-rooted conditioning. Love is all inclusive and does not need attachment to anything or anyone, for once having touched that love, everyone and everything is inclusive in it.

When we feel lonely, we are prone to get attached to somebody or something that will give us satisfaction. Our conditioning creates in us the need to feel secure and therefore the feeling to depend on something or someone. We all work in this way, more or less. Some get attached to their spouse, children, cars and so on. Attachment comes because of the feeling of loneliness that then is covered by whatever we are attached to. Attachment always brings pain, as we know from looking at our own life and experiences and seeing how they play out. Love with no attachment is true Love. Where there is attachment, love cannot flow. It is restricted by the ego and therefore the individual is never happy except for brief and temporary periods of satisfaction.

Why do we feel lonely? Why are we always attached and identify ourselves with a group, with a person, with an idea, with an object? It is because in our inner life we are not at peace; we struggle then we tend to run away from the inner turmoil most of us live in. We actually live two lives – external and internal. For most of us, the internal life is personal, and we very rarely share it with anyone else. When we ourselves cannot deal with our internal life, we may share it in part with a friend, counsellor, psychologist and so on. Even married people do not always share their inner life fully. Few are those who do and very rare are the ones where the inner and outer are merged into one. In this state of equanimity – which is not equality – we can begin to start to grasp reality.

> *The Lord is called light, life, resurrection and truth (cf. John 8:12; 11:25; 14:6). He is light because He gives lucidity to the soul, dispels the darkness of ignorance, illumines the intellect so that it can grasp what is unutterable, and reveals mysteries perceptible only to the pure. He is life because He gives souls who love Him the activity proper to the divine*

realm. He is resurrection because He raises the intellect from its lethal attachment to material things and purifies it from all decay and mortality. He is truth because He gives to those found worthy an unchanging state of sanctity.

-St Maximos the Confessor

Saint Maximos the Confessor here describes how with faith we are helped by the Lord of Love in cutting all attachments to the material world and in doing so the mind becomes purified. Once that is done, we receive the mysteries of life seen only by the pure in mind and heart.

Also there exist others who, being attached to their own personal ideas and interpretations, Become fettered by these attachments and so do not perceive the Clear Light. The Śrāvakas and the Pratyekabuddhas are (mentally) obscured by their attachments to subject and object. The Mādhya-mikas are (mentally) obscured by their attachments to the extremes of the Two Truths. The practitioners of the Kriyā Tantra and the Yoga Tantra are (mentally) obscured by their attachments to sevā-sādhana practice. The practitioners of the Mahāyoga and the Anuyoga are (mentally) obscured by their attachments to Space and Awareness. And with respect to the real meaning of nonduality, since they divide these (Space and Awareness) into two, they fall into deviation. If these two do not become one without any duality, you will certainly not attain Buddhahood. In terms of your own mind, as is the case with everyone, Samsāra (state of wondering) and Nirvāna (Enlighten state) are inseparable. Nonetheless, because you persist in accepting and enduring attachments and aversions, you will continue to wander in Samsāra.

-Padmasambhava

The great master Padmasambhava explains that even the monks or practitioners of any yoga can fall into being attached to ideas and precepts, and points out that the fall can be prevented by being aware of any attachment or resistance within. Only in that way can one transmute the world of duality and become liberated by being aware of duality.

In these times, with the advance in technologies, we tend to share our inner life less and less. Most of the struggles are internal; the inner war is happening as the forces of good and evil fight for supremacy within us. This psychological war starts from childhood between the ideas, experiences and beliefs that have been imposed on us and what we then make out of them, as well as what we add through the experiences we have. This war will never end unless we can harmonize the inner and outer life into a single one and this is not an easy task.

This is where Christ stated:

> *If two make peace with each other in a single house, they will say to the mountain, "Move from here!" and it will move.*

-Gospel of Thomas: 48

Christ is telling us here that when the ego merges into the real self then the inner war is finished, and we can live in peace regardless of the circumstances and conditions that arise in life. In order for us to live in that state of equanimity of mind, we have to live only in the present moment. This does not mean we should erase our memories, but rather erase our attachments to the memory, for memory is still needed to function. We can look at memories, but we should not be affected by them.

The Munduka Upanishad states:

> *Like two golden birds perched on the self-same tree, Intimate friends, the ego and the Self Dwell in the same body. The former eats the sweet and sour fruits of the tree of life While the latter looks on in detachment. As long as we think we are the ego; we feel attached and fall into sorrow. But realize that you are the Self, the Lord Of life, and you will be freed from sorrow. When you realize that you are the Self, Supreme source of light, supreme source of love, you transcend the dualistic mind and enter into oneness.*

-Munduka Upanishad

Like Christ, the Upanishads point to the same truth, for when the realization of one true self arises, the ego relinquishes all power and the being enters into full union with all existence in the same way a glass of water becomes the ocean when poured into it, the same way anyone who realizes the self becomes one with all life and transmutes the world of dualistic view, seeing everything as one movement. In the Upanishads, the second bird is freely detached from the material world. It is the real self and when we realize it, all else is realized.

When the inner and outer life of an individual are merged into one, relating to another takes on a different meaning. For example, in a relationship, in love, everything is fine for a little while because both lovers are covering their loneliness with each other's so-called love, but after a while this so-called love fades and the inner struggles the individuals had prior start to resurface and run havoc. In many cases, people end up separating, then may search for another partner, often entering the same pattern of thought again and being bound by it. The goal could be to enter a relationship without any struggle – inner or outer – which, of course, does not mean that we do not have any problems in life but when we bring the inner and outer life into harmony, accepting whatever comes and goes, then we are at peace and can act the right way and thus flow with life, with nature, with love. Still, very few are in this position to accept if someone has dumped us, no matter the reason. For one who is free, there is no need to find a reason, it is what it is and then love can continue its play in the stream of life, the same as a river finds its way to the sea despite the interruptions it encounters, so the soul in the end will find its way home.

To be in that position, we have to be detached not only from people, things, places and so on but from the fruits of our actions. When we act without any selfish motive, we do not expect anything in return and therefore sorrow is left behind. Sorrow cannot be where love is. In the case of two individuals in an intimate relationship who have not awakened to reality but have the intention to help each other in life and stick with one another, loving one another, then the two can make it into oneness. In doing so they will scatter the feathers of illusion. The nearest love to true love is to be found in intimate relationships. Even the saints have found this in their previous lives before being born as saints.

This inner war, as we mentioned in previous chapters, was described in the Kurukshetra battle by Arjuna and in David's battle in the Bible. This is the inner war we fight in ourselves all the time until we realize that there is nothing to fight, and there is nothing to cry for; it is all a projection of our own mind. It is our beliefs, ideas and concepts that keep us from seeing reality as it is without the ego intervening. A child immersed in playing with a toy will feel some pain if that toy is taken away because of his attachment to the toy. If given a different toy, the same child can forget the pain and be happy playing with the new toy. As adults we still work more or less in the same way. We are attached to things that give us pleasure and detached from the ones which cause us pain. We memorize the pleasures and try to rid our memory of bad experiences that bring us pain. But the question arises here why we store memories. On the physical plane, memory is indeed necessary, as without it we cannot function in the world. Psychological memory is not needed but we are conditioned to store these memories too. Bringing up memories of bad or good experiences can let us relieve the hurt or be hurt by good memories that are no longer alive, but what we want to somehow relive; this is an illusion. Revisiting hurts that have been stored in memory is like living with death because memory is death. It is of the past and has no life in it. We can remember them but if we are attached to them, bringing painful memories into the present can cause us to experience that same pain again.

If we do not have any conditioning, attachments or beliefs, then memory has no effect on us. We recognize the memory but do not compare it or judge it; we do not overthink it or need to change what was, into what we would like to have happened, then the memory has no effect and therefore there is peace and love can flow.

> *Detachment is the mark of a perfect soul, whereas it is characteristic of an imperfect soul to be worn down with anxiety about material things. The perfect soul is called a 'lily among thorns' (S. of S. 2:2), meaning that it lives with detachment in the midst of those who are troubled by such anxiety. For in the Gospel the lily signifies the soul that is detached from worldly care: 'They do not toil or spin ... yet even Solomon in all his glory was not arrayed like one of them' (Matt. 6:28–29). But of those who devote much anxious thought to bodily things, it is said: 'All the life of the ungodly is spent in anxiety' (Job 15:20. LXX). It is indeed ungodly to spend one's whole life worrying about bodily things and to give.*

-St Diadochos of Photiki

Saint Diadochos of Photiki tells us that detachment from things is a necessity in order for us not to live with worries and anxieties. Here, of course, physical detachment has to be practiced for a while till we can get rid of all psychological attachments that cripple the mind with anxiety and depression. All attachments will strengthen the identification with body and mind.

> *Understand that the greatest fortune is to be inwardly detached, and that there is no greater misfortune than being attached to worldly things.*

-St Shri Samartha Ramdas

Here the master points out that inward detachment is the key to living a free life and if inward detachment is achieved then attachment to worldly things disappears on its own accord. We cannot just give away our spouse and kids and let them starve because we want to detach from things and places – that is running away from what is and is not the correct way. Yes, we may have to retreat for a bit in isolation to meditate, contemplate and observe how it is not, to be close to our loved ones, to everything we cherish in life, and to understand how one becomes attached and who is doing the detachment.

The basic identification that needs to be recognized is identification with the body and mind. Each of us identifies deeply with our body and our own ego – the *I* thought – because *I...* is prior to any other thought. Everybody uses the I thought. It is not a private thought, but it seems to be private because our basic identification with the body and mind. When we think of I, what we think about is in reality the ego, which is an accumulation of all our conditioning – memories, habits, belief systems – and a label as name. Ramana Maharshi, a great Indian saint, explained in his teachings that if we can get to the source of where the I thought arises and where it resides, we are transformed from a living being into a divine being: this is what he calls the awakened state. All humans are using I thought. Once the identification with the little personal I is broken, then the universal I which is everybody's birthright is revealed with no effort at all. It is there as it has always been, free from time and space, free from thought.

The 'I'-thought is said to be the sum total of all thoughts.
Enquire into the source of this 'I'-thought.
This investigation is Self Enquiry, and not pouring over
scriptural texts. When the Source is searched for, the 'I'
notion merges into that Source.
The 'I-thought' is only a semblance [or reflection] of the
Self. When that thought dissolves, there remains the undi-
luted primary Self, the Reality, Perfect and Full.
The result of self-enquiry is the cure for all sorrows. It is
the highest of all results. There is nothing greater than this.
Wonderful mystic powers may be had through other means.
Even when they are obtained, bliss can be had only through
Self Enquiry.

-Sri Ramana Maharshi

Here, Ramana Maharshi points out a way out of illusion and he states that when the ego dissolves, the true Self can be experienced and this can only come about by enquiring into our own reality.

The disciples said to Jesus, "Tell us how our end will be."
Jesus said, "Have you discovered, then, the beginning, that
you look for the end? For where the beginning is, there will
the end be."

-Gospel of Thomas: 18

Here, Christ makes a clear statement that if you bring time and space into the mind, there the I thought will be also, but if you stay with the present moment then the I thought will never arise. Buddha also has pointed out the same essential truth, as have the Upanishads, the Vedas and all other religious traditions. They have all pointed to this truth: self-knowledge will bring wisdom, and wisdom will cut through ignorance and therefore only the True-Self will remain, and this cannot be described, only lived.

Another statement by Christ:

> *A man said to him, "Tell my brothers to divide my father's possessions with me." He said to him, "O man, who has made me a divider?" He said to his disciples, "I am not a divider, am I?"*

-Gospel of Thomas: 72

Christ here clearly states that God is not a divider; he is one with oneness therefore he does not divide, for there is nothing to be divided when everything flows in oneness, and nothing is apart from it.

We then may ask how we can come to know ourselves, through what method we may be capable of doing so.

All methods, whatever we practice, will only help in harmonizing the energies of the body and mind but only through self-knowledge, one can become liberated from all bonds. Effort is needed till you get rid of what you are not. After that a state of effortless will remain, which is bliss, love, truth – whatever one may call it for it is nameless and responds to all names. It is eternity itself.

> *The true value of a human being can be found in the degree to which he has attained liberation from the ego-self. The ancients knew something, which we seem to have forgotten.*

-Albert Einstein

For us to cut all identification with our ego is not an easy task for the fear of annihilation will take over; the fear that I will be nothing is not easy to overcome. Here is where yoga and methods from all religious traditions such as meditation, prayer etc. have their place. We have to realize that we have been conditioned to identify and therefore attach to different objects or ideas that we think will give us security, but all attachments and identifications will only strengthen the ego, thereby keeping us in an illusory state of mind where there is always conflict and therefore suffering.

> *Stillness alone engenders knowledge of God, for it is of the greatest help even to the weakest and to those most subject to the passions. It enables them to live without distraction and to withdraw from human society, from the cares and encounters that darken the intellect. I mean not simply worldly cares but also those that appear insignificant and sinless. As St John Klimakos says, "A small hair will irritate the eye." And St Isaac says, "Do not think that avarice consists simply in the possession of silver or gold; it is present whenever our thought is attached to something." The lord Himself has said, "Where your treasure is, there will your heart be also" (Matt. 6:21) – either in divine or in worldly thoughts and concerns. For this reason, all should be detached and should devote themselves to God. If they live in the world, they can in this way attain at least some measure of understanding and spiritual knowledge.*
>
> -St Peter of Damascus

Saint Peter of Damascus points out also that detachment from worldly concerns is a must in order for us to be able to unveil our true reality as the identifications we have with all their attachments will give strength to the ego. As long as we work from an ego there will never be peace, harmony, and love on this earth, we only need to look around and see it for ourselves.

In the Sutra *The Way to the Beyond* (Parayanavagga), Ajita asked Buddha:

> *By what is the world enveloped? Why does it not become clear? What do you say is its defilement? What is the world's great fear?*
> *"The world is enveloped by ignorance, because of heedlessness and meanness it does not become clear. Hunger is its defilement, I say; suffering is the world's great fear."*
>
> -Buddha

Here, the Buddha states that ignorance smothers the world and because of it suffering is the greatest fear. It is not an easy task to live life with no attachments, with no fear, always accepting whatever life brings to you and whatever life takes from you. We tend to cling to the things that give us the most pleasure and satisfaction and push away anything else. The secret unveiled to us by the masters of old is to always accept what it is. If we cannot change it, we should enjoy life but always be ready for what else life has to offer – not only pleasures but pains too – and we will see a different state of mind come about, a mind not moved either by pleasure or pain. We also have to move from a state of mind that is always ready to receive in order to be happy in a state that is ready to give with no expectation of any reward. We now should look at fear and desire and how they affect our lives.

CHAPTER 10

FEAR & DESIRE

The greatest fear of all is the fear of Death; the fear that after we die there is nothing left of us as individuals. Fear has many branches – fear of darkness, fear of snakes and so on – but all fears go back to the root which is just *fear*. Because of this humanity has suffered a great deal. Leaders of the past and present have control, and many maintain their position by instilling fear in society by their own conditioning. Fear can be personal or communal depending on the origin. Fear is created by our own minds; it does not come from an external source. It is our inability to perceive reality that produces fear in us and the inability to see reality is due to our conditioning, which then puts us into a state of ignorance.

This conditioning is based on memory, then from experience. Knowledge arises and is saved in memory and the response of memory is thought. This process is explained over and over again in Jiddu Krishnamurti's talks. Then thought and time are the root of fear because of the past transmuted into the present by thought. One may be afraid that what happened yesterday may happen tomorrow, and thus thought in time produces fear. The thinker is the thought; they are not separate. As long as we believe the thinker to be separate, we live in the world of duality of thought and time. The thinker is the ego, is the observer, and the observed the experiencer and the experience. When we are angry, we are the anger itself. The anger is not coming from outside. The trigger may be there, but the anger is one with the one being angry. This is how fear arises.

> *When one realizes the Self, in whom All life is one, change-less, nameless, formless, then one fears no more. Until we realize the unity of life, we live in fear.*
>
> -The Upanishads

> *Dear disciple, Self-Knowledge is itself the attainment of contentment. With Self-Knowledge the bondage of the fear of worldly life is seen to be false at its root.*
>
> -St Shri Samartha Ramdas

The Upanishads and the master in *Dasbodh* point out that with the realization of the self, all worldly fears disappear. The light of self-knowledge dispels the darkness of desires and fears.

We may be prone here to look at any particular fear, but this does not solve fear itself. Fear is when peace and love are not. Fear is when one is insecure and when trying to find security in anything, fear arises on the spot. We can see that in insecurity – whatever the object or subject that triggers the insecurity may be – it does walk step by step alongside with fear. The question here arises: is there any permanent security in the world? Again, we just have to look into our own life, and we can see that permanent security is an illusion created by the mind. For example, think of a stellar disruption in the universe that could make earth disappear in the blink of an eye: where is security then? Is it in the country, army, religion, money, wife, husband and so on….

Countries have signed pacts and treaties with each other for centuries in order to feel secure, but can one find security in any document? It is just a piece of paper and can be ripped at any time. History has proven over and over again that peace accords can be broken. If we observe what is happening in the world today, we see for ourselves that there is no security in anything. Peace and security in the world happen only when all individuals find it in themselves. As Christ has said, the kingdom of heaven is within us, and thus peace can be found within, once found, the world is at peace and is perfect as it is.

Physical security is necessary for most people; only a few do not need any security, and these are the souls who have no desire for anything and therefore no fear. They live in a world driven by a universal will for their personal will has been extinguished.

This is a state that has existed in all of us from the beginning of time, but because of our fears, insecurities, desires etc., this state cannot be recognized and lived. So here we have introduced another player – desire – which, along with fear and insecurity, plays an important role in keeping us ignorant of the true reality. The basic desire is to be in our natural state, which, according to the Vedas, is *Sat-Chid-Ananda* (Truth, Consciousness, Bliss). Because of our ignorance and the lack of knowledge of who we really are, this basic desire cannot be easily fulfilled and in fact even this desire in the end has to be given up, for we are already the children of the living Father as Christ has stated, as has the Buddha and all masters of all traditions.

> *God, who created all nature with wisdom and secretly planted in each intelligent being knowledge of Himself as its first power, like a munificent Lord gave also to us men a natural desire and longing for Him, combining it in a natural way with the power of our intelligence. Using our intelligence, we struggle so as to learn with tranquility and without going astray how to realize this natural desire.*

Impelled by it we are led to search out the truth, wisdom and order manifest harmoniously in all creation, aspiring through them to attain Him by whose grace we received the desire.

-St Maximos the Confessor

Saint Maximus the Confessor points out the natural desire that exists in all created beings from the beginning of creation. This desire is the basic driving force in us all but because of our ignorance we do not recognize it and we therefore attach to lower desires according to our conditioning and impressions of the mind. Fear and desire therefore are like the two faces of the one coin.

How desire works in general works from memory, and it is born out of the five senses, sight, touch, taste, hearing and smell. One of these sensations arouses and, in many cases, is inflated by memory of past sensations and pleasures, then thought comes and makes it into a desire. After the fulfillment of the desire, the feeling of pleasure and relative happiness is there. With the arising of desire, the fear of not having the desire fulfilled arises then sorrow is born if the desire is not fulfilled.

The other afflictions, like greed, anger, jealousy and hate, are born when we try to pursue the desire at any cost. Most people who do not have the ability to fulfill their desires are in pain and suffer and will always look for a way to fulfill their desires. The only remedy to these afflictions of the mind is for us to stop getting attached to desires. This is not to say stop living, but to live in such a way that we accept what comes and goes and enjoy it without endlessly pursuing the fulfillment of desires we cannot fulfill. The one who can live and flow with life without any clinging or aversion has crossed the ocean of life.

In living this way, true humility, compassion, discipline and morality are born. Not the humility, compassion, discipline, morality that is cultivated by thought and thus limited to the conditioned mind or any societal norms, which is conditioning at the group level. We have this tendency of attachment due to our fears but also due to the fact that we are consciously or unconsciously seeking unity with all existence, any attachment becomes a hindrance to letting go. True surrender to what is, is the way of being free. If we can surrender with all our heart, then the grace of God and his love will be recognized in ourselves and all around.

Speaking of the senses, there are people who believe that reality is only what is tangible to the senses and can be proven and described by them. But as we have shown in earlier chapters, the senses are very limited and today we have the capacity in science to prove that subtle energies exist that our normal senses do not have the ability to perceive. If we are bound by the senses, we will never perceive reality and will be restricted to only seeing the transient reality, which is an illusory state of mind.

It is not an easy task to give up desire for the desire to give up all desire is still a desire, is it not? We might find it easier to live in the world by just accepting life without trying to distort it. For example, if a problem arises, solve it if possible; if not, accept what it is without resistance because resistance will give you pain and sorrow, as you will be in conflict between what is and what you would like it to be. We think we know what's best but accepting what it is, may turn out to be actually better even though at first glance it may not look that way. Everyone will encounter some situations that are not favorable when they arise but from every situation something good will come if one just has patience to wait and observe.

Every bad situation can turn into a good one and every good situation also has the potential to turn into a bad one. These two energies may seem different and opposing but to an awakened person they are the same. It is one energy in movement, and how we see it depends on our perception and the insight we have of life.

Life – which is Love, Truth, God, Intelligence – knows what an individual needs to encounter in life; what is good for us, how much and when. This intelligence operates from the beginning of time and this we call life. We may see a problem that human beings encounter, like war for example. Life sees it from a different perspective, holistically, not restricted by thought or judgement. For life war is just an energy in movement, in transformation, even though from our human perspective war seems horrific. If we could see life holistically, wars would be out of the question because we would act in the right way and never take up arms to kill each other, even if our life would be in danger, for we would know that life is a movement in continuous transformation and the physical body is just one form through which life moves and if the body is not, life still goes on in other forms in a subtle body.

This is why, in all traditions of yoga and in other religions, it is advised to give up attachment to desires for they are the one cause of all mischief in the world. This is not to say that we cannot enjoy life and what life has to offer. If we cannot eradicate desires in life, at least we should try to only have what we need without pursuing what we want. In general, a human being needs three things: food, clothes and shelter. If these needs are fulfilled, we can be content and happy. What we consider the "need" of anything else is not a need but a want, a desire. We have to understand that fear is illusory; it is our own creation and only we can get rid of it. Nobody can do it for us. We have seen how many troubles, war and suffering are born from fear. In the end, we come again to see how the ego creates fears, attachments and identifications in order to sustain itself.

So far, we have looked at how masters of all traditions point to ego; we explained how the ego operates and how we are being kept prisoners of our own doing. The question arises: Is there an entity that can save us, or is it still up to us to dispel ignorance which keeps us in darkness and therefore creates so much suffering for ourselves and the world around us?

Christ did not solve the problems of Lazarus even though he gave him a little longer to live in order to instill faith in the nonbelievers and doubters. Still, Lazarus had to die again for he was not absolved of death. The people Christ healed still had to face life and the problems in life, of course, after he touched them. They attained higher wisdom, and it might have been a little easier for them to grasp reality but the faith they had in him was the most important factor in the physical and spiritual changes that occurred in them. It is not Jesus the man who saves us; it is the Christ consciousness that is in us all – the pure energy of love, which if we touch, makes us becomes immortal and thus will not taste death as Christ has stated. Jesus was the body that carried the Christ consciousness.

But not those who are free from desire; they are free because all their desires have found fulfillment in the Self. They do not die like the others; but realizing Brahman, they merge in Brahman. So, it is said: When all the desires that surge in the heart Are renounced, the mortal becomes immortal. When all the knots that strangle the heart are loosened, the mortal becomes immortal, here in this very life.

-Brhadaranyaka Upanishads

The Brhadaranyaka Upanishad states that one who is desire free and only has one desire – to know the self – that one will not be reborn in suffering but will be reborn in love and bliss supreme and become one with the absolute reality God.

Do not love the world or the things in the world. If anyone loves the world, the love of the Father is not in him. For all that is in the world – the desires of the flesh and the desires of the eyes and pride of life is not from the Father but is from the world. And the world is passing away along with its desires, but whoever does the will of God abides forever.

-John 2:15–17

It is clearly said here that any desire for worldly things can become a trap and can transform into a habit, and any habit will keep the intellect in darkness. All desires and pride are not of God for all these stop love. God is only love, therefore if we have the intent to find God, we have to look at how desires and attachments imprison us and dropping our personal will so that we can align with the universal one is a must.

In *Surah Al-Jathiyah* 45:23, the prophet states:

> *Have you seen ‹O Prophet› those who have taken their own desires as their god? ‹And so› Allah left them to stray knowingly, sealed their hearing and hearts, and placed a cover on their sight. Who then can guide them after Allah? Will you ‹all› not then be mindful?*

> -Muhammad

Surah Al-Jathiyah also states the same truth: that whoever has desire as their guide cannot know reality, for they are under the veil of illusion.

From the *Dhammapada*, verse 39:

> *For one who is awake,*
> *Whose mind isn't overflowing [with greed],*
> *Whose heart isn't afflicted [with hatred]*
> *And who has abandoned both merit and demerit,*
> *Fear does not exist.*

> -Buddha

Buddha also states that fear goes along with desire; in desiring something there is always fear of not being able to have it or of losing it. Fear is where desire is, and desire is where fear is; they go hand in hand following each other.

If a man keeps dwelling on sense-objects, attachment to them arises; from attachment, desire flares up; from desire, anger is born.

-Lord Krishna

Krishna tells Arjuna that if we keep our attention on sense objects, attachments to them will surface and desire will be born out of that. Then anger also arises if the desires somehow cannot be fulfilled. This shows us how, from worldly attachments, all afflictions flare up like a domino effect.

We will talk about desires and attachments to them in the upcoming chapters because desire is the root of all suffering and all the masters have stated the same fact in their teaching as we have seen so far. Next, we should look at death, for this is the greatest fear, the greatest unknown, for most of us. Some people never ask the question what death is or if there is life after death.

CHAPTER 11

DEATH &
REINCARNATION

What is death? Most of us are reluctant to talk about death because we are afraid and not willing to face it. We live with death every second for our bodies are born and die. Every moment, millions of cells die and are born in us. Every moment our thinking and ideas change. Everything is a continuous transformation; nothing is eternal though we might like it to be. If we are willing to observe, we can see that each of us walks hand in hand with decay and death and this is the cycle of life. Christ clearly stated that those who understand his words will not taste death. Those who merge fully in the pure consciousness will not have to go through death for there is nothing to die, in someone with no attachments to anyone or anything who is therefore free. In that freedom is pure love, bliss, creation and as Christ has resurrected his body so is one who has overcome the world with all its desires and fears.

At the moment of death, we go through death and will go to a place of our own imagining – into a heaven of our own choosing depending on our level of spiritual growth – or to a hell also of our own making depending on our works while alive in a body.

Krishna gives a pointer of where we go after death.

> *THE BLESSED LORD SAID: Freedom is union with the deathless; the Self is the essence of all things; its creative power, called action, causes the whole world to be. About beings, know that they die; about gods, know the Supreme Person; and know that true worship is I myself, here, in this body. Whoever in his final moments thinks of me only, is sure to enter my state of being once his body is dead. Whatever the state of being that a man may focus upon at the end, when he leaves his body, to that state of being he will go.*
>
> -Lord Krishna

He clearly states that whatever the state of being one focuses on at the time of death, one will go to a similar place. If we are attached to our spouse, children and so on, we will go to a heaven where family members are there too. If we are attached to drugs or other addictions, we will go to a hell that emulates the pain of not having our drugs or of having too much. Everything is a possibility. We create our own heavens and hells depending on our purity of heart and mind at time of death.

> *Our spiritual nature, which had become dead through wickedness, is raised once more by Christ through the contemplation of all the ages of creation. And through the spiritual knowledge that He gives of Himself, the Father raises the soul which has died the death of Christ. And this is the meaning of Paul's statement: "If we have died with Christ, we believe that we shall also live with Him" (cf. 2 Tim. 2:11).*
>
> -Evagrius the Solitary

The real death is to die the death of Christ, for he never died, and so do we never die if our egos are no more. Then there is nothing to hang onto; there are no fears, no attachments, no ideas, no concepts. In the death of Christ there is only purity of mind and heart where only love is, and there we can live with him in the awareness of being.

This is why he stated:

> *Whoever discovers the interpretation of these sayings will not taste death.*
>
> -Gospel of Thomas: 1

Whoever understands and discovers their own self will not have to die. Death is just a part of life. There is never an ending, just a transformation from one form to another. Many people today do not believe in reincarnation because they have been conditioned to a contrary belief; others, even if they believe, do not grasp the process of it. Some believe in the soul and some not. The question arises: which is the entity that reincarnates if reincarnation exists?

Let's look at some of the sayings of great masters. Jesus says:

> *This heaven will pass away, and the (heaven) above it will pass away.*
>
> -Gospel of Thomas: 11

Here, Christ gives us a hint on reincarnation in showing that even heavens are born and die and so they are as us, included in this cycle of birth and death, unless we go beyond it, for God is beyond heaven and hell and is beyond our imagining.

*For all the Prophets and the Law prophesied until John.
And if you are willing to accept it, he is the Elijah who was
to come. Whoever has ears, let them hear.*

-Matthew 11:13–15

*And he will go on before the Lord, in the spirit and power
of Elijah, to turn the hearts of the parents to their children
and the disobedient to the wisdom of the righteous – to
make ready a people prepared for the Lord.*

-Luke 1:17

Here again, Christ is relating how John will go before the Lord
in the power of Elijah, which clearly indicates that the power of
Elijah is also the power of John, thus the same nature or spirit that
works through Elijah and John. This is why Christ was speaking
in parables: he always ends a statement with whoever *has ears, let
them hear.* Only one who hears such a statement with no judgement and with pure perception can understand what he was
saying.

*When harmed, insulted or persecuted by someone, do not
think of the present but wait for the future, and you will
find he has brought you much good, not only in this life but
also in the life to come.*

-St Mark the Ascetic

Saint Mark the Ascetic also refers to the life to come whereby
what we do also has a bearing on the next life. Christian scholars
have come with many interpretations and even John will not
have known at that time that he was Elijah for he was only the
messenger. Only Christ knew the past and present for he was one
with God and therefore all knowing. Our life is just like a fragment of all life and the purpose can actually never be seen from
only a fragment; it has to be seen wholly. When people die as
children or very young, they have not yet come to grasp deep

wisdom. Only an awakened master would know what is behind their fast departure from this plane of existence.

Krishna in the *The Bhagavad Gita* tells the same:

Those who are without faith in my teaching,
cannot attain me;
they endlessly return to this world,
shuttling from death to death.

Here, Krishna tells Arjuna that we are bound to come back in this world over and over again until we have faith and when that faith is complete, we will understand the teachings of the great masters and break free from the cycle of birth and death.

Buddha in one of his discourses said:

Oh, Bhikshu, every moment you are born, decay, and die.

-Buddha

If we look at our own selves, we observe this statement is true in every aspect of life. What reincarnation means is that we incarnate every moment while in the body and this is a process of life that does not end with the body: after the body is no more, the process of life continues if the individual clings to anything and has unfulfilled desires (tendencies, impressions, believes, desires) that will continue in consciousness till that content is exhausted and there is no need to be reborn or continue in the stream of life, for one is then whole and in union with life.

What need is there then to be reborn? When a person has attained the awakened state, he has no more desires for what desire will be left, when one is one with everything and is in everything. We can now see that whether we believe in a soul or not, the process of life is not interrupted by any belief we may have. The tendencies, imprints and desires of an individual will continue in the process of life regardless, if he reincarnates as human or any other being because these tendencies carry the momentum. They are the individual, the content of the consciousness we have at moment of death, and that is what constitutes the individual. Nevertheless, the identification of that individual dies with the body, much as in dreams where the body is asleep and resting, but mentally we still exist.

Another statement of Christ that gives us a clue is this:

> *Jesus said to them, "Truly, truly, I say to you, before Abraham was, I am."*

-John: 8:58

Here, Christ clearly stated that he existed before Abraham, telling us that not only is he omnipresent but also omniscient, for he knew all the previous forms in which he existed. Buddha also knew all his previous forms, as do all other enlightened masters coming after them. Absolute knowledge comes to the ones who have awakened fully from the ignorance that smothers our reality, as Buddha states.

Here we realize that we are *Sat-Chid-Ananda* (Existence, Consciousness or Knowledge, Bliss or Happiness), which is the immortal God who does not have a beginning or an end and is infinite. We can then see that thought does not touch God and can only exist in the cycle of life where everything is subject to birth, decay and death. As Einstein stated, nothing in the universe is lost; everything is in a continues transformation. The (Chid) Consciousness is pure awareness, intelligence where thought can operate but can never affect that intelligence, much as the sky is unaffected by the clouds.

We can then say that even if we believe in a personal soul united after enlightenment with God the universal, the individual soul loses its identification (personal self) if it had any, like the drop of water poured into the ocean, which is no longer a drop but becomes the ocean. But if we do not realize reality at the moment of death or before, the content of our consciousness will continue to exist and will incarnate in order to burn all desires, tendencies and so on. That content will incarnate in a suitable body in a suitable universe in order to burn that which one may call karma.

Here we go back to the Gospel of Thomas:

And he said, "Whoever discovers the interpretation of these sayings will not taste death."

-Gospel of Thomas: 1

Here, Christ does not say that things do not decay and die but rather that the one who understands his sayings will realize his own reality of being and will not taste death, for how can God die?

"It is I who am the light which is above them all. It is I who am all. From me did all come forth, and unto me did all extend. Split a piece of wood, and I am there. Lift up the stone, and you will find me there."

-Gospel of Thomas: 77

Here, Christ not only refers to himself but also to the father who is the only one God revered by all. He is clearly inviting us to find our own divinity, as do all the masters who walk the earth. Until we do so we will be in the cycle of life, of time, of becoming and of death.

Reincarnation is an inaccurate term; it would be better to call it *incarnation* for there is nothing that reincarnates. It is rather a continuum of a subtle form of the tendencies and desires – the content – of each individual, that we may call soul. When all content has been burned away, then one is one with all (God), no longer apart from everything and working from a little center but rather one with everything with no need of anything. The soul is not something apart from God, it is God but, in our ignorance, we think we are something apart and thus produce suffering for ourselves and others.

The union with God is what Patanjali in the yoga sutras called Nirvakalpa Samadhi where all the subtle tendency of the mind has been burnt. This is what in yoga is the final union with the absolute God.

Even science has looked into the possibility of reincarnation and studies have been done on it; of course, all this is prone to a lot of debate given that the nature of thought is always prone to conflict and each party sees reality from the comfort of their own conditioning.

Over a period of 40 years, psychiatrist Ian Stevenson from the University of Virginia, recorded case studies of young children who claimed to remember past lives. He published twelve books, including Twenty Cases Suggestive of Reincarnation a contribution to Ethology of birth marks and birth defects (a two-part monograph), European Cases of the Reincarnation Type, and Where Reincarnation and Biology Intersect.

-Science and Reincarnation: Wikipedia

There are also many references in the Upanishads, the Hindu scriptures, on reincarnation:

As a caterpillar, having come to the end of one blade of grass, draws itself together and reaches out for the next, so the Self, having come to the end of one life and shed all ignorance, gathers in its faculties and reaches out from the old body to a new.

-The Upanishads

In a similar vein:

> *All things whatsoever ye would that men should do to you,*
> *do ye even so to them.*

-Matthew 7:12

This is simply restating the Law that whatever you do to others will in turn be done to you. And since *"he that soweth to his flesh shall of the flesh reap,"* to incarnate therefore is an absolute necessity, to provide us the body in which to reap what we have sown, good or bad. Reincarnation only happens in illusion, as discussed before. At any given moment you are not the person who was here an hour ago. Millions of cells have died, and others were born, and thoughts and idea have changed the state of your mind. What we think of as ourselves is just a continuum; therefore, incarnation is a continuum.

We have seen some examples and could give more but that would take a book on its own so let's keep things simple and direct. Now if reincarnation exists – and it makes sense that it does but not in a way we think – then death is only a transformation from the gross to the subtle, but most humans are scared of death because for most of us death is the unknown. Each of us form an idea, a belief on death, corresponding to our conditioning. The Asian world believes in doing good in order to have a better life in the next one. Christians today are confused for with the advent of the internet, the church cannot hide the essential teachings of Christ. The Gnostics and even the Jews knew that reincarnation is a possibility, for in God's eyes everything is possible.

The idea of resurrection is right from Christian and Muslim perspectives, but we can also look at resurrection from a different perspective whereby resurrection means that there is no more death, and every human who has become one with God and found the kingdom of heaven within is resurrected, for the Lord has stated that the one will not taste death if one can align to the highest teaching of Christ: "Love you neighbor like your life and protect him like the apple of your eye." This Love is preached in all traditions and until we are full of that love, how can we expect to be resurrected if we go with a heart of steel?

Resurrection means an awakened being; the one who, as Buddha states, does not become anymore for when becoming has stopped, desires are no more, and the individual is merged in the universal pure consciousness Braham or Father. This is what Buddha calls Nirvana, Hindu call Moksha and Christian and Muslims call it one with the father or Allah.

We see here that if we understand the essential teachings of one religion with a real conviction, then we will comprehend all, and the most important factor is how wide is our heart and how open our mind to the Love of God. We should share this love with all, regardless of their beliefs or ideas, for these beliefs and ideas are the primordial factor in not allowing love to flow to our neighbor.

Real death occurs when one dies every moment of yesterday and therefore is then able to live in the present moment which is God, Love, Intelligence, whatever one may wish to call it.

If one touches divine love, one has transmuted from the world of duality and who then is there to be resurrected? Christ resurrected himself because he was one with God. He did it for us that we may believe in his teachings and follow him but how many can follow him? Sadly, very few. He even said, "Destroy this temple and I will rebuild it in three days (John 2:19).

So, we need to understand that nobody can do it for us, so we need to do it ourselves. Power is in us and if we surrender, that power will guide us towards liberation, for this is the final destination of all beings. There is no death for one who understands and has reached the highest wisdom and love. One who can recognize unity in all the diversity of forms is free of all troubles. We have been conditioned to look at death as something horrific and we have also been conditioned to avoid it, and when we come near it, not many of us can face it with Love. Instead, we are all bound to attachments – ideas, money, family – and we cannot let go and thus death becomes a horrific experience. But if we are free from all attachments without clinging or aversion, instilled in Love, we will never taste death, as the Lord and many masters have pointed out. The real death is to die every day of all attachments, thoughts of me and mine, and live in the present moment in the awareness of being where one being is in love with being.

Here we have touched on reincarnation and death, for if we grasp the wisdom imparted to us by the masters, we will touch reality and life becomes simpler. In this way, in realizing our true nature we gain our true freedom. All religions and traditions have preached the highest Love but in the present day, sadly, we see it not. This love comes from the fullness of joy, and it flows to all and through all and it does not ask for anything in return. God, love, life is not an authoritarian power as some religious institutions have expressed it. God does not rule by any power apart from Love. This love is all pervading and exists in everyone and everything. Next, we should look at what may happen after death. Note, I do not call it "after life" for life and love are eternal.

Chapter 12

AFTER DEATH

We call this chapter "After Death" because death and birth are just a beginning and an end, but life is infinite and eternal. It is Love and God absolute; it is form and formless.

The question now arises: what happens to us after we die? Where are we going? In a previous chapter, we have touched on reincarnation and death. We came to understand that death exists only in terms of matter, as the body, but we continue to exist in subtle form as the content of our consciousness and as long as we have content that content will go on until it has been extinguished. We could call the content the soul or atman. The moment the content is extinguished, the soul merges into the super soul (God) and becomes one with all. The process is the same if one believes in the existence of a soul or not; it does not make any difference actually.

In order for continuum to exist, it needs matter, and experience therefore needs to continue in some form depending on what the content contains. Dependent on the desires, tendencies, impressions from previous lives and so on, we may continue to exist in different forms. In the Upanishads, we find references to this continuum that we may call the wheel of life.

Well then, O Gautama, I shall tell thee this mystery, the old Brahman, and what happens to the Self, after reaching death. 'Some enter the womb in order to have a body, as organic beings, others go into inorganic matter, according to their work and according to their knowledge.

-Katha Upanishad

If a man could not understand it before the falling asunder of his body, then he has to take body again in the worlds of creation.

-Katha Upanishad

The wheel of life (Samsara) cycle of life given in the Hindu and Buddhist view (called the *Bhavachakra* in Sanskrit), represents the cycle of birth and rebirth and existence in samsara as is depicted by the six realms (worlds).

The outer wheel depicts a blind man or woman (representing ignorance); a monkey (consciousness); two men in a boat (mind and body); a house with six windows (the senses); an embracing couple (contact); an eye pierced by an arrow (sensation); a person drinking (thirst); a man gathering fruit (grasping); a couple making love (becoming); a woman giving birth (birth); and a man carrying a corpse (death). The Lord of Death controls the wheel, the same as in the Christian tradition. Lucifer is seen as the bad angel but if we contemplate a little more, we could also say that he is still a good angel with a job to keep us in the wheel of life. This is how Buddhists and Hindus see Lord Yama or Mara, respectively. Lord Mara or Yama was the one who tried to deflect Buddha from his awakening, offering him the world, same as Lucifer tried to pursue Christ.

These are the six realms depicted in Hindu and Buddhist perspectives.

The Gods Realm

The Realm of the Gods (Devas) sounds like a nice place to live, but even the Realm of the Gods isn't perfect. Those born in the Gods Realm live long and pleasure-filled lives. They have wealth and power and happiness. Because of their blessings, they do not recognize the truth of suffering. Their happiness is, in a way, a curse, because they have no motivation to seek liberation from the Wheel. Eventually, their happy lives end, and they must face rebirth in another, less happy, realm. This realm on earth depicts people who are wealthy and have all the pleasures of the world at their feet but still something is missing: they still have not awakened fully to the reality of who they are.

The Asuras Realm

Asuras are hyper-competitive and paranoid beings. They are driven by a desire to beat their competition – and everyone is competition. They have power and resources and sometimes accomplish good things. But, always, their first priority is getting to the top. We can think of powerful politicians or corporate leaders when we think of Asuras.

The Human Realm

Liberation from the Wheel is possible only from the Human Realm. The Human Realm is marked by questioning and curiosity. It is also a realm of passion; human beings (Manushyas) want to strive, consume, acquire, enjoy, explore. Here Dharma is openly available, yet only a few seek it. The rest become caught up in striving, consuming, acquiring, missing the opportunity.

The Animal Realm

Animal Beings (Tiryakas) are solid, regular, and predictable. They cling to what is familiar and are disinterested, even fearful, of anything unfamiliar and go through life seeking comfort and avoiding discomfort. The Animal Realm is marked by ignorance and complacency. Animal Beings may find contentment, but they easily become fearful when placed in a new situation. Naturally, they are bigoted and likely to remain so. At the same time, they are subject to oppression by other beings – animals do devour each other.

The Hungry Ghosts Realm

Hungry Ghosts (Pretas) are wasted creatures which have huge, empty stomachs, but their thin necks don't allow nourishment to pass. Food turns to fire and ash in their mouths, so they are constantly hungry. Greed and jealousy lead to rebirth as a Hungry Ghost. The Hungry Ghost Realm is often, but not always, depicted between the Asura Realm and the Hell Realm. It is thought the karma of their lives was not quite bad enough for a rebirth in the Hell Realm but not good enough for the Asura Realm. Psychologically, Hungry Ghosts are associated with addictions, compulsions and obsessions. People who have everything but always want more may be Hungry Ghosts.

The Hell Realm

The Hell Realm is marked by anger, terror and claustrophobia. It is depicted as a place partly of fire and partly of ice. In the fiery part of the realm, the hell beings (Narakas) are subjected to pain and torment; in the icy part, they are frozen. Interpreted psychologically, Hell Beings are recognized by their acute aggression. Fiery Hell Beings are angry, abusive and drive away anyone who would befriend or love them. Icy Hell Beings shove others away with their unfeeling coldness. Then, in the torment of their isolation, their aggression increasingly turns inward, and they become self-destructive.

Human beings fluctuate in these states of mind depending on their level of spiritual growth and actions performed. We have seen how Christ pointed out how even heavens come and go. From his statement, we can see that nothing is everlasting aside from the Father (God) and so we are in Narakas world when frustrated and in torment, in Pretas world when chronically frustrated, in a human world when in a state of equanimity, or even mindlessly in Devas world when deliriously happy, in Asuras world when furious and angry and in animal world when dumb. If we are observant, we will realize that at one stage or another in our lives, we have been more or less in each of these states of mind.

The wheel of life also depicts Buddha and a door that he points to as a way out of the cycle of existence, for all life is a cycle, from the time, the hours, the days, the cycle of planets and so on. An awakened being is one who has come out from this cycle, this state of mind.

The world and societies at large are also subject to these states. We can look at the seven chakras we discussed in the creation chapter or the seven churches. The goal is to reach the seventh state and, if reached, that is the door to liberation, the crown chakra on top of the head.

At the time of death, each individual, according to the actions performed and the level of spiritual understanding they have achieved, will be reborn as animal, plant, or human being again depending on what experiences they still have to go through in order to find their true reality. The end goal of all is the same but many see it in different ways. Some may see it as happiness, others as union with God. Regardless of our perception, this union with the absolute will happen for everyone in their own time.

Christ says:

> *This heaven will pass away, and the (heaven) above it will pass away.*

-Gospel of Thomas: 11

This saying is in accordance with Hindu and Buddhist thought whereby we create and sustain these states of mind. These states are but illusions and not a true reality but a platform from which awakening can happen. An awakened being is beyond any of these states and can see all these states in each being.

Krishna explains this in the *Bhagavad Gita* in the chapter "Absolute Freedom":

> *Closing the nine gates of the body, keeping the attention in the heart, drawing the breath to the forehead, with the mind absorbed, one-pointed, uttering the sacred Ôm, which itself is freedom, focused on me as you leave the body, you attain the ultimate goal. For men whose minds are forever focused on me, whose love has grown deep through meditation, I am easy to reach, Arjuna. Reaching me, these great souls attain supreme perfection and no longer are reborn in this fleeting world of sorrow and pain. All realms, up to the realm of Brahma, are subject to rebirth; but those who attain me, Arjuna, will never be reborn again.*

-Lord Krishna

Here, Krishna specifies that all states (realms) are subject to the cycle of existence apart from Brahma, the God state/realm. The human state is the foundation from which we can catapult ourselves into the God realm. Krishna also specifies one of the ways this can be achieved: when one is full of devotion and faith and has gained insight from meditation, has opened fully the heart to the love supreme, then they can find freedom in absolute love.

Buddha states that the human realm is very rare and is the only state where enlightenment can happen because it is the grosser of all other states and from here all other states can be experienced for oneself. Buddha has expressed in one of his talks how rare is to obtain a human form.

> *"Bhikkhus, suppose that this great Earth had become one mass of water, and a man would throw a yoke with a single hole upon it. An easterly stream would move it eastward. A westerly stream would move it westward; a northerly flow would move it northward. A southerly stream would move it southward. There was a blind turtle that would come to the surface once every hundred years. What do you think, bhikkhus, would that blind turtle, coming to the surface once every hundred years, insert its neck into that yoke with a single hole?"*
>
> *"It would be a rare occurrence, Bhante (Lord), that the blind turtle, coming to the surface once every hundred years, would insert its neck into that yoke with a single hole."*
>
> *"So too, bhikkhus, how extremely rare that one is born a human. You have this rare chance now, bhikkhus, to be not only born a human but be born while a Tathāgata has arisen in the world. While the Dhamma and Discipline proclaimed by the Tathāgata shines in the world."*
>
> -Buddha

Most of us are wasting our lives in the pursuit of happiness in this world but here we can only find the temporary and elusive happiness where the everlasting one is to be found here in this world but with the knowledge that is not of this world. What is stopping us really from getting to the everlasting happiness is our ego, as we seen in the preceding chapters. The five senses running after the pursuit of pleasures and therefore throwing us in the five poisons (ignorance, attachment, aversion, pride, envy). These energies run riot in the world producing all the mischief and stopping the flow of divine love in our hearts.

With the advent of the internet, we see all sorts of stories, some true some false, regarding people dying and then returning to the body, all have different experiences depending on the level of condition or culture they lived in. From all that information available, one can form a closer view in line with the Hindu and Buddhist views depicted in the wheel of life. All these heavens and hells are no more than our imaginations; because of this imagination we have actually projected this world as it is.

Most of us are wasting our lives in the pursuit of happiness in this world but we can only find temporary and elusive happiness. Meanwhile, the everlasting one is closer than we think but we are too scared to look within, to die of everything that we are not, to die of all our attachments, habits, imagining. Only when we die of all that can we say that we have died of ourselves and, in doing so, are allowing the Lord of Love to take over and live a life guided by the universal will.

At this point, we should look in detail at the five poisons and see how they affect our lives.

THE FIVE POISONS
(Ignorance, attachment, aversion, pride, envy)

In preceding chapters, we have touched a bit on the five poisons. They are important for they are at the root of all pain and suffering in the world. What makes these poisons arise in our minds? Who is responsible for their birth and death? I think if we are observant and aware we will clearly see that they are our own creation; we are giving birth to all these energies and not God, though some would like to blame God for all the suffering in the world. He is only Love, nothing else. He has nothing to do with the suffering we undergo. It is all due to our ignorance and we have to uproot it in order to touch his love.

THE FIVE POISONS

Poisons	Description	Alternate words used
Ignorance	Lack of discernment; not understanding the way things are	Confusion, bewilderment, delusion, illusion
Attachment	Attachment or desire for what we like	Desire, passion, greed
Aversion	Aversion to what we don't like, or to what prevents us from getting what we like	Anger, hatred
Pride	Having an inflated opinion of ourselves and a disrespectful attitude towards others	Arrogance, conceit
Envy	Being unable to bear the accomplishments or good fortune of others	Jealousy

God has provided us with the needed environment, with the intelligence and intellect to create our own reality, and if we observe, we have done a marvelous job regarding the technological realm, but we are lacking in our personal and spiritual realms. From time immemorial, we have had wars. The causes can be political, religious or expansional, but wars are still wars. And no matter how moral they may appear to their advocates, morality has nothing to do with love, intelligence and life, for it goes against the teachings and what the masters have taught us, to love and help each other. Even today the powerful want to enslave the weak. Whether economic or territorial, exploitation of the masses still exists, and it exists because as long as the five poisons are fed, we will still have conflicts in families and societies and the world at large. Special children are exploited more so now than in the past.

In order for humanity to exist in harmony, each individual has to extinguish these poisons for themselves. Firstly, we have to be aware and observe how we are conditioned to always have more and be better, to compete with others. Any competition creates conflict between individuals and society. In each of us, one of the poisons will be more prevalent than another. Some are greedier, others more jealous or angrier, but regardless, the poisons all arrive in us in similar ways. The way they get to us is through our ego, which always creates mischief and is responsible for sustaining and creating the five poisons depending on our individual desires and attachments.

For example, say we have a girlfriend and are passionately in love with her. The ego-self will produce jealousy, and we might think she is my girlfriend, and I want to possess her only for myself, for my own happiness, for my own satisfaction, therefore nobody should interfere with my happiness. If she talks with another or pays attention to another, I might become jealous or frustrated. This means we are in a state of jealousy produced by the ego and in doing so closing all the avenues where love can flow. If we are observant and look carefully, we see that our lives are not without judgement, we will see how these poisons and afflictions create havoc in our own lives.

When we are angry, we might wonder if anger is in us or if it comes from an external factor. It is obvious in us, created by our own inability to use our intelligence when our intelligence is hijacked by the desire to be better or have more. My anger is internal. We may also say that I am rightfully morally angry at someone who made me angry. Does that anger free me or, on the contrary, do I become a prisoner of it? As we saw earlier, the monk Shantideva, in the same way as Christ and all the masters, warned us about these afflictions of the mind. Christ warns us to guard our senses because through them the robbers will come in and steal our love and peace.

It is fair to say that these poisons are of our own doing and because we create them as illusions, when we realize this fact, they will disappear in the same way we created them, for they do not have any real existence on their own. Any emotions and feelings we may have are based on these poisons, stealing our love and peace of mind. This is why the ego must die, so to speak, and then the self can function in the world as God has ordained it and fulfill the will of the Father as Christ stated.

> *Gird your loins with great strength, so that the robbers will not find a way to get to you.*
>
> -Gospel of Thomas: 21

Above, Christ is telling us to be watchful for the five poisons can easily hijack our consciousness and make us act in a selfish way that is destructive towards ourselves and others. In his parables, Christ has revealed the union with the absolute as he mentions in the following.

> *Take my yoke upon you, and learn from me, for I am gentle and lowly in heart, and you will find rest for your souls. For my yoke is easy, and my burden is light.*
>
> -Matthew 11:29–30

By *yoke*, Christ means union: for my union with the father, take it up yourself for I am gentle, and I do not force anyone to do anything against their will, but if you take this union, whatever you need to go through in life you can easily then carry the burden, for it will be made light in the light of the father. Christ is inviting us to learn from his life, which was full of wisdom and love. Whatever he had to endure, he did it because of his union with the father, the energy we call God, Allah and many other names for that is the absolute supreme reality.

> *Therefore, my dear son, since through the grace of Christ you possess natural understanding, continue always to occupy your mind with such meditation. Do not let yourself be overcome by destructive forgetfulness or by the laziness which paralyses the intellect and turns it away from life; do not allow ignorance, the cause of all evils, to darken*

your thinking; do not be lured by the corrosive vice of negli-
gence; do not be seduced by sensual pleasure or defeated
by gluttony; do not let your intellect be taken prisoner by
lust through assenting to sexual thoughts, defiling yourself
inwardly; do not be overcome by the anger which causes you
to hate your brother and for some pathetic reason to inflict
and suffer pain, leading you to store up malicious thoughts
against your neighbor and to turn away from pure prayer.
Anger enslaves the intellect, and makes you regard your
brother with bestial cruelty; it fetters the conscience with
uncontrolled impulses of the flesh and surrenders you for
a time to be chastised by the evil spirits to whom you have
yielded.

-St Mark the Ascetic

Saint Mark the Ascetic here clearly describes the five poisons and points out ignorance as being the worst. All the teachings point out that we must overcome these afflictions of our minds and stop creating them by not identifying with the thoughts that pass through our minds. Buddha also stressed in his teachings that all our problems lie in our own minds, and, as the wind that brings in the clouds, they are also taken away by the same agency. So it is with all the problems that are created by us. It is we who can solve them with the clear light of wisdom.

These energies are not easy to get rid of unless we uproot them and in doing so put the ego in its place. This is where various spiritual practices can help us get rid of some of the accumu-lated unwelcome energies in our bodies and minds. The most potent spiritual practice is – as all masters have pointed out and acknowledged – the way of self-knowledge (the true knowledge of our own being).

By being free of clinging to anything whatsoever, you are purified of objects perceived externally. Objects being purified does not mean that you stop perceiving. It means not to hold and cling while being bright and empty. Like the example of reflections in a mirror, they appear but are empty in that there is nothing to grasp, and your perceptions are known as perceptions occurring to yourself. By means of the inner perceiving mind being purified, here is the instruction in liberating no clinging awareness in itself: No matter what occurs in your mind – the flow of thoughts, memories, or the five poisonous emotions – when you do not focus upon them, the movement vanishes by itself; thus, you are untainted by the faults of thinking.

-Padmasambhava

In the above, Padmasambhava points out how the emotions created by the five poisons are just mirages and do not have any real existence. If we are established in awareness with no focus on any thought or emotion, these will clear on their own accord. He does not say, not to perceive and withdraw our perception from objects; he only invites us not to perceive with attachment and thus be purified of everything we perceive. If we can live with that perception, we are on the right path towards liberation. Perception is the ability to listen without the filter of conditioning.

For when the soul has been overlaid by pernicious forget- fulness, by destructive laziness, and by ignorance, the mother and nurse of every vice, the afflicted intellect in its blindness is readily enchained by everything that is seen, thought or heard. For instance, when we see a beautiful woman, our intellect is at once wounded by sensual desire. Then we recall what we have seen, heard, or touched with impassioned pleasure in the past, and so our memory forms sinful images within us. These defile the intellect that is still impassioned and afflicted through the activity of the demons of unchastity. Then the flesh, too, if it is well fed, full of youthful spirit, or flabby, is easily roused to passion by such memories, and moved to lust; and it performs acts of uncleanness either in sleep or awake, even though it does not have intercourse physically with a woman. Although such a man is regarded by others as chaste, pure, and virgin, and may even have the reputation of being a saint, yet he is condemned as defiled, dissolute and adulterous by Him who sees into the secrets of men's hearts.

-St Mark the Ascetic

Saint Mark goes on and gives a natural example of how the mind plays with images and how, on seeing the beautiful image of a woman, the mind recollects the past pleasures and images and forms a new sensation, which then gives birth to a new desire for the woman seen, so the mind is defiled by trying to project new images and acting on them. But if we are mindful and vigilant, we can stop at the point where the beautiful woman is seen, recognize the beauty and leave it there. This way of living and thinking has not been taught to us in any school, therefore we do not know how to stop the mind from causing havoc in our lives and sending us along the road of suffering and misery.

Just as ignorance divides those who are deluded, so the presence of spiritual light draws together and unites those whom it enlightens. It makes them perfect and brings them back to what really exists; converting them from a multiplicity of opinions it unites their varied points of view – or, more accurately, their fantasies – into one simple, true and pure spiritual knowledge, and fills them with a single unifying light.

-St Maximos the Confessor

Saint Maximos the Confessor clearly states that ignorance is overcome by spiritual knowledge, which equals self-knowledge. When that is done, the light of the soul will be seen.

Therefore, the solitary ought to guard this Hock night and day, making sure that none of the lambs is caught by wild beasts or falls into the hands of thieves. Should this happen in some valley, he must at once snatch the creature from the mouth of the lion or the bear (Sam. 17:35). What does it mean for the lambs to be caught by wild beasts? It means that when we think about our brother we feed on hatred; when we think about a woman we are moved with shameful lust; when we think about gold and silver we are filled with greed; and likewise, when we think about gifts received from God, our mind is gorged with self-esteem. The same happens in the case of other intellections if they are seized by the passions.

-Evagrius the Solitary

Evagrius the Solitary explains how the passions that run through the senses give rise to the five poisons and when that happens, we are enslaved by these emotions and feelings, which make us act in foolish and selfish ways, giving strength to the ego in us and also in others. Passions are the satisfactions we derive from the senses and any thought directed towards any satisfaction will strengthen and feed the ego.

For if one associates with materially minded people involved in worldly affairs, one will certainly be affected by their way of life and will be subject to social pressures, to vain talk and every other kind of evil: anger, sorrow, passion for material things, fear of scandals. Do not get caught up in concern for your parents or affection for your relatives; on the contrary, avoid meeting them frequently, in case they rob you of the stillness you have in your cell and involve you in their own affairs. "Let the dead bury their dead," says the Lord; "but come, follow me" (cf. Matt. 8:22).

-Evagrius the Solitary

Evagrius here advises us to be vigilant with things of the world and people who can easily deflect us from the right path. He also advocates detachment even from families and loved ones because any attachment will stop love from flowing naturally.

Saying that oneself is "I" or "me," is ego. The sense that one is an individual is what is meant by ego. Ego is ignorance, which means having attachment to the sense of an independent "I." When attachment is given up, there is unity with That which is unattached. This is the authority of the attainment of That which is without imagination. When one does not know one's Self, it is called ignorance. When ignorance is removed by Self-Knowledge, one realizes oneself as Parabrahman. Understand that body-identification is not important in Parabrahman. There, the sense of "I" has no place.

-St Shri Samartha Ramdas

In *Dasbodh,* the teacher explains to the students that the biggest ignorance of all is identification with the body – the ego sense of "I"; of being an individual – and only by detaching from this wrong identification and by gaining self-knowledge is ignorance removed.

Our fourth struggle is against the demon of anger. We must, with God's help, eradicate his deadly poison from the depths of our souls. So long as he dwells in our hearts and blinds the eyes of the heart with his somber disorders, we can neither discriminate what is for our good, nor achieve spiritual knowledge, nor fulfill our good intentions, nor participate in true life; and our intellect will remain impervious to the contemplation of the true, divine light; for it is written, "For my eye is troubled because of anger" (Ps. 6:7. LXX).

-St John Cassian

Saint John Cassian points out that the poison of anger must be eradicated, lest it keep us in a prison of our own making and rob us of the intelligence and insight which is the divine light.

> *With pride comes envy, and with envy comes hatred. This hatred then breeds anger, which continues to grow stronger. In this way, one becomes spoiled and full of desire and anger, and the false ego affects one's attitude. This can be clearly seen in one's behavior. How can it be said that one who is overwhelmed by desire and anger can be considered a good person? In ancient legend, even Rahu the demon died after drinking the immortal nectar because of being evil-mindedness.*
>
> -St Shri Samartha Ramdas

Here the master explains to the students how envy and anger come from pride and one's intellect is overwhelmed by desire and anger. We see clearly how the ancient sages from all spiritual traditions point to the five poisons and how they affect our minds, making us ignorant of our true nature. Without getting rid of the afflicted states the poisons create, we never will be at peace and function in love.

> *Freedom from anger, from dejection, self-esteem and pride also contributes to purity of soul in general, while self-control and fasting are especially important for bringing about that specific purity of soul which comes through restraint and moderation.*
>
> -St John Cassian

Here, Saint Cassian points out that pride and anger need to be relinquished in order to purify the soul or heart and to attain a pure mind where the heart can manifest its purity in love. This is what Buddha refers to as *moderation* or the middle way.

The true sanyasi is one who has completely given up the six afflictions of the mind (desire, anger, arrogance, lust, jealousy, enticement). Only those who inquire into their true nature and are deeply thoughtful can be true renunciates. One's spiritual progress is dependent upon one's spiritual practice.

-St Shri Samartha Ramdas

The master here states that one who has the intention to find their true nature with the help of spiritual practices and a deeply thoughtful state of mind can aim to give up the poisons that afflict the mind. If the passions aroused by the senses are kept in check and understood, then we can live with them and use them for the purpose for which they were given to us. We will not be attached to them but rather ready to forsake them at any moment. Then the ego, which only relies on them for its survival, will have no power to enslave us through them and will find its own death.

Of the demons opposing us in the practice of the ascetic life, there are three groups who fight in the front line: those entrusted with the appetites of gluttony, those who suggest avaricious thoughts, and those who incite us to seek the esteem of men. All the other demons follow behind and in their turn attack those already wounded by the first three groups. For one does not fall into the power of the demon of unchastity, unless one has first fallen because of gluttony; nor is one's anger aroused unless one is fighting for food or material possessions or the esteem of men. And one does not escape the demon of dejection, unless one no longer experiences suffering when deprived of these things. Nor will one escape pride, the first offspring of the devil, unless one has banished avarice, the root of all evil, since poverty makes a man humble, according to Solomon (cf. Prov. 10:4. LXX). In short, no one can fall into the power of any demon, unless he has been wounded by those of the front line. That is why the devil suggested these three thoughts to the Christ: first he exhorted Him to turn stones into bread; then he promised Him the whole world, if Christ would fall down and worship him; and thirdly he said that, if our Lord would listen to him, He would be glorified and suffer nothing in falling from the pinnacle of the temple. But our Lord, having shown Himself superior to these temptations, commanded the devil to "get behind Him." In this way He teaches us that it is not possible to drive away the devil, unless we scornfully reject these three thoughts (cf. Matt. 4:1–10).

-Evagrius the Solitary

Evagrius and the early fathers did not write these teachings only for the ascetic who has to withdraw from the world, but for everyone who has the intention to discover the reality of our own being. True asceticism is in the mind and if it is practiced there, the body will follow suit. We can agree that times of solitude are needed in our lives, but the real practice is to find this peace in the midst of the world, for only there we can test ourselves. To be a monk inwardly is what is required today: to have a chaste mind, anew and afresh every moment. An innocent who has this kind of mind is living the real religious life.

Evagrius explains that the demons (afflictions) that attack us first are Greed, Desire and Pride and he makes a correlation with why the devil tempted Christ in the same way, and why Buddha was likewise tempted by lord Mara. So, evil does not live outside but is a product of our own thinking and is produced by the five poisons. This means that when we uproot these poisons from our minds, evil is actually non-existent. It is as the Buddhist masters have stated: these evils are merely apparitions of the mind like mirages in the desert. Everything we see, think and do is happening in the mind; nothing is out of it.

There is no venom more poisonous than that of the asp or cobra, and there is no evil greater than that of self-love. The winged children of self-love are self-praise, self-satisfaction, gluttony, unchastity, self-esteem, jealousy and the crown of all these, pride. Pride can drag down not men alone, but even angels from heaven, and surround them with darkness instead of light.

-St Neilos the Ascetic

Saint Neilos points out that pride is a poison in our hearts that is not easy to uproot, for it is very subtle and can bring us down from our awareness into the deceit of arrogance and conceit.

The passion of pride arises from two kinds of ignorance, and when these two kinds of ignorance unite, they form a single confused state of mind. For a man is proud only if he is ignorant both of divine help and of human weakness. Therefore, pride is a lack of knowledge both in the divine and in the human spheres. For the denial of two true prem-ises results in a single false affirmation.

-St Maximos the Confessor

Conceit is a truly accursed passion. It is a combination of two vices, pride and self-esteem. Pride denies the Cause of virtue and nature, while self-esteem adulterates nature and virtue itself. A proud man does nothing that accords with God's will, and a man full of self-esteem achieves nothing that accords with nature.
The mark of pride is to deny that God is the author of virtue and nature; the mark of self-esteem is to make divisions in nature and so to treat some things as worthless. Conceit is their natural offspring, being an evil state composed of a voluntary denial of God and ignorance of the equal dignity that things possess by nature.
Conceit is a mixture of pride and self-esteem. In its contempt

for God It blasphemously maligns providence; while in its alienation from nature, it treats everything belonging to nature in an unnatural way, and thus corrupts its beauty by misuse.

-St Maximos the Confessor

Saint Maximos the Confessor explains how pride, ignorance and self-esteem give birth to conceit, meaning we do not work in accordance with life and nature but rather in contrast to them by making a division between nature and all things: where there is division, there is always conflict. Our pride makes us ignorant of our true reality – of our unity with all existence – and in doing so we are afflicted in such a way that we always think that nature exists only to be exploited for our selfish benefits, not realizing that we are a part of that same nature. This is why humanity always treats nature as an object to be manipulated and used for our own benefit, not realizing that it is a living being.

These eight passions should be destroyed as follows: gluttony by self-control; unchastity by desire for God and longing for the blessings held in store; avarice by compassion for the poor; anger by goodwill and love for all men; worldly dejection by spiritual joy; listlessness by patience, perseverance and offering thanks to God; self-esteem by doing good in secret and by praying constantly with a contrite heart; and pride by not judging or despising any one in the manner of the boastful Pharisee (cf. Luke 18:11–12), and by considering oneself the least of all men. When the intellect has been freed in this way from the passions we have described and been raised up to God, it will henceforth live the life of blessedness, receiving the pledge of the Holy Spirit (cf. 2

Cor. 1:22). And when it departs this life, dispassionate and full of true knowledge, it will stand before the light of the Holy Trinity and with the divine angels will shine in glory through all eternity.

-St John of Damascus

Saint John of Damascus lists in the above how, if we have the intention to uncover our true reality, we can destroy the passions (afflictions) of the mind and body and in doing so become free from the prison of this world and can align the body, mind and spirit with the universal one. In doing so, we discover its own nature by the divine knowledge that is in us all.

So, pride is one of the passions that needs to be watched, for it can fool us into being awakened or being masters, it can fool us into doing charity with the sense of expecting praise for doing so. When we are doing charity, we should do it in a secret way and it should be known only by the giver; the receiving party should not know where it is coming from, only that it arrived by providence. That is true charity.

All these poisons that are afflictions of our minds are produced by us, but most of us will never accept this truth and will search outside ourselves where we fall into ignorance, for nothing outside the whole of existence is in one mind, not yours or mine. The mind, like space, welcomes everything and everyone. Because we desire, we become attached to objects of desire and allow the poisons to create havoc in our inner world and outer world where everyone is affected by them so we should not forget that we are the world, and the world is us. Only by watching how these afflictions arise in the mind, by what means they arise and how they try to corrupt our hearts, only in that pure observation can we, if we are adamant to stop the creations of such hosts in our minds, purify the mind, the heart and the world we live in.

All the realized masters have pointed out that the way these afflictions come in us is through our five senses and when we do not use them appropriately for the purpose they were created for, then we are prone to fall prey to them, giving in to the desires they produce. One can, for example, enjoy a drink with a few friends, but one should not fall prey to drink and drink till one loses consciousness because then all other afflictions like lust, pride and so on will easily take over our minds. We can see that if we do not watch what is not intelligible, we fall out from the intelligible power of the intellect and succumb to ignorance and the desires of the senses. This is the fall from grace from the original one till now. We should become like children and walk with innocence and when we fall, we should get up again and find the right path. It is not an easy road to travel; the road to freedom is marked by much adversity and travail. Everyone has their own path to travel. That is why Christ said, "Take up your cross and follow me" in the walk of truth, peace and love. Nobody can do it for us; we need to do it alone with faith, prayer, meditation, contemplation and by our spiritual practices we surely can overcome all obstacles. If we have pure intent, we will transform the heavy cross into love, peace, harmony and bliss. At that point, we will never have to travel, to seek anymore, because we are home. Whatever form we have or wherever we are, we will discover the mysteries of love and life supreme.

> *Therefore, my son, he who wishes to take up the cross and follow Christ must first acquire spiritual knowledge and understanding through constantly examining his thoughts, showing the utmost concern for his salvation, and seeking God with all his strength. He should question other servants of God who are of the same mind and engaged in the same ascetic struggle, so that the does not travel in the dark without a light, not knowing how or where to walk.*

-St Mark the Ascetic

All realized masters have told us that thoughts are the root of all problems. We should develop the capacity to discern thoughts which harm ourselves and others for they are not good and all thoughts that promote love, compassion and truth are good. In simple terms, all selfish thoughts are detrimental and all unselfish are good. In the observing practice, we should be vigilant not to be fall into selfishness, pride and so on, and by keeping vigil, we will thread the right path.

To go further into this, we should be aware of the afflictions of body and mind and what we should always be watchful of in our everyday existence.

> *Something should also be said about the vices or the passions of the soul and the body. The passions of the soul are forget-fulness, laziness and ignorance. When the soul's eye, the intellect, has been darkened by these three, the soul is dominated by all the other passions. These are impiety, false teaching or every kind of heresy, blasphemy, wrath, anger, bitterness, irritability, inhumanity, rancor, back-biting, censoriousness, senseless dejection, fear, cowardice, quarrelsomeness, jealousy, envy, self-esteem, pride, hypocrisy, falsehood, unbelief, greed, love of material things, attachment to worldly concerns, listlessness, faint-heartedness, ingratitude, grumbling, vanity, conceit, pomposity, boast-fulness, love of power, love of popularity, deceit, shameless-ness, insensibility, flattery, treachery, pretense, indecision, assent to sins arising from the soul's passible aspect and dwelling on them continuously, wandering thoughts, self-love, the mother of vices, avarice, the root of all evil (cf. 1 Tim. 6:10) and, finally, malice and guile.*
>
> *The passions of the body are gluttony, greed, over-indul-gence, drunkenness, eating in secret, general softness of living, unchastity, adultery, licentiousness, unclean-ness, incest, pederasty, bestiality, impure desires and every passion which is foul and unnatural, theft, sacri-lege, robbery, murder, every kind of physical luxury and gratification of the whims of the flesh (especially when the body is in good health), consulting oracles, casting spells,*

*watching for omens and portents, self-adornment, osten-
tation, foolish display, use of cosmetics, painting the face,
wasting time, day-dreaming, trickery, impassioned misuse
of the pleasures of this world and a life of bodily ease, which
by coarsening the intellect makes it cloddish and brute-
like and never lets it raise itself towards God and the practice of the virtues. The roots or primary causes of all these
passions are the love of sensual pleasure, love of praise and
love of material wealth. Every evil has its origin in these.*

-St John of Damascus

These are, more or less, the afflictions destroying our love, peace
and bliss. If we watch them with naked awareness in a pure state
of mind, all can be uprooted from our minds and then we can
have the right relationship with ourselves and the world at large.

*With pride comes envy, and with envy comes hatred. This
hatred then breeds anger, which continues to grow stronger.
In this way, one becomes spoiled and full of desire and
anger, and the false ego affects one's attitude. This can be
clearly seen in one's behavior.
For now, let this talk end. Everyone takes according to
one's own capacity. However, the reader should know that
the best thing is to give up all pride.*

-St Shri Samartha Ramdas

Saint Shri Samartha points out that pride is one affliction that
needs to be got rid of, for there we fall into greater afflictions
and our attitude and behavior is determined by how much these
afflictions affect our bodies and minds. The teachings of our
great masters from all traditions are not merely philosophies but
strict actualities that deal with all factors of life. We deal with our
attachments, our habits, our deep-rooted desires, feelings and
emotions, which are all created by these afflictions or passions, as
the earlier fathers of Christianity call them.

Brahman cannot be realized by those Who are subject to greed, fear, and anger. Brahman cannot be realized by those Who are subject to the pride of name and fame Or to the vanity of scholarship. Brahman cannot be realized by those Who are enmeshed in life's duality. But to all those who pierce this duality, whose hearts are given to the Lord of Love, He gives himself through his infinite grace; He gives himself through his infinite grace.

-The Tejobindu Upanishad

In the Tejobindu Upanishad, the master is pointing out that God can't be realized as long as we are under the spell of the five poisons and therefore in the world of duality which cannot be penetrated unless we are free from the poisons and completely surrender to the Lord of Love.

It is said that after God created all the universes, before creating man he asked his archangels to advise him on where he should hide all the wisdom and knowledge so that man could not find it too easily. Rafael, one of archangels, said "hide it in the deepest ocean"; God said "no, they will find it for they will use my intelligence." Then Gabriel said, "hide it on the furthest planet" then God said "no they will eventually get there for they will use my intelligence." Then God said, "I will place it deep in their own hearts, they will be too immersed in the world outside and will not have any time to look into themselves," and so indeed very few have or will have the tenacity and intention to look within.

The living father and all knowledge is revealed to the one who enters the union with God, for all knowing then is known. It is imperative for us to understand how we are shaped by our feelings, emotions and desires and how the poisons shape our psyche and determine our behaviors and actions, based on the level of hold they have on our hearts. We have to arrive at an understanding that self-knowledge is the only true practice in order to be free and therefore to be one with existence/ consciousness/ bliss.

We will devote a chapter to self-knowledge but first we should look at and understand yoga and its values, practices, and benefits.

CHAPTER 14

YOGA

All spiritual practices – yoga, meditation, prayer, contemplation – are just methods of clearing some of the negative energies from our bodies and minds in order to be able to tap into the wisdom and intelligence that can lead to self-knowledge. We will not write a thesis on yoga here, because many good books have covered the topic already, but we will give a description of yoga and the practices that are helpful in our times in order to lead more loving and peaceful lives. All of this book so far is about the union with the absolute reality which is inherent in every living and non-living being.

Yoga is a Sanskrit word that comes from the root, "yuj" which means "to join together." Simply put, yoga means "union." In many ways the term yoga is similar to the English term, "communion." It refers to the state of union with God, one's true Self. Yoga also refers to the philosophies and practices that may be undertaken in order to achieve a state of union. It brings attention to the conditions necessary to experience inner peace and enlightenment. Two main aspects of yoga practice focus on how to bring flexibility to the body and how to bring tranquility to the mind.

In the state of yoga, the body, mind, emotions and soul are all in balance – a state of equanimity. The Bible talks about this same principle in terms of "purity of heart." So, what is the one quality necessary to enable us to see God? It is purity of mind and heart.

In the Beatitudes, Jesus says:

> *Blessed are the pure in heart, for they shall see God.*
>
> -Matthew 5.8

That same principle is behind yoga. It is the foundation of all religions that purity of heart should be our way of life. This purity is our essence: when we get rid of the five poisons, we unveil our true reality, which is pure and divine. Yoga has been classified into six branches but in fact it is only one yoga as the union incorporates all of them. One may be inclined to practice one particular branch but in fact all branches support and overlap each other. Some level of devotion is needed to practice any other branch. Some pranayama is needed in all and some mantras are used in others. The six branches are as follows:

1. Raja Yoga

Raja yoga focuses on meditation and contemplation in order to fully realize the self. Known as the royal (Raja) or king path of yoga, it is based on the eight limbed path towards self-realization outlined in Patanjali's *Yoga Sutra* and tends to attract the more spiritually devoted practitioners. The eight limbs also include other yogas.

2. Bhakti Yoga

Bhakti yoga is the path of devotion, emphasizing devotional love for and surrender to God. By seeing the Divine in everyone and everywhere, Bhakti yoga cultivates acceptance, tolerance, and love for all beings. Bhakti yoga also involves a lot of devotionals, singing and chants that evoke feelings of love, connection, and bliss. Without devotion and faith, one cannot practice any yoga.

3. Jnana Yoga

Jnana yoga is the path of wisdom and knowledge (Jnana), involving disciplined study of scriptures and constant inquiry into the nature of self. Often called the yoga of the mind, Jnana yoga is well suited to the more intellectually inclined. The yoga of self-knowledge has been regarded as the culmination of yoga and the most direct path. All yogas bring one to self-knowledge, which is self-realization.

4. Karma Yoga

Karma yoga is the path of selfless action, the yoga of doing. Remaining completely detached from the outcome of their actions; Karma yogis are in continual service to the betterment of all beings with no intention of physical gain.

This yoga is the surrender of the fruit of action to the supreme without any expectation of reward. That is the best charity in the world. Everyone can practice this yoga every day in one form or another, through secret charity.

5. Mantra Yoga

Mantra yoga is the yoga of sound. Considered sacred utterances, mantras are syllables, words or phrases representing a particular attribute of the Divine. Mantra yoga is the practice of becoming centered through the repetition of mantras. Even this yoga plays an important role in all other yoga's. It can help many become established in meditation or contemplation.

6. Hatha Yoga

Hatha yoga is the practice of yoga postures, or asanas, using the body as a vehicle for self-transformation. Without a sound body, nobody can practice any yoga. This is why this is essential yoga for the body.

All six branches have spread outward from India but also have been practiced by other traditions all over the world, though not as a system as is depicted in Patanjali's Yoga sutras. He was the first of the rishis Indian (seers) who composed yoga and wrote it down in a scientific way. Before him, yoga was passed on as an oral tradition, as were other scriptures from their beginnings passed from one generation to another in an oral form.

In the *Bhagavad Gita*, Krishna exposes all yogas to Arjuna as the way to become liberated from the cycle of existence. One of the yoga he exposes is devotional yoga.

> *ARJUNA SAID: One man loves you with pure devotion; another man loves the Unmanifest. Which of these two understands yoga more deeply?*
> *THE BLESSED LORD SAID: Those who love and revere me with unwavering faith, always centering their minds on me they are the most perfect in yoga.*
>
> -Lord Krishna

In these statements, Krishna tells Arjuna that one who is immersed in God with full devotion and surrenders all to him is perfect in the union with God. One in such a state is guided by the universal will, acting always right for all beings.

Christ gave the same message of surrender and devotion.

> *Then Jesus said to His disciples, "If anyone wishes to come after Me, he must deny himself, and take up his cross and follow Me. For whoever wishes to save his life will lose it; but whoever loses his life for My sake will find it."*
>
> -Matthew 16:24–25

Here, Christ not only encourages us to take his cross and follow, but he states beforehand that we have to deny ourselves, meaning deny the ego, for whoever wants to save the life of the ego will lose the real self and whoever losses the life of the ego will gain eternal life.

In the *Dhammapada* it states:

> *The one who protects his mind from clinging to desire, anger and aversion and unawareness, is the one who enjoys real and lasting peace.*

> -Buddha

Buddha here talked about surrender in a different way. He states that in order to get everlasting peace, we have to neither cling to nor reject anything but surrender to what it is. All the masters and teachers have thought this way: it is the only way. Either surrender to Love, to the present moment, to Christ or Krishna, etc. They are all the same avenues that will take us to freedom from the clutches of the ego.

Depending on the tendencies, impressions on the mind and the ego, we have to find for ourselves which yoga may be suited for us or if any practice or no practice is better. Even no practice is still yoga. It comes by the grace of God but rare are these souls to whom the grace of God descends without them pursuing or practicing anything. The purpose of any spiritual practice – either yoga or not – is to transcend the world of dualistic view and become wholly, one with all existence and as Buddha said extinguish all energy but Love.

> *He who has let go of hatred, who treats all beings with kindness and compassion, who is always serene, unmoved by pain or pleasure, free of the "I" and "mine," self-controlled, firm and patient, his whole mind focused on me – that man is the one I love best.*
> *He who neither disturbs the world nor is disturbed by it, who is free of all joy, fear, envy – that man is the one I love*

best.
He who is pure, impartial, skilled, unworried, calm, selfless
in all undertakings – that man is the one I love best.
He who, devoted to me, is beyond joy and hatred, grief and
desire, good and bad fortune – that man is the one I love
best.

-Lord Krishna

Above, Krishna exposes the qualities which transform a human being into a divine being, one who is at home wherever he may be and is unaffected by the adversities of life. That is the one who, though in a human body, knows God. These qualities are not to be cultivated: they are our inborn nature, and in order to get to them, we have to get rid of what we are not and here yoga has its role in helping us unveil our true reality, which is our true nature.

Hatha Yoga helps in keeping the body in a healthy state, for if we are sick, it will be much more difficult to concentrate and keep the mind on God in meditation or on self-enquiry. This is why we need a healthy body. Even if we do not practice any yoga, a healthy body is a necessity to achieve a healthy mind and when a healthy mind is there then a healthy being will be there too.

Even a non-religious person who does not practice any yoga can actually achieve a healthy state of being, but their practice may be done unconsciously and therefore the process goes on naturally. Nevertheless, as we stated earlier, such human beings are exceedingly rare. Among them are only Christ, Krishna and some others unknown to us who were born holy and who only incarnate in order to burn the Karma of others and help humanity rise to higher sates of consciousness.

The Practice of yoga brings us face to face with the extraordinary complexity of our own being.

-Sri Aurobindo

Yoga is a scientific approach to the mysteries of life and should not be taken as a religion, for all the core teachings of all religions are in fact yogas. Jesus or Buddha and all the awakened beings have not founded any religion, they were founded after they were long gone by others. If we practice the real fundamental teachings of any faith with all our hearts, we will in the end discover reality for ourselves.

One of the Masters of Yoga describes beautifully the purpose of yoga:

> *The yoga we practice is not for ourselves alone but for the Divine. Its aim is to work out the will of the Divine in the world, to effect a spiritual transformation and to bring down a divine nature and a divine life into the mental vital and physical nature and life of humanity. Its object is not personal Mukti (liberation) alto Mukti is a necessary condition of the yoga, but the liberation and transformation of a human being, It is not personal Ananda but the bringing down of the divine Ananda Christ's kingdom of heaven Satya-yuga (divine era) – upon the earth.*
>
> -Sri Aurobindo

Kriya Yoga is an ancient science. Babaji revealed to Lahiri Mahasaya:

> *The Kriya Yoga which I am giving to the world through you in this nineteenth century is a revival of the same science which Krishna gave, millenniums ago, to Arjuna, and which was later known to Patanjali, and to Christ, St. John, St. Paul, and other disciples.*
>
> -Lahiri Mahasaya

Here, Lahiri Mahasaya points out that the yoga he teaches is the same yoga that all spiritual masters have practiced in one way or another, in order to enter in union with the absolute reality, God.

There are many types of yogas: Buddhists have their types and Hindus have theirs, Christians also theirs and so on. Any spiritual discipline we may call yoga. Sage Patanjali in the yoga sutras describes yoga as follows:

"Yogas chitta vritti nirodha" is Patanjali's definition of yoga. It means that yoga is the removing of the fluctuations of the mind. Yoga is the stilling of the mind until it rests in a state of total and utter tranquility, so that we experience life as it is: as Reality. We experience life through the clearest of lenses – lenses not colored by thoughts of good or bad, mine or yours. When the fluctuations of the mind are totally removed, we are at one with everything, the absolute.

> *Performing all actions for my sake, desireless, absorbed in the Self, indifferent to "I" and "mine," let go of your grief, and fight! Men who constantly practice this teaching of mine, Arjuna who trust it with all their heart, are freed from the bondage of actions.*
>
> -Lord Krishna

In the above statement, Krishna is teaching Arjuna the yoga of action, saying that all actions performed for him without any desire for oneself and only acting for the benefit of all are the right actions and one who also gives up the fruit of any action is performing the yoga of action. Right action comes only when we perform any action for others never thinking about ourselves. Before we can come to such practice, we have to have pure faith and a strong intention to please the Lord or self in any action we perform. Some people are more inclined to practice this yoga and do it through charity or performing work for the benefit of others. This is Karma Yoga.

In Hindu yoga, the actions performed by an individual have three natures (Gunnas):

- *Tamas* (darkness, destructive, death)
- *Rajas* (energy, passion, birth)
- *Sattva* (goodness, purity, light)

Roughly, individuals act within these qualities depending on their spiritual maturity and the level of control the ego has over them. An individual who has raised the consciousness to a pure level, acts always in the Sattva where one only shares with others goodness, purity and light. These are the beings who have reached the state of equanimity and humanness of mind, and their ego is only used as a tool to function in the world, but they are not under the control of the ego.

Krishna explains:

> *Actions are really performed by the working of the three gunas; but a man deluded by the I-sense imagines, "I am the doer." The wise man knows that when objects act on the senses, it is merely the gunas acting on the gunas; thus, he is unattached.*
>
> -Lord Krishna

Here Arjuna asks Krishna, what makes people perform evil actions. Krishna explains:

> *ARJUNA SAID: What is it that drives a man to an evil action, Krishna, even against his will, as if some force made him do it?*
> *THE BLESSED LORD SAID: That force is desire, it is anger, arising from the guna called rajas; deadly and all-devouring, that is the enemy here. As a fire is obscured by smoke, as a mirror is covered by dust, as a fetus is wrapped in its membrane, so wisdom is obscured by desire. Wisdom is destroyed, Arjuna, by the constant enemy of the wise,*

which, flaring up as desire, blazes with insatiable flames. Therefore, you must first control your senses, Arjuna; then destroy this evil that prevents you from ever knowing the truth. Men say that the senses are strong. But the mind is stronger than the senses; the understanding is stron ger than the mind; and strongest is the Self. Knowing the Self, sustaining the self by the Self, Arjuna, kill the diffi- cult-to-conquer enemy called desire.

-Lord Krishna

Krishna is telling us that without understanding desire – which comes through the senses and is born in the mind, sustained and then inflamed by the ego – such desires can be uprooted only by the Self, which is stronger than the ego. This is why it is so important for us to find our true reality because then the ego has no more power over the self. This is helped by all the yogas, but the most profound is the yoga of wisdom according to Krishna and all other masters. Below, Krishna explains that wisdom is the final goal of every action and every action that is performed with wisdom will liberate.

Thus, many forms of worship may lead to freedom, Arjuna. All these are born of action. When you know this, you will be free. Better than any ritual is the worship achieved through wisdom; wisdom is the final goal of every action, Arjuna.

-Lord Krishna

Wisdom is the quality of virtue that will abolish desire, and this wisdom comes with the practice of yoga with the understanding of the self and of others as we have seen through the teachings of Christ, Krishna and many others. Wisdom comes from expe- rience; from pure observation without thinking. Wisdom will always be followed by the right action, because only one who has wisdom can act rightly in an unselfish way. Wisdom will always regard the self as it does others, as we see in the lives of great souls. Wisdom is there when the ego is not. Wisdom is pure intelligence operating without thought. Wisdom is God.

The next yoga Krishna explains is the yoga of renunciation. But what is one to renounce?

> *The man who has seen the truth thinks, "I am not the doer" at all times when he sees, hears, touches, when he smells, eats, walks, sleeps, breathes, when he defecates, talks, or takes hold, when he opens his eyes or shuts them: at all times he thinks, "This is merely sense-objects acting on the senses." Offering his actions to God, he is free of all action; sin rolls off him, as drops of water roll off a lotus leaf. Surrendering attachment, the sage performs all actions, with his body, his mind, and his understanding, only to make himself pure.*

> -Lord Krishna

As Krishna states, the true renunciant is one who renounces any attachment and in doing so acts with wisdom, performing the right actions, as we have stated earlier. There is yoga of action, of renunciation, of wisdom and all this comes together in the yoga of meditation.

The yoga of meditation starts with concentration as Krishna explains:

> *He looks impartially on all: those who love him or hate him, his kinsmen, his enemies, his friends, the good, and also the wicked. The man of yoga should practice concentration, alone, mastering mind and body, free of possessions and desires. Sitting down, having chosen a spot that is neither too high nor too low, that is clean and covered with a grass mat, a deerskin, and a cloth, he should concentrate, with his*

whole mind, on a single object; if he practices in this way, his mind will soon become pure. With torso and head held straight, with posture steady and unmoving, gazing at the tip of his nose, not letting his eyes look elsewhere.

-Lord Krishna

Next, Krishna shows us that with the practice of yoga we will develop attention and awareness, and they will lead to meditation which by itself can bring liberation.

He should sit there calm, fearless, firm in his vow to be chaste, his whole mind controlled, directed, focused, absorbed in me. Constantly mastering his mind, the man of yoga grows peaceful, attains supreme liberation, and vanishes into my bliss. He who eats too much food or too little, who is always drowsy or restless, will never succeed in the yoga of meditation. For the man who is moderate in food and pleasure, moderate in action, moderate in sleep and waking, yoga destroys all sorrow. With a mind grown clear and peaceful, freed from selfish desires, absorbed in the Self alone, he is called a true man of yoga.

-Lord Krishna

The man of yoga is greater than ascetics, or the learned, or those who perform the rituals; therefore be a man of yoga, my son. Practice yoga sincerely, with single-minded devotion; love me with perfect faith; bring your whole self to me.

-Lord Krishna

If we have the intention and are steady in the practice of any kind of yoga with total devotion, we will undoubtedly reach the state of great bliss, as Buddha calls it; the state of Brahman Vihara (free state). Meditation is a subject that is somehow misunderstood in the modern world, and we will look into it later.

Meditation is the portal that opens new dimensions to be seen, and they are ever fresh and new, not new because the new is different from the old but really new every moment without the past. All yoga and spiritual practices will lead one who practices into meditation, which is like everyday activity but can make every activity that seems boring be fresh again, and can bring a new energy that heals the sickness of being bored.

The yoga of Christ is similar to the yoga of Krishna or Buddha. All the yogas that all masters of all traditions have exposed may come in different forms – in different symbols or ideas – but in fact the same energy is making its play into the diversity of forms. In the Gospel of Thomas is written the whole yoga of Christ and if someone has the ear to hear it, they will grasp reality and will become one with the absolute, intelligence, bliss, and love.

We can define yoga as any practice that helps any individual to arrive at home in their own selves, for it is there where we find the kingdom of heaven and when we find it, the kingdom of heaven will be wherever we are. The real home will be where we are at any moment in time.

In the following, we see the same truth exposed by Krishna restated by a Kryia Yogi master of our times.

> *Yoga is not just a practice of asanas. Yoga is that which takes you from the ordinary to the extraordinary. This is the potential of Yoga.*
>
> -Sri M

> *What is spirituality? To find the truth, to find yourself, to find your true nature and your link with the Supreme Being. This is the only aim of spiritual practice. And if you are with a spiritual teacher, this is exactly what he or she would like to inculcate in you.*
>
> -Sri M

Then the goal of yoga as Krishna exposes is as:

> *ARJUNA SAID: What is this absolute freedom, Krishna? What is the Self? What is the true nature of action, the nature of beings and of gods? Teach me the way of worship: what it is, here, in the body. And how at the hour of death can a man be with you in spirit?*
>
> *THE BLESSED LORD SAID: Freedom is union with the deathless; the Self is the essence of all things; its creative power, called action, causes the whole world to be. About beings, know that they die; about gods, know the Supreme Person: and know that true worship is I myself, here, in this body. Whoever in his final moments thinks of me only, is sure to enter my state of being once his body is dead. Whatever the state of being that a man may focus upon at the end, when he leaves his body, to that state of being he will go.*
>
> *Therefore, Arjuna, meditate on me at all times, and fight; with your whole mind intent on me, you will come to me — never doubt it. Strong in the practice of yoga, with a mind that is rooted in me and in nothing else, you will reach the Supreme Person that I am. Meditate on the Guide, the Giver of all, the Primordial Poet, smaller than an atom, unthinkable, brilliant as the sun. If you do this at the hour of your death, with an unmoving mind, drawing your breath up between your eyebrows, you will reach the Person that I am. I will teach you about the state called the eternal, the absolute, which those who strive toward me enter desireless, freed from attachments.*
>
> -Lord Krishna

Krishna, Christ, Buddha and all other masters have revealed this truth in a different way in different language but in fact it is the same truth. Whatever yoga one is inclined to practice consciously or unconsciously will lead to the absolute state of freedom and union with the absolute. Only that ultimate union will give perfect freedom. We can learn from all the perfect teachers, we can learn from all beings and nature, and if we have the intention to find the truth, we will be guided by the hand of God with a book, a teacher, an experience, a wisdom and slowly we will lift the veil of illusion and unveil our true reality, not as we imagine it to be but as it is, perfect in its own state, because all is perfection in that state. The state of mind of any of us is affected by the quality of actions we perform as described in yoga and, depending on these qualities, the mind will then be in a state accordingly low as hell or high as heaven or, even better, beyond all in the realm of absolute reality, God.

There are many paths to reach the divine and everyone must find the path for themselves. Intention arises and will arise at the perfect time and the perfect place; just as not all fruits ripen at the same time and in the same spot, so intention to find the truth will come to us in our own time and in our own place. The truth cannot be sold at the altar of demand but each being has to find it on their own, assisted by the environment and the world we live in, according to the circumstances and conditions that arise in our lives though they are not in our control as some would like to believe: we have very little control.

Life itself is a web of relationships and how we act in these relationships with people, with nature, with all things is based on our level of dependence on our ego. If we act directed by the ego, our actions and the results of our actions will be selfish no matter how moral. On the other hand, if actions are directed by the self, then these actions will be the right actions, and everyone will benefit either directly or indirectly. This is why Krishna mentions that all actions performed without expecting any result and done fully for him who is in all beings, will be right actions. This is where yoga is beneficial for it helps us in getting to the right action.

Intelligence can operate and perform actions without thinking and that action will always be the right action. The thought is the thinker, and the thinker is the thought. Everything we experience in life, we do it through the mind and we act accordingly. Through the senses, as discussed before, we get in contact with the world (objects of the senses) and by our reasoning we take from the senses the sensations, depending on our conditioning, and we give rise to our desires based on these sensations. Whether fresh or accumulated in memory, from these sensations we respond or react to them, giving rise to feelings that create further responses and reactions and innumerable states of mind. So, all these sensations may give birth to pleasure or pain, and we always try to find the happy states and run from suffering and pain.

We have discussed this before, but it is worth mentioning again for it does help to see it in the context of yoga. By running away from pain and by suppressing suffering, we put ourselves into a state of never-ending conflict and of eternal running or seeking. Here, if we intend to find the truth, instead of running away from any form of suffering, we have to stay with it, without any aversion or clinging to anything. In that state of stillness, we realize that suffering is not something alien but is actually the self. Then perhaps we realize that suffering is self-made, regardless of the avenue by which we may think it arrived. In that realization, the suffering is no more, for we realize is just a creation of our own mind. The same applies to pain. This is why the great masters who were going through sickness were never affected by pain; they bear it with fullness of love.

Yoga will help if we practice with our whole heart to be in that original state. This is not a state induced by the mind: it is the clear light, a light where silence is unaffected by noise just as space is unaffected by the clouds or the flight of a plane; so the mind should not be affected by thoughts. That light is the eternal light from which all beings come, as Christ pointed out:

> *If they say to you: Whence have you come? say to them: We have come from the light, the place where the light came into being of itself. It [established itself], and it revealed itself in their image. If they say to you: Who are you? say: We are his sons, and we are the elect of the living Father. If they ask you: What is the sign of your Father in you? say to them: It is movement and rest.*

-Gospel of Thomas: 50

Forgive the writer, but it is essential to repeat statements like the above in different contexts for truth is multidimensional and cannot be expressed in linear terms; it is holistic. In the above statement, Christ is reminding us that we are the sons of the living father God. We only need to have faith and look into ourselves, observe how the agitation which is the manifestation of God and the rest which is the essence of God both exist in us. Therefore, we are gods also, as he stated many times throughout his teachings and as all masters of all traditions have shown us as well the same truth.

> *Yoga is on how to expand one's potential and take you to its highest. It could be work, Karma yoga, it could be understanding or intelligence which is Jnana yoga, it could be spiritual, Raja Yoga or it could be your heart, devotion and compassion, Bhakti Yoga.*

-Sri M

In Indian and other traditions, there are a number of yogas but all the teachings and the practices they employ take us to the one fundamental truth: that God is oneness, he is all Love, and we are all part of him. Everyone, regardless of whether they are practicing yoga or not, will grasp in the end this fundamental truth and then the kingdom of heaven will reveal its glory by being seen all around. If we grasp this fundamental truth, we can change society and the world we live in. We will now look at what society is and who makes society, and the effects society has on everyday living.

CHAPTER 15

SOCIETY

What is society and why is it so important to understand that society is not something apart from us, but it is us?

> *A society is a group of people participating in continuous social connection, or a broad social group occupying the same social or spatial territory, normally exposed to the same political power and cultural standards that are dominant.*
>
> -Wikipedia

From the above statement we see that society is a group of human beings living in a close network of relationships with each other. These connections increase in complexity from individual connections (husband and wife) to complex connections like families, then to more elaborate connections like religious or large organizations, then societies, which grow into regions, countries and the world at large.

Society is made up of humans and humans create society. If humans are happy and have wisdom and love, society will reflect that. Today, if we observe as Christ suggested, we see that societies, families and individuals are in much turmoil and conflict with themselves and others. These conflicts produce war, destruction and misery for all parties involved directly or indirectly, for we all live on the same earth and under the same sky, so we also breathe the same air.

These conflicts come up because of our selfishness, our egos, which are always in the five poisons of ignorance, attachment, aversion, pride, envy.

This selfishness is reflected and works at the individual level, family level and then in society at large. The fundamental fact is that it starts with the individual. If we want society to change, we need to change as individuals for we are society, we are not apart from it. If we are waiting for the society to change us – as is happening today, then we rely on politicians, religious leaders, psychiatrists and the knowhow people to change us – whereby they are actually shaping us consciously or unconsciously into a mold according to their conditioning. This comes from their understanding, the conditioning they are exposed to, and the end result will be in accordance with that mold.

We can see that any change in society that is made from an external factor is only the past with a sugar coating in the present to somehow be changed in the future and changes made like that are not changes at all. It is the past and the past is always a dead thing, never alive and with no potential to express love. Love is always fresh and new, and it is always in the moment. In order to change society, we need to change ourselves and this is a very arduous task. A society might change from outside only through a leader or leaders with wisdom, who have reached the awakened state. Unfortunately, in our present times, such souls are rare and even more extremely rarely are they involved in politics.

This is why Christ has stated:

> *I stood in the midst of the world, and I appeared to them in the flesh. I found them all drunk; I found none of them thirsting, and my soul was afflicted for the sons of men; for they are blind in their heart, and they do not see that they came empty into the world, (and) empty they seek to leave the world again. But now they are drunk. When they have thrown off their wine, they will repent.*

-Gospel of Thomas: 28

Christ in the above statement clearly mentions how he found humanity and the society in turmoil with our hearts closed and too drunk on our own ignorance and he stated that only when we shake up the vine (ignorance) will we repent and find our way. If we observe, we have not yet found the way, we are still ignorant and therefore our hearts are still closed to the love of God, and we will leave this world empty instead of living this world with our hearts filled with love.

In times of old, leaders have relied on divine providence, and they had guidance from awakened beings such as priests, shamans, philosophers, medicine men and so on. Today society is much corrupted by the greed, power, ignorance, hate and anger and in order for society to change, we need to understand that society is us and it will not be better unless every member looks within and finds the truth, for we are all a part of a whole and we never can be apart from each other no matter how fragmented we believe ourselves to be. Unless we have undergone an inner revolution in our being, we can never have a loving and caring society. The Chinese master Loa Tzu has given us three weapons of change and they are as he states.

Simplicity, patience, compassion.
These three are your greatest treasures.
Simple in actions and thoughts, you return to the source
of being.
Patient with both friends and enemies,
you accord with the way things are.
Compassionate toward yourself,
you reconcile all beings in the world.

-Lao Tzu

If we take a closer look at the lives of our great spiritual teachers, they all have practiced simplicity, patience and compassion, which sums up Love. Are we living like them today? Intellectually we may understand what they are trying to convey to us, but practically it is hard to follow these teachings for it takes tremendous energy to drop all that we think we are, all the accumulated habits, experiences and attachments, all the content of our consciousness.

It is very important to understand that change has to come from within. There is a natural order as found in nature and this order comes with its own intelligence. This order is also inherent in us, but we have lost touch with it. We lost touch with nature since the industrialization of the world and moving from a village life into a city life. More and more people today are attracted back to nature, but it is this nature in us which we should aspire to get to, for nature outside is just a pointer to our inner nature. We live with fictions of our imaginations and everyone's imagination is different, according to their conditioning, senses, objects they are attracted to and what the mind makes up of all that. We are lost in the world of our own creation. There is nothing wrong in enjoying the world, but it has to be enjoyed and shared with all.

If today's leaders would look to the leadership of Christ, we would definitely live in a different world. In the fourteenth century, the church had power over the masses. In the eighteenth century power went to nations with powerful armies and now power is in the hands of people and organizations with more assets and money. Still, real true power lies in our hearts. If the power in our hearts is unlocked, all nations, organizations, armies will become redundant and money will have no value, not because money won't still exist, but we will not give it any intrinsic value. Gold will also be of no value when we have found our inner nature and aligned the body, mind and spirit into a single unitary movement in love.

Many problems in the world come from control; from an authoritarian process conducted whereby authority comes down through the hierarchy to the masses. Most businesses today have an authoritarian system of management, as do the churches and the Temples and all corporations. Authority of any kind carries with it great negativity and conflict. None of the great masters conducted their lives and teachings in that way. We have not found a better system because most of us just follow without questioning; as long as we can fulfill our desires, all is fine. What need is there to question anything then? We can observe that everywhere people compete and are in much conflict and stress. These tensions between individuals, families and nations create divisions and where there is division and conflict there is no love.

For centuries, we have been trying to establish peace and to no avail. Whatever we do, it does not work. We sign agreements, but they are broken all the time. There is never to be any security on a piece of paper. Also, there is never security in having an atomic bomb. In actuality, the nation that does not have any arms, any armies, is the most secure from all conflicts, because the nation that bows its head is greater than the one that conquers and has more power. It is like the sea. All rivers run to the sea. Why? Because the sea is lower. The sea has lowered itself and in doing so become vast and loving, accepting all rivers to flow into love. The one who conquers is insecure, always wanting more, never satisfied and never at peace: always restless and selfish.

Because our consciousness has not evolved enough to be done with such authoritarian structures, we continue to use them and in doing so we create a lot of conflict in the world. These structures are our society. They are not apart from us and when each individual recognizes this fact, perhaps then a natural change will take place in society where equanimity, wisdom and intelligence will prevail and not the cunningness of the politicians or of the businessmen who do a lot of mischief in order to succeed because of the competitiveness nature they have been conditioned too. When humanity comes to a level of consciousness whereby an individual will use intelligence which is not corrupted by thought, then we will not have a need for politicians to tell us what to do. Unfortunately, we are still far away from that state of living.

This is why it is very important that each one of us strive to get to that state of intelligence, love and compassion after which the natural order of things will take care of family, society, state, country and the world. Life itself is just a web of interdependent relationships. Each of us depends on the relationships we have with other individuals to actually exist. None of us can exist on our own while in the body, and not even after unless we have awakened fully to our reality. This is why we have to understand that life is unity. It is the yoke (union) Christ, and all the realized masters of all traditions have spoken of in a multiplicity of forms.

How are we to bring an inner revolution? Where do we start? We may look at being simple and always doing the right thing. Christ said:

> *But seek ye first the kingdom of God, and his righteousness;*
> *and all these things shall be added unto you.*

> -Matthew 6:33

What he means here is to find for ourselves the kingdom of heaven which, of course, is within us and also outside of us: it is everywhere. The kingdom is the state of mind where one is living in righteousness and having only what one needs. This is the right thing to do, for this allows others to have also what they need. Being patient is another virtue to cultivate in order to flow with life without being anxious about tomorrow. Compassion is Lao Tzu's third virtue and allows us to be able to act for the benefit of all beings. All the passions one person has, when they are gathered together, makes for Common passions (compassion), and all these simple but most powerful virtues (simplicity, patience, humility) will propel one into LOVE for all beings.

Self-knowledge can unveil our true nature. Most of us live in ignorance of who we are and are so busy running after the pleasures the world has to offer. There is a big difference between seeing the world and experiencing it by running after pleasures without having self-knowledge and enjoying what the world has to offer, after we gain self-knowledge. After we awaken to our true reality, we stop running after pleasures. This does not mean that if they present themselves, we will reject them: we will still enjoy them but will do it with no attachments and therefore whatever life has to offer one will welcome, in the same way, without any clinging or aversion which will bring about the right action in any given situation for wisdom will show the way.

> *Teachers and scriptures can stimulate spiritual awareness. But the wise disciple crosses the ocean of ignorance by direct illumination, through the grace of God. Gain experience directly. Realize God for yourself. Know the Self as the one indivisible Being and become perfect. Free your mind from all distractions and dwell in the consciousness of the Self. This is the final declaration of the Vedanta: Brahman is all; [It is] this universe and every creature. To be liberated is to live in the continual awareness of Brahman, the undivided Reality.*

> -Adi Shankara

In the above statement, Adi Shankara is pointing out that only through our own effort and by direct knowledge can we gain our true freedom from ignorance and therefore be what we have always been. He also states that teachers and scripture are of help but, in the end, we have to do it alone. We need to find out for ourselves. Buddha told his disciples to find out for themselves the truth: he only could just point to it. Christ and others after them have said the same. We can see that authority in psychic or spiritual aspects of ourselves has no place here at all. Here most important is that we come to our own truth through our own experiences and our own observations; we really need to penetrate for ourselves into the truth. Truth cannot be pinned to a board with a statement that one has it: one who says he knows does not really know. The real truth is a living thing in a continuous transformation. One has to observe it every moment and stay with it and this is the most difficult task.

The truth is simple: unless each one of us lets go of all our conditioning – all so-called accumulated knowledge regarding truth – we can never have a society based on Love. Society will always reflect our inner being. If our inner being is at peace with much Love, society will reflect it accordingly. Every society and individual aspires to be happy. We should next investigate happiness and its intricacies.

CHAPTER 16

HAPPINESS

Happiness pertains to emotions and is usually a response to something which pleases us. But emotional nature is dual, and where there is happiness there is also sadness. Because just as one thing may please us and we feel happy, so something else may displease us and we feel sad. Joy pertains to the Soul or Consciousness. Joy arises spontaneously from within each moment and does not depend on anything external. Joy is an ever-present quality which is felt in the heart when we become still enough to find space within.

Bliss pertains to Spirit or Being. This is not bliss in the sense of overwhelming ecstasy. This is simply the freedom of knowing the Self to exist without limits, the bliss of an uncontained Being. Every being in the universe wants to be happy, to be fulfilled, to be healthy and we can all accept this fact. But we should make a distinction between an induced happiness and natural happiness. Happiness that comes about by any reason is never permanent happiness. The happiness that does not need a reason is natural happiness which is joy. We may call it joy to distinguish between man-made happiness and a natural one, which, by the way, is inherent in us all. Joy is the path.

> *One who acts on truth is happy in this world and beyond.*
> *Thousands of candles can be lighted from a single candle,*
> *and the life of the candle will not be shortened. Happiness*
> *never decreases by being shared.*

-Buddha

For example, observe an animal. Animals also have the ability to express happiness, and pain or pleasure as we do. The difference is only in the sense faculties they were endowed with. Likewise, in an infant, joy is more prevalent than happiness because the infant does not need much to smile and be joyful. It's why we call them bundles of joy. As we get older, that inherent joy quality is covered and forgotten and is substituted by the happiness that always needs a reason and an object of desire to come to fruition. If the object of desire is not acquired, happiness turns to sorrow and we live in a world of duality where there is pleasure accompanied by pain always.

What has changed us from joyful little creatures into creatures of habit and creatures of desire always wanting more, always wanting to be better, always becoming something? A child has the ability to learn through direct experience but as we get older that learning is inhibited by our accumulated knowledge of the world and its workings and we are always told how to behave, what to do, what to think, etc.., by parents, teachers and others in our lives. Rare are the moments when we as children learn by direct perception and this only happens when we are very small, about the age we learn to walk. At that age, we are attracted by objects, colors, movement and as our curiosity about the world enhances, we are attracted by the outward sensations to learn from the external world. This is a natural process found in all animals, plants, and beings.

These sensations then are stored as memory, pleasant and unpleasant, and we naturally run from the unpleasant to the pleasant. As we are conditioned to what is good and bad, slowly that simplicity we had as a child becomes burdened by complexity that carries with it confusion, conflict, and sorrow. By adulthood, moments of joy in life are rare. We may have temporary moments of happiness, but joy is forgotten by many.

We have been conditioned to always chase happiness through the senses but this happiness – regardless of how it comes about – is only temporary and we have to work very hard to maintain it. Here work does not mean only physical work but also psychological work. We acquire happiness, work to maintain it and, if somehow it is lost and gone then we look for a new source of happiness. It is always a vicious cycle, and we are never really happy. Is this elusive happiness what makes us do all the mischief which we see in the world from time immemorial? Desire is the moving energy that makes us always chase happiness. We have only to observe for ourselves that this is the case. In that observation, we may find the real danger in wrong and selfish desires.

According to the Buddha, desire is the root of all sorrow and freedom from desire is freedom from sorrow for all mankind, which he defined as nirvana.

-Sri M

It is desire that is the root of our problems. Buddha's disciples ask him then how to get rid of desire and he sent them to meditate. After some time, one disciple came back and said, "Even if I got rid of all desires, the desire is still there in the form of desire trying to get rid of desires. It is the same as the mind trying to kill the same mind." Buddha smiled and said to him. "You have understood then." We still can live with desires and chase them, but we should not pursue them at any cost and get attached to them trying to relive them repeatedly time and time again and creating habits which then construct patterns of thoughts in our minds conditioning the mind even further.

> *All that we are is the result of what we have thought. It is founded on our thoughts. It is made up of our thoughts. If one speaks or acts with an evil thought, pain follows one, as the wheel follows the foot of the ox that draws the wagon. All that we are is the result of what we have thought. It is founded on our thoughts. It is made up of our thoughts. If one speaks or acts with a pure thought, happiness follows one, like a shadow that never leaves.*

> -Buddha

Happiness in this world is created by us, by our thinking and actions. As Buddha has stated above, it is dependent on our thinking, so it is our happiness or sorrow. All our thinking is dependent on circumstances and conditions which present themselves and our ability to respond negatively or positively depending on our state of mind given the desires and attachments we have.

The moment we stop chasing happiness of any kind by any means and remain always with what it is, then there is the possibility for joy to arise from the depth of our being. If this happens then happiness is a second-hand affair. Of course, it is not an easy task to remain with what it is, always in the moment. We can remain with what it is when the mind is silent with no chatter, no judgements, no fluctuations of any kind. In Chapter five, we used the analogy of the chariot to explain how the mind runs after the senses and is caught in the world of objects, imprisoned in the cycle of existence. A child has the power to observe and learn in pure awareness but that power is hijacked by the teacher, by the parent and so on, and the child then relies less and less on the inherent awareness, and becomes more and more conditioned by the accumulative knowledge, therefore relying on that knowledge and in doing so conforming and building a mind structure on ideas and concepts from where one cannot escape with ease and the human being becomes a robot in a prison of our own doing.

Direct knowledge is knowledge that comes from pure awareness, pure observation, where the seeing and the acting are without any interference, and without the observer getting involved with what was learned or known from the knowledge in memory. Direct learning is always new, fresh, untouched by the thinker. Physical knowledge may involve the thinker and the thought, but spiritual knowledge is a direct experience where only the experience is, and the experiencer is one with the experience, in a state of continuous experience from moment to moment fresh and alive, without the burden of the past or anxiety for the future.

Buddha called it mindfulness; others called it full encompassing attention or pure observation, choiceless awareness or pure consciousness. This is the key to teaching us about our inner and outer life. We have to do it alone – to observe, to enquire. Not everyone is meant for this but if we have the intention to see the truth by staying in a state of choiceless awareness we can find out how to live a joyful life in love with all beings. All spiritual practices were designed in a way to get us here, to this energy that moves and maintains all creation and to which we also are a part.

Awareness is all inclusive. One who is aware of the inward movement of life and outward movement is blessed. One who stays in that awareness – not corrupted by thought or memories or any image, by any projection of the past changed in present and projected into the future – the one who lives this way every moment is free to really see reality as it is without any distortion. Divine Love manifests in that fully aware state and it is there where real meditation starts. Joy is found where there is no thought to corrupt it, where there is intelligence, bliss and love. When we are in that state, we will know, for this state cannot be reached or got to it, does not come from somewhere, it is our true nature, and, in that state, we are at home. From there, we will always act in the right way and intelligence can then operate in freedom. When we can see that thought can never bring everlasting happiness but only brings illusory happiness, a superficial happiness according to the tendencies, desires, and the conditioning we have been exposed to through our lifetimes, in that understanding there is freedom.

We may run after happiness through sex, drink, entertainment, yoga; through work, power, status, etc..., but have we ever questioned what we are doing in the process? These are just ways of escaping from our true reality, are they not? We constantly run to new experiences, new ways to improve ourselves. We are in a state of becoming all the time with no end in sight. We are doing this because we do not know any better, we just follow the norm because our minds have been conditioned to function in a direction where there is more happiness or a better self. Even yoga is a deterrent if there is not a wise teacher to help us.

Whatever happiness one pursues is done through effort. Always we need a reason to be happy and that reason is our own projection according to our desires. The reasons can change but the goal is an illusory happiness and if we do not achieve the desired results then we are on the other side of happiness, which is sorrow. That sorrow can turn into anger, frustration or disappointment and we then create conflict in ourselves, and this conflict will exteriorize somehow in many different ways depending on the desires, circumstances and conditions that have arisen. This is how we tend to flow against the flow of life.

For example, we are looking forward to a holiday. We have prepared for it, imagined where we will go and what we will do and on the way the car breaks down and all our imaginations, all our projections have shattered. We might then become angry with ourselves, or our mechanic. We are extremely disappointed and so on. A problem has arisen in the mind which is now affected by the car breaking down. The holiday has been spoiled and this leads to disappointments. Here we see a case of working with images and projections and when the desired result is not met then anxiety, disappointments and even anger arise in us. We always cling to the results of our actions and reject what is not in favor of them. Here when the car breaks down the thinker makes it into a problem. Problems are in the mind; they are born there. For one who is not attached, who does not cling or reject to what is, there are no problems, only different actions. For example, okay the car is down: fix it if we can, if not, go back and enjoy a holiday at home. A different course of action will present itself if one is in that state of pure awareness.

Next, we should investigate clinging and aversion because if these are understood we can then find a state where equanimity is present, a state which will take us out of the world of duality and from that state we can see life with different eyes. This is the state where meditation can occur.

CHAPTER 17

CLINGING & AVERSION

We look at what Longchenpa, a Buddhist master of non-duality, has said regarding duality.

> *To apprehend duality where there is no duality Is like looking at a mirage. Do not let yourself be caught by clinging, by taking or rejecting what has no reality. Watch your mind, Itself not different from a mirage. This is the wisdom of the Conquerors past, present, and to come.*
>
> *-Longchenpa*

In the above, Longchenpa is saying that either clinging or aversion are just an illusory state of mind regardless of the way is produced either by craving or aversion. And he explains further:

Chapter The fifth Vajra Point

Just as in a pool of clear water the reflections of the stars and planets appear, likewise, within the clear water of the mind, and through the doors of the limpid sense powers, outer and inner phenomena (form and the other five sense objects) appear in the manner of reflections. But the mind is deluded and takes such objects to be really existing. In the terms of the comparison, the mind and the sense powers are like the pure water, whereas the appearance of the sense objects – which are the awakening of the habitual tendencies stored in the mind from time without beginning – are represented by the stars and planets. These sense objects are neither the mind nor some thing other than the mind. Manifesting in the manner of reflected images, appearing objects come before the dualistically oriented mind. And reacting to them with craving and aversion, as things to be accepted or rejected, beings are caught thereby.

-Longchenpa

Longchenpa also states that the mind's nature is always pure but if the sensory objects are not recognized as reflections in the mind and if one reacts by either aversion or clinging, then the mind is in the dualistic view, therefore the mind is deluded by these objects by taking them to be real.

It is most important to understand this and see where our inner practice lies and pay attention to how the mind operates and clings to pleasures; to just watch what happens and how we fit in this play of life. It does take tremendous energy to just patiently watch and even keep watching while participating in our daily activities. To be in that state of awareness is not easy at all and each of us must find our own helping tools to stay in that choiceless awareness. When we are praised, we respond quickly, for it gives us a sense of achievement and therefore pride. When blame comes, we reject it as quickly, and our pride is then hurt. If we do not react either to being blamed or praised, then the self is not affected either by clinging or aversion.

How we are inclined to cling or resist, to like or dislike, to see good or bad is according to our conditioning. If all our conditioning and all our traits of personality are no longer clinging to the ego, then we will see much more, hear much more, feel much more, taste much more. Then the senses will take us to a new dimension of existence; where the senses become extraordinary in their perception, becoming very astute and sensitive.

Nissagarata Maharaj, a Vedanta master of non-duality, states that clinging and aversion are the cause of all suffering. If we really observe how the process unfolds within ourselves, we will discover the truth of this statement. The non duality cannot be overcome by saying it is only an illusion. The illusion is there if we look at it with aversion or clinging, but if we just look with no judgement or comparison, with no filter of our conditioning then duality disappears. When we are living every moment in that state, we are in a state of equanimity of mind, and it is this state where true meditation is and not the meditation which is induced by thought. Then there is no exclusion or inclusion of anyone or anything; there is always what it is and that is Love. When we are in that state, we are present in the flow, between pleasure and pain.

In the Middle Length Discourses the Buddha said:

> *On seeing a form with the eye, one does not lust after it if is pleasing and one does not dislike it if it is displeasing. Having thus abandoned,*
> *favoring and opposing, whatever feeling one feels, whether painful or pleasant, or neither painful nor pleasant, one does not seek gratification through feeling or remain attached to it. As one does not do so, craving for feeling ceases. With the cessation of craving comes cessation of clinging; with the cessation of clinging, cessation of being with the cessa-*

tion of being, cessation of birth; with the cessation of birth, aging and death, sorrow, lamentation, pain, grief, and despair cease. Such is the cessation of this whole mass of suffering.

-Buddha

Here Buddha clearly states a way out of duality. It is not that we are not involved in the play of life, but rather that we are aware and observant of every feeling and emotion and do not react with either clinging or aversion. In doing so, we put an end to suffering and rise above that impoverished state of mind.

Buddha says in the *Dhammapada*:

All conditioned things are impermanent – when one sees this with wisdom, one turns away from suffering.
The root of suffering is attachment.
Change is never painful, only resistance to change is painful.
Every experience, no matter how bad it seems, holds within it a blessing of some kind. The goal is to find it.

-Buddha

Like it or not, change always comes, and the greater the resistance, the greater the pain.

-Alan Watts

Letting go gives us freedom, and freedom is the only condition for happiness. If we still cling to something in our hearts, we cannot be free.

-Thich Nhat Hanh

The art of living... is neither careless drifting on the one hand nor fearful clinging to the past on the other. It consists in being sensitive to each moment, in regarding it as utterly new and unique, in having the mind open and wholly receptive.

-Alan Watts

These quotes all point to the same energy: any attachment to anything is a cause of suffering, but one should not fall in ignorance because as Alan Watts states, the art of living is being sensitive to each moment and having a mind and heart open as the sky and operating in that intelligence which always promotes the right action. We could read thousands of quotes but if we do not really pay full attention and stay in the present moment, the quotes will only give an intellectual orgasm and nothing more. This will not in any way lead to the opening of the mind and heart to the one reality of oneness. When there is no clinging or resisting without effort then a state of equanimity unfolds. In the present moment there is no room to play with images and project them in future, therefore if they do not unfold as we have projected them, we suffer according to the intensity of the attachment.

Christ also says this, as we have seen in the previous chapter. We should look again at his statement:

Jesus said to them: "When you make the two into one, and when you make the inside like the outside and the outside like the inside and the above like the below - that is, to make the male and the female into a single one, so that the male will not be male and the female will not be female — and when you make eyes instead of an eye and a hand instead of a hand and a foot instead of a foot, an image instead of an image, then you will enter [the kingdom].

-Gospel of Thomas: 22

He clearly points out the same state of equanimity as Buddha has done. And when one lives in this state and this state alone, one will discover the mysteries of life, love, and truth and this is the highest meditative state.

Jiddu Krishnamurti stated in his talks that, "Meditation is the understanding of all movement of life" and this is the meaning of true meditation. The Upanishads also has pointers to overcoming the world of duality and entering the state of equanimity. In that state, love flows and is not corrupted by thought. In that state, thought is powerless. There is only intelligence, wisdom and compassion operating, where love flows uninterrupted.

Fear is another cause of suffering and because of fear we tend to cling or resist. Feelings of loneliness or insecurity are all due to our conditioning and how we approach and see life. Fear also lives in duality for the one who has no fear, has Love and Love is whole, never divisible, never dualistic. As the Sun's rays do not discriminate a criminal from a saint, so Love does not discriminate at all. Divine Love flows through the saint and so through the criminal. The only difference is that the saint allows it to freely manifest where a criminal cannot manifest that love fully because he still lives in duality with all the fears, clinging and aversion according to his conditioning. Love is restricted to flow where conditioning prevails. Alternatively, we can say that love flows there fully but the criminal is not aware of that flow and is limited in his awareness of that love.

From what we have discovered so far, we can observe that clinging and aversion both have to be abandoned, and it is the fears and desires which are the cause of both clinging and aversion. Where desires are fulfilled, automatically attachment arises. It is the pleasures which any object of desire provides that allow us to create attachment to that object and because of that pleasure we try hard to hang onto it and to repeat that pleasure numerous times. We give in to a new more pleasurable sensation and then get into a pattern of thought called a habit.

Desires cannot be given up, but attachment to our desires should be given up and the fulfillment of any desire should not be stored in memory. We can enjoy something and let it go, moving on with life, for life is a movement of Love. If we try to hang on to anything, we are in illusion, but if we flow with life – never resisting or clinging to anything – we will be out of suffering. Suffering is caused by the attachments we make and the more we cling, the more pain and suffering increases.

We can look at and observe our habits and attachments to things, places, people ideas, concepts, and observation is the greatest tool at our disposal, observing the inner movement and outer movement of life. If we can stay in that awareness, we will transmute the inner and the outer by merging both in one movement. The energies of lust, greed, ignorance, envy and anger never sleep for they are also a part of that movement of life, and they reside in us, in our being. They are a product of our own ego in attachments, desires and producing feelings, sensations and so on. We can enjoy life only if we live with no attachments to wife, son, daughter, friend and so on. The moment we become attached, control is there, and conflicts arise. Then love cannot flow; it is restricted by the negative energy produced by clinging or aversion which may result in guilt. We just need to observe this in everyday life, and we will see the truth of the statement as all masters pointed out that it is imperative for us to see.

We may think that in order to overcome all desires, we have to be as monks and denounce all the joys of everyday life. There is not only one road to truth for freedom is, here and now. If we are observant, we will be aware of our own attachments and in that awareness, will find a way of overcoming them. We may sit in silence, we may write a book, we may work; whatever we do, as long as we function with full awareness of the moment, we cannot go wrong because that moment is our guide supreme, which lies in our own hearts. It is our guru supreme.

If we can live in full awareness, we are always in the present moment. It is now, which is alive, full of life and love. The past is a dead thing, and the future does not exist. Therefore, the future is now. It is determined always by what we do now. Eckart Tolle in *The Power of Now* touches on the eternal now, just as all masters have beautifully presented the power of the moment which is in the mind, for it is the mind which can bind, and it is the same mind which can liberate.

A true monk is the one who does not cling to anything and does not reject anything, just flows with life. But in order for one to flow with life, one requires faith in the unknown where there is no so-called security, there is nothing to hang on too, or nothing to be supported by and one is really alone.

Most of us fear loneliness but the one who is alone is never lonely for in that state of being alone everything is, and one therefore is never apart from the whole. If we observe being lonely without running away from it through entertainment or chattering, we will see that loneliness is no longer there. It is there only in the moment of flight, of trying to escape, but if we stay with it, in that awareness, that loneliness is dissolved and if we are so blessed, the benediction comes uninvited, full of love and bliss supreme. Here we have introduced loneliness, which topic we discuss next in order to grasp how loneliness comes about and how it is affecting us.

CHAPTER 18

LONELINESS

Everyone at one point or another has encountered loneliness. We may call it boredom and a feeling of anxiety or depression may come with it, or a combination of the two most likely. This loneliness arrives in our lives in order to awaken us to the reality of being. Everyone, either from a relationship breakdown, a death, a loss of something or someone, has been faced with this feeling of being alone or lonely. Being alone with this loneliness is what most of us cannot endure and therefore are trying to escape, whether through music, looking to be in someone's company, watching tv, or any kind of entertainment through food, shopping and so on. Few are those who can actually stay with it and face it until that feeling dissipates and is understood finally as just an illusory state of mind of our own making, which keeps us from finding reality.

These states of anxiety and depression are sometimes very strong and therefore create so much pain for the individual. These states are created by our inability to understand how these feelings are produced in the first place. If we stay with that feeling of loneliness as much as we can every day, little by little we will overcome it and realize that loneliness is a fabrication of our mind, shaped by conditions, habits, ideas, attachments and so on, which are also products of our mind. But we will not overcome it only by an intellectual understanding; we have to go through it like a ship goes through the eye of a great storm. We have to stay with that moment, not allowing the mind to flee to sensory objects or get in any direction of thought. In staying with it, surrendering to it fully, we will eventually cross the ocean of the world of duality. This is the key to gaining our own true freedom. We always try to flee from this feeling and in doing so fuel this loneliness and allow it to grow. This loneliness then enforces the ego for it will try to escape from it by any means and in that escape, the ego is sustained and grows, keeping us in a prison of our own making.

The yogis, the monks of all traditions and all people of a spiritual discipline have learned to stay with this loneliness, and some have overcome it, pointing out to us that we also can do it if the intention is there. It takes a mind with no judgement, one free of ideas or concepts, a mind that stops creating images about self and others, a mind with patience, simplicity and humility to be able to face this loneliness, from this feeling all other feelings arise and if we overcome this great feeling, we have gone beyond it all. Staying with that loneliness is the key to opening new dimensions of existence, a great space where the mind expands and is no longer confined to any attachment to ideas, to concepts, to anyone or anything. Then the little center – the "me" we work from – disappears.

Most of us try to flee and in doing so remain caught in the cycle of birth and death. It is not an easy task to escape the cycle. It requires faith and courage to surrender our own little center, our ego. Our minds are conditioned to the universal mind, which has been also conditioned since time immemorial and this conditioning is like layers of a gigantic onion, joined one by one with the glue of attachment and desire for the things that give us pleasure, the more the pleasure, the stronger the glue. The Rishis of India and enlightened teachers from all religious traditions have shown that it is possible to transcend this conditioning and if we are eager to shed this conditioning ourselves it can be done, but it is not an easy task. Jesus Christ has exposed this difficulty.

Jesus said, "I shall choose you, one from a thousand and two from ten thousand, and they will stand as a single one.

-Gospel of Thomas: 23

Here, Christ mentions how great is the task to overcome the world with all the desires and how rare it is to be the chosen one. For the beings which have pure intention to gain freedom from the cycle of worldly existence, the benediction will come, and they will merge back into the father, into oneness. When we have understood the world and developed our full intention to be really free of all sorrows and misery then we will fully surrender to the mysteries of life, to the qualities of love such as intelligence, compassion, wisdom, humility, simplicity and patience. All these qualities are embedded in Love, and they show up as required, working their magic all around.

It is clear so far that faith is a requirement. Faith is the ability to fully surrender to the unknown, to life, which is carried by the innate intelligence of the absolute. Only true love can have a true relationship with all beings without conflict and without any shadow of control over the other. In that relationship with others, there is no condition; there is no exclusion of one over another; there is no connection to being severed for in oneness connection does not exist. One who is free has a free relationship with every-thing, meaning he is one with (Sat, Chit, Ananda) truth, existence, bliss.

Christ, and many other awakened masters, have stated that when we see this world as a corpse, we will realize that in it we never find everlasting peace. Not that the world is literarily a corpse and ugly: rather, it is only that when we realize fully that we are not apart from it, but we are virtually a part of it, a unitary movement with the whole of manifestation – the seen and the unseen. This is a unitary movement of love. It is all encompassing when we are in deep meditation where all sounds and movements have been incorporated into oneness: the being is not something separate. It is one with the oneness where all sounds, movements and whatever is manifested come into being and go back to it, if one grasps it one can then really see the beauty of nature and the world and will never do anything to hurt it.

The root of all problems is attachment, but then we may ask how we can live with no attachments to wife, possessions, children and so on. It is one thing to see at the intellectual level, but different to really grasp it at the heart level. It is not an easy task to cut all attachments, for the more pleasure things give, the more our attachment to them is. If, for example, we cut all attachments, one may wonder how we are to function in life, and how we are to have a loving relationship with others, here fear arises; it is the fear that we will be left alone with nothing and nobody to love. Here the thinking mind confuses love with attachment, but for the one who is free, there is no confusion. It is just love regardless.

Christ has stated regarding this.

> *Anyone who loves their life will lose it, while anyone who hates their life in this world will keep it for eternal life.*
>
> -John 12:25

The Middle Length Discourses of the Buddha, has stated:

> *Acquisition (attachment) is the root of suffering.*
>
> -Buddha

These statements clearly point out that if one clings or has attachments to or desire for anything in this world, they cannot have everlasting joy and in loving this kind of life – immersed in pleasures and attached to them – they will lose the real life and taste death, being in the cycle of life and never free. In the second part,

Christ clearly states that to die to the life of desires and attach-ments to things, places and people is the key to gaining eternal life. He means to die a psychological death – the death of the ego, where we are free from it – and in that freedom we will find the eternal life.

What Christ refers to above goes hand in hand with his statement, "Seek the kingdom and everything will be added onto you." Once we see the truth of these statements, we can gain total freedom from all illusory states of existence, and can then surrender to life, enjoying and seeing the world with a different eye, therefore enjoying even the life of the senses if they are offered, but not be bound in any way by them. Many contemporary masters have come and gone, but each in their own way has pointed to the same truth. Swamy Vivekananda was an ascetic; Lahiri Mahasaya was a householder: neither had a problem in finding the truth. Each worked in life accordingly, because they fully surrendered any idea or concept, and both have touched the supreme love, showing us that wherever we are in life, it can be done from right there and we do not have to copy others for if we copy another, we fall into illusion.

The teachings of the great masters cannot and should not be taken literally or they will give rise to many contradictions and conflicts in the individual and society at large. These teachings have to be understood by heart and lived in our everyday life. Meditation is one of the tools to help us stay with this loneliness and the more we sit in it, the more we will transcendent it. Some beings do not mean to encounter this loneliness in this lifetime and go through life with not many problems but most of us will encounter it because it is said:

Blessed are the poor in spirit: for theirs is the kingdom of heaven.
Blessed are they that mourn for they shall be comforted.
Blessed are the meek: for they shall inherit the earth.
Blessed are they which do hunger and thirst after righteousness: for they shall be filled.
Blessed are the merciful: for they shall obtain mercy.
Blessed are the pure in heart: for they shall see God.
Blessed are the peacemakers: for they shall be called the children of God.
Blessed are they which are persecuted for righteousness' sake: for theirs is the kingdom of heaven.
Blessed are ye, when men shall revile you, and persecute you, and shall say all manner of evil against you falsely, for my sake.
Rejoice, and be exceeding glad: for great is your reward in heaven: for so persecuted they the prophets which were before you.

-Matthew 5: 3–12

Here, the Lord shows that all who suffer in one way or another will find a blessing in every suffering, if they are able to stay with that suffering. Every suffering will put us face to face with this loneliness where there is great fear and sorrow. If we have the power not to flee but to accept suffering, we will find in it there is great blessing and freedom and with every suffering something in us is transformed.

Most of us are not able to face it; we always try to find a way to escape it and always look for pleasures that give us small gratification: this leads us into losing our life, as Christ mentions. In that loneliness we can see our pains, our fears, our attachments. In that pure observation, if we are there totally, we may transcend it all, realizing that this loneliness is the gate to the other side, so to speak, and when that loneliness has been obliterated by the clear light of wisdom which is pure awareness there is no longer the other side and only oneness remains.

We talked about fears which have accumulated throughout a lifetime – or many lifetimes. Often, we have not had the courage to face them, always running when faced with them. Only when life pins us down and we have no more avenues of escape do we look at it, but in resisting or suppressing fear or feelings there is the potential for great pain because one day these fears and feelings will come up in our consciousness with a force which is too problematic for most of us.

Facing loneliness can come with the feeling of not been able to escape it, a feeling of being powerless over the circumstances and conditions in our life which have got us to the stage we are in. It is a blessing to be put in such a position, not to be able to escape from it and to be forced to face it with all our being. The more we are able to face it, the more we unveil our true self. The more we unveil, the more we expand ourselves into oneness and come to the realization that we are all the children of the living father, as Christ stated. In this facing of our fears, we are really looking within. When we start to look within, we will initially see only darkness, the same as when churning milk all the bad stuff comes out first before we can get the goodness out. So, before we find the light, we see our own attachments, desires and so on as darkness.

This loneliness comes about when we have understood the five poisons as we discussed earlier; when we have stopped being in the pleasures of the world and the attachments that come with it which cause us to fall prisoner to the trappings of the five poisons. In the imprisonment of the five poisons, we are ignorant regarding our true nature and will always create mischief for ourselves and others, therefore living in conflict, never having a loving relationship with the world and others because the ego will do anything to keep us in that state of imprisonment. In that state, we are thrown from anxiety into depression therefore oscillating between the two. If we look for an escape, we are then back in the world and lose our life, for true life is found in true love where there are no attachments, fears or ignorance.

Here we look at what the Paramahamsa Upanishad points to us.

Narada enquired of the Lord of Love: "What is the state of the illumined one?" The Lord replied: "Hard to reach is the state of the illumined one. Only a few Attain it. But even one is enough. For he is the pure Self of the scriptures; He is truly great because he serves me, and I reveal myself through him always." He has renounced all selfish attachments and observes no rites and ceremonies. He has only minimum possessions and lives his life for the welfare of all. He has no staff nor tuft nor sacred thread. He faces heat and cold, pleasure and pain, Honor and dishonor with equal calm. He is not affected by calamity, pride, jealousy, status, joy, or sorrow, greed, anger, or infatuation, excitement, egoism, or other poisons; For he knows he is neither body nor mind. Free from the sway of doubt and false knowledge He lives united with the Lord of Love, who is ever serene, immutable, Indivisible, the source of all joy and wisdom. The Lord is his true home, His pilgrim's tuft of hair, his sacred thread; For he has entered the unitive state. Having renounced every selfish desire, He has found his rest in the Lord of Love. Wisdom is the staff that supports him now. Those who take a mendicant's staff while they are still at the mercy of their senses Cannot escape enormous suffering. The illumined man knows this truth of life. For him the universe is his garment, And the Lord does not separate from himself. He offers no ancestral oblations; He praises nobody, blames nobody, Is never dependent on anyone. He has no need to repeat the mantra, no longer need to practice meditation. The world of change and changeless Reality are one to him, for he sees all in God. The aspirant who is seeking the Lord Must free himself from selfish attachments to people, money, and possessions. When his mind sheds every selfish desire, He becomes free from the duality of pleasure and pain that rules his senses. No more is he capable of ill will; No more is he subject to elation, for his senses come to rest in the Self. Entering into the unitive state, He attains the goal of evolution. Truly he attains the goal of evolution. OM shanti shanti shanti."

-The Upanishads

In this Upanishad, it is pointed out that the goal of evolution is the entering into the unitive state with all existence, the Lord of Love, God or whichever name we assign to oneness. In order to enter such a state, we have to give up all selfish desires, to deny ourselves to find our true nature and wisdom is the only support we have. Once all selfish desires are given up, we become free from the world of duality, of pleasure and pain. We are not afflicted by cold and heat, pride or blame, like or dislike. We are ever free from all practices of meditation, traditions and the like. We have freed ourselves from all attachment to money, possessions and pleasures. We are one in union with the Lord of Love and see all existence as one God.

Christ also points out the same as the Upanishads: that we need to understand that this life is not our true reality; it is only a relative reality we need to be in for the process of our awakening to take place.

While anyone who hates their life in this world will keep it for eternal life.

-John 12:25

We must renounce all selfish desires and in doing so, enter the state of equanimity of mind where we transmute the world of duality and surrender to the Lord of Love (God) and thus enter the supreme state of being which is the home of every sentient being. The Paramahamsa Upanishad relates the wisdom needed in order to find our own reality: with the knife of wisdom, we are capable of cutting through the dualistic view of life which is ignorance as illusion.

It would be easy if we had a golden pill to take us there but unfortunately the golden pill is a pill full of sorrow and suffering, for only through that may we be inclined to ask the question if there is more to life than meets the eye. When the world goes through wars and natural crises, a feeling of unity, love and compassion arise. It is only through hard times that families unite and come together as a unitary movement, and it is unfortunate that only suffering brings about unity in diversity. Unless we have the intention to find the kingdom, the state of great bliss, we can only find it on our own, and no guru, no saint can do it for us. We need to walk the path. They may walk with us, but nobody will carry us there – no politician, no institution, no money – nothing can help us. Only one who has done it, can show the way or show a glimpse of the eternal, but even that is still an experience which lives in time and must be killed. Buddha has stated, "if I came in your dream or in a vision take the teachings from me but kill the image you see," meaning do not get attached to it. This is why going through this loneliness, misery, and suffering must be done by us alone. With the help of wisdom which will come if we have the intention to find the truth, we will find freedom in love. We are conditioned to run from any form of suffering. It is an animal instinct to do this at the physical level of existence, which is fine, but at the psychological level we need to stay with whatever is there, for all the inner pain and suffering is only caused by our own ignorance; from our inability to see what is in front of us. A wife or husband is cheating and when the other finds out, they are in a state of shock, pain and suffering because all the images they have created throughout the relationship come crashing down and do not agree with what the actuality is. If one in that pain stays with the fact, with the actuality, without trying to change anything, they will transmute the pain and can accept the other as a cheater, no matter the reason for it. In that acceptance, a solution to the situation will present itself and either one forgives the other or they part ways, therefore changing the role of the relationship but never changing the love they have for each other. But who can do that? Only one who is in the state of equanimity and can see with the eye of wisdom the desires of the one who cheated, in that seeing the wise can forgive and that is forgiveness, which is not cultivated by thought, then there is Love.

This state of equanimity has no fears, no anxiety, no stress, no frustrations, no anger or feeling of guilt or being sorry, no attachments of any kind, no selfish desires. It has only compassion and wisdom and the desire for all beings to be happy, all prerequisites for love to descend in the heart and make the union of the being with the supreme Lord of Love.

To stay with the loneliness with the present moment it is not an easy task for the ego is always trying to take us out of that state of equanimity of mind, from the state of awareness of the present moment, and it does that by thinking and makes us cling to any thought, in doing so takes us out in some kind of action for we always look for action, in doing something. We rarely have a moment of rest and even if physically tired and we sit, the mind is never at rest in silence, it is always thinking of something which lures us out into the world. We also do this by building images for this building of images is the mechanism which keep us in ignorance and produces so much mischief for ourselves and others. Because we create images which then give hope, either we bring them from past images and change them in the present then project them into the future, or we create new ones in the present and project them into the future. It is all the same. We live with these images, about the wife, the boss, and so on and if they do not fit reality, we are in inner conflict which then can be felt by others, and we are never resting and never in peace.

Christ told the disciples:

> *If they ask you, "What is the evidence of your Father in you?" say to them, "It is motion and rest."*

-Gospel of Thomas: 50

Here, Christ is telling us we are creatures of action but also of rest, though most of us only find pleasure in action and very rarely in rest. He also suggests that the father is action, and rest at the same time, for he is the manifestation and the essence of everything from which everything springs and into which it returns. We also have to find this balance and learn how to rest, how to find the essence of our being and only in rest can we find it, in that silence where there is noise and no noise. This is the most arduous task, and it is the goal of all beings. We are to find our reality; as the Upanishads shows, it is the natural goal of evolution.

It is very important, as Jiddu Krishnamurti has stated, that the mind stops creating and storing images by giving full attention to what is.

> *We all have suffered psychologically in various ways, either with great intensity or to a lesser degree – we have all had suffering of one kind or another. When we suffer, instinctively we want to run away from it – through religion, through entertainment, reading books, through anything to get away from the suffering. Now if the mind is attentive and does not move away from suffering at all, then you will see that out of total attention comes not only energy – which means passion – but also that suffering comes to an end. In the same way, all images can end instantly when there is no preference for any image; this is very important. When you have no preference, you have no prejudice. Then you are attentive, then you can look. In that observation there is not only the understanding of the building of images, but also the ending of all images. So, I see the importance of*

relationships, and there can be a relationship without any conflict, which means love. Love is not an image; it is not pleasure; it is not desire. Love is not something that can be cultivated; it is not dependent on memory.

-Jiddu Krishnamurti

Above, Jiddu Krishnamurti is clearly showing us a way out of the patterns of thought by purely observing, by being mindful. Buddha also states this.

Do not dwell in the past, do not dream of the future, concentrate the mind on the present moment. … It is a man's own mind, not his enemy or foe, which lures him to evil ways.

-Buddha

Similarly to Buddha, Christ is pointing to the same approach in:

Know what is in front of your face, and what is hidden from you will be disclosed to you.

-Gospel of Thomas: 5

In all these sayings of the awakened ones, we see the secret of coming out of suffering, sorrows, and feelings of loneliness. This ability to observe without judgement or prejudice, without any idea of what we may know about what is presented to us, in that state of pure awareness the truth reveals itself with no effort.

Jiddu Krishnamurti has pointed out that for as long as we are in the world of pleasure and projecting of images, we can never find true love and can never have a loving relationship with one another for we will always be in attachments and trappings of our own mind, as Buddha states. The projecting of images creates hope – the hope that the images we created and projected will come to fruition. If they do, we are happy; if they do not, we are in sorrow and suffering is produced. There is nothing wrong with imagination and visualization. It is actually of importance in Yogic practices, especially in the tantric practices where one visualizes the deities and the world and at the end of the visualization dissolves it all into the clear light with no attachment to any, thereby transforming and cleansing the body and mind in the process. There is also nothing wrong with creating images about your life and the direction to take, as long as one is not affected if these images become reality or not; as long as one is not attached to such images and understands how to use them in a constructive way.

We will talk about Love in chapters to come, for all chapters will start to be intertwined together into a dance, for the teachings of the awakened masters are never linear, never straight. One of their statements can be comprehended and respond to a multiplicity of questions. Next, we will look at awareness, for it is this energy that can get us out of the patterns and habits of our own minds.

CHAPTER 19

AWARENESS

This is a topic of immense importance, for this awareness is the pure energy where one can find Love and all the qualities that love incorporates: Peace, Compassion, Silence, Humility, Simplicity, Patience, Sensitivity, Intelligence and Wisdom. All the masters of all traditions have pointed to this energy – we can call it mindfulness, total attention or spirit – and they have iterated that in this awareness of being we will find what we are not and then we remain with what we are, then the self will be discovered with no effort. The only effort needed is to drop all that we are not.

> *I am a mass of awareness and of consciousness. I am not a doer nor an experiencer. I am the very Self, indestructible and changeless.*
>
> -Adi Shankara

Above, Adi Shankara declares that awareness or consciousness is the very substratum where the self dwells. In this pure awareness, the experiencer is not, only the state of experience remains. This awareness is like space and is the very essence where everything comes and goes. In the previous chapter, we have seen how one works with images, and we have mentioned that by giving total attention to that process we see how it unfolds without any prejudice or judgement. We go for a walk and instead of staying with what we encounter – the nature around, the noises, the color of the sky, the smells and so on – we are thinking and worrying about different things therefore never able to stay in the joy of walking, never being able to fully stay with the present moment as it arises. We live like this most of the time and by doing so we are all fragmented, the mind is always running after the things we are attracted to and in which we find more pleasure and satisfaction.

In this pure awareness we are looking at the outer expression of life as well as the inner with all its intricacies, responses, and reactions. When we are able to stay in this awareness without any control over what life has to offer or what life has to take, we are in the natural state of being. We call this awareness with no choice or naked awareness as described by Padmasambhava, a fully awakened master whose arrival as a fully awakened one was predicted by Buddha Shakyamuni; in his book Self Liberation through Seeing with Naked Awareness, Padmasambhava points out how one can liberate oneself from the cycle of birth and death.

> *This self-originated Clear Light, which from the very*
> *beginning was in no way produced by something*
> *antecedent to it, is the child of awareness, and yet it is*
> *itself without any parents, amazing!*
> *This self-originated primordial awareness has not been*
> *created by anything, amazing!*
> *It does not experience birth, nor does there exist a cause for*
> *its death, amazing!*
> *Although it is evidently visible, there is no one there who*
> *sees it, amazing!*
> *Although it has wandered throughout Samsara, it has*

come to no harm amazing!
Even though it has seen Buddhahood itself, it has not come
to any benefit from this, amazing!
Even though it exists in everyone everywhere, yet it has
gone unrecognized, amazing!
Nonetheless you hope to attain some other fruit than this
elsewhere, amazing!
Even though it exists within yourself (and nowhere else),
yet you seek for it elsewhere, amazing!
How wonderful!
This immediate intrinsic awareness is insubstantial and
lucidly clear: Just this is the highest pinnacle of all views.
It is all encompassing, free of everything, and without any
conceptions whatsoever: Just this is the highest pinnacle
among all meditations. It is un-fabricated and inexpress-
ible in worldly terms: Just this is the highest pinnacle
among all courses of conduct.
Without being sought after, it is spontaneously self-per-
fected from the very beginning:
Just this is the highest pinnacle among all fruits.

-Padmasambhava

These verses show how everything arises from this clear light and this light does not have any support in anything but supports everything. It is eternal in itself. Christ refers to that light in the same way in the following verses.

If they say to you, "Where have you come from?" say to
them, "We have come from the light, from the place where
the light came into being by itself, established [itself], and
appeared in their image." If they say to you, "Is it you?"
say, "We are its children, and we are the chosen of the
living Father." If they ask you, "What is the evidence of
your Father in you?" say to them, "It is motion and rest."

-Gospel of Thomas: 50

Here in one statement, Christ refers to the clear light of awareness; that which Padmasambhava referred to as being the nature of reality, being God. Both refer to it as having no need to be supported by anything for it came into being by itself. Also, both refer to it being the nature of rest and movement and existing everywhere including in ourselves.

Ramdas also refers to the same light of consciousness:

> *It is this one Consciousness, or "knowingness," that is dispersed around in all living beings, and being of the nature of awareness, it protects all bodies everywhere. The name of it is the "Light of the Universe" and all living beings are alive because of this Universal Light. The actual experience of it is evident and can be seen directly for oneself.*
>
> -St Shri Samartha Ramdas

If we recognize the reality to which these statements point and live there with all our hearts, we will be liberated in an instant. I am sure all readers at one point or another have experienced this awareness when they were looking at something which took their breath away, where the little center, the me, disappeared and we were established in that oneness where the experiencer, the experience and the object of experience become one, in that awareness of being. Adi Shankara also points out the same truth in the statement "I am the mass of awareness and consciousness". Here both awareness and consciousness refer to the same immensity of being.

Awareness of being is self-explanatory in the next quote from *Dasbodh* where an awakened master gives teachings to aspirants.

Being, Pure Awareness, and Oneness are all one's own form. When all of the elements, which are non-essence, have been left to disappear, what remains is Essence and there is the realization that one's true identity is formless.

-St Shri Samartha Ramdas

When we can sit in that awareness without any judgements or prejudices, any ideas or concepts about anything or anyone then we are at home, and there is the start of meditation. In that meditation, we recognize the whole movement of life, which is eternal. In that state, the body is not felt even though we know the body is there and the light eternal is the formless oneness. The whole purpose of yoga, prayers, tantras and all such systems is to make the mind silent, at peace and to be established in that awareness which sees with the clear light of wisdom allowing God to manifest in us. Then from there we will act the right way; we will know what love is and we will work for the benefit of all beings. As discussed in previous chapters about the mind, here everything comes together; if we have understood the mind and the limitations then we can see the ego with its intricacies which keep us in misery and suffering.

If we are really serious then we will be established in that awareness of being and will live life as the universal will dictates, not how our little will (me and mine) dictates. It is not easy to surrender that little me, as mentioned before, but there is no other avenue, I am afraid the road is narrow, and it is like walking on a razor's edge.

All spiritual practices are designed to help us stay in that state of universal will of love, peace and oneness.

Longchenpa says this about the mind:

> *This mind that estimates appearances as dreams, If now and then you really search for it — Out or in or somewhere in between — There's no way to identify it, No point on which to set your bearings. There is a state of openness like boundless space. Devoid of the wild frenzy of your memories and plans, Awareness luminous and empty, Free of all conceptual construction, Arises of its own accord. When the apprehender ceases, the apprehended also is no more. When the subject has withdrawn, all holding of an object vanishes. Then there is no link with an appearing object. The framework of discernment falls away. Then there's simply primal wisdom, Nondual, self-arisen.*

-Longchenpa

Another awakened master refers to the mind as it is constructed; as nothing but an illusion. As it gives up all the grasping of objects and surrenders to the naked awareness, then the mind is one with the clear light of wisdom and sees reality as it is. We can give a simile that awareness is like space where everything appears and disappears, and the space is not affected by any of the appearances for that space is reality and all appearances are illusory and never have an independent origination or support, whereas the light of awareness has its own support and its own light. Everything is dependent on other things: this is a truth that Buddha exposed in the dependent origination.

For example, the Buddha has said the flame in an oil lamp depends upon the oil and the wick. When the oil and the wick are present, the flame in an oil lamp burns. If either of these is absent, the flame will cease to burn. This example illustrates the principle of dependent origination. Let us take another example: the sprout, which is dependent upon the seed, earth, water, air, and sunlight in order to arise. There are in fact innumerable examples of dependent origination because there is no existing phenomenon that is not the effect of dependent origination. All phenomena arise dependent upon a number of causal factors. We can conclude as a fact that the entire universe and the like are subject to this law of dependent origination. Everything depends on other things and so the whole universe is a complex matrix of relationships, it is in fact a living entity.

We will not dive in depth into the subject of dependent origination but only to understand the simple fact which the awakened masters understood: the fact that all reality and all phenomena in the universe are but a construct which has as its basis the essence of all existence. As Christ has stated, the light of awareness is everywhere and in everything and whatever appears and disappears came from that light.

When we understand that we are all part of this universal movement of God in awareness, which is also God, then perhaps we will stop killing one another or hurting one another for we will realize that we only hurt ourselves in the process of life. The ego may attempt to turn us away from this truth but if we stay in the clear light of awareness of being, we will realize the truth not just as a mere statement but as an actuality. This is why Christ has stated:

> *This heaven will pass away, and the (heaven) above it will*
> *pass away.*
> *And the dead are not alive, and the living will not die.*
> *In the days when you consumed what was dead, you made*
> *it alive.*
> *When you are in the light, what will you do?*
> *On the day when you were one, you became two.*
> *But when you become two, what will you do?*
>
> -The Gospel of Thomas: 11

Whoever finds his own reality in God will not die, but Christ also mentions that even heavens are just states of mind, coming and going and nothing is everlasting. When we are in that light of awareness there is nothing to be done, for we are one with the father and not apart from him. On this, Padmasambhava has stated:

> *Thus, we speak of the Middle Way where one does not fall into any of the extremes, and we speak of intrinsic awareness as uninterrupted mindful presence. Since emptiness possesses a heart that is intrinsic awareness, therefore, it is called by the name of Tathagata-garbha, that is, "the embryo or heart of Buddhahood." If you understand the meaning of this, then that will transcend and surpass everything Else. Therefore, it is called by the name of Prajnaparamita, that is, "the Perfection of Wisdom." Because it cannot be conceived of by the intellect and is free of all (conceptual) limitations from the very beginning, therefore it is called by the name of Mahamudra, that is, "the Great Symbol." Because of that, in accordance with whether it is specifically understood or not understood, since it is the basis of everything, of all the bliss of Nirvana and of all the sorrow of Samsara, therefore it is called by the name of Alaya, that is, "the foundation of everything." Because, when it remains in its own space, it is quite ordinary and in no way exceptional, this awareness that is present and lucidly clear is called by the name of "ordinary awareness."*

> -Padmasambhava

The great masters have all explained the meaning of what we call intrinsic awareness, or pure awareness or naked awareness and they point out that even Samsara and Nirvana are just manifestations of the same energy of God which is the essence of all things.

The book *Day by Day with Bhagavan* is the diary of Devaraja Mudaliar, a long-term devotee of Sri Ramana Maharshi, recording conversations and events that took place during the years 1945 to 1947.

A young man from Colombo, Ceylon, said to Bhagavan:
"J. Krishnamurti teaches the method of effortless and
choiceless awareness as distinct from that of deliberate
concentration. Would Sri Bhagavan be pleased to explain
how best to practice meditation and what form the object of
meditation should take?"
Ramana Maharshi: "Effortless and choiceless awareness is
our real nature. If we can attain that state and abide in it,
that is all right. But one cannot reach it without effort, the
effort of deliberate meditation.
All the age-old vasanas (inherent tendencies) turn the mind
outwards to external objects. All such thoughts have to be
given up and the mind turned inwards and that, for most
people, requires effort. Of course, every teacher and every
book tell the aspirant to keep quiet, but it is not easy to do
so. That is why all this effort is necessary.
Even if we find somebody who has achieved this supreme
state of stillness, you may take it that the necessary effort
had already been made in a previous life. So effortless
and choiceless awareness is attained only after deliberate
meditation. That meditation can take whatever form most
appeals to you. See what helps you to keep out all other
thoughts and adopt that for your meditation."

-Sri Ramana Maharshi

Here the great Sage Ramana Maharshi explains the teaching of Jiddu Krishnamurti on choiceless awareness and points out, as Christ and Padmasambhava have done, that in that state of pure awareness we find our true nature and indeed that is our true nature. Unlike Krishnamurti, who wanted listeners to reach that state while he was speaking, Ramana, and all other Yogic traditions, show that effort is necessary in order to reach that state, but as Christ mentioned, turning within is a must for all our conditioning and tendencies are turning the mind outward, not allowing it to turn within and the treasure is to be found within our hearts.

Every Yogic tradition teaches that the mind has to be turned inward in order to be able to abide in that state of bliss and love supreme, not the love and happiness one knows about or has been told about, for that is merely a projection, a seeking for something one has lost. That love and bliss cannot be expressed in words in the same way as God cannot be a word or an image, for the God which has been told is not the real one, but just a fiction created by the ego. As we mentioned before, the mind has the power to keep us in bondage or to liberate us, and in order to liberate us, we really need to be aware of its workings by the way of self-knowledge, when we get to know ourselves, we will be known, as Christ has stated.

Because everything arises in the mind, we should see what the great master Padmasambhava has pointed out regarding mind.

Appearances are not erroneous in themselves, but because
of your grasping at them, errors come into existence.
But if you know that these thoughts only grasp at things
which are mind, then they will be liberated by themselves.
Everything that appears is but a manifestation of mind.
Even though the entire external inanimate universe
appears to you, it is but a manifestation of mind.
Even though all of the sentient beings of the six realms
appear to you, they are but a manifestation of mind.
Even though the happiness of humans and the delights of
the Devas in heaven appear to you, they are but manifesta-
tions of mind.
Even though the sorrows of the three evil destinies appear
to you, they are but manifestations of mind.
Even though the five poisons representing ignorance and
the passions appear to you, they are but manifestations of
mind.
Even though intrinsic awareness, which is self-originated
primal awareness, appears to you, it is but a manifestation

of mind.
Even though good thoughts along the way to Nirvana
appear to you, they are but manifestations of mind.
Even though obstacles due to demons and evil spirits
appear to you, they are but manifestations of mind.
Even though the gods and other excellent attainments
appear to you, they are but manifestations of mind.
Even though various kinds of purity appear to you, they
are but manifestations of mind.
Even though (the experience) of remaining in a state
of one-pointed concentration without any discursive
thoughts appears to you, it is but a manifestation of mind.
Even though the colors that are the characteristics of
things appear to you, they are but manifestations of mind.
Even though a state without characteristics and without
conceptual elaborations appears to you, it is but a manifes-
tation of mind.
Even though the non-duality of the one and the many
appears to you, it is but a manifestation of mind.
Even though existence and non-existence, which are not
created anywhere, appear to you, they are but manifesta-
tions of mind.
There exist no appearances whatsoever that can be under-
stood as not coming from mind.
Because of the unobstructed nature of the mind, there is a
continuous arising of appearances.
Like the waves and the waters of the ocean, which are not
two (different things),
Whatever arises is liberated into the natural state of the
mind.
However, many different names are applied to it in this
unceasing process of naming things,
With respect to its real meaning, the mind (of the indi-
vidual) does not exist other than as one.
And, moreover, this singularity is without any foundation

and devoid of any root.
But even though it is one, you cannot look for it in any
particular direction. It cannot be seen as an entity located
somewhere, because it is not created or made by anything.
Nor can it be seen as just being empty, because there exists
the transparent radiance on its own luminous clarity and
awareness.
Nor can it be seen as diversified, because emptiness and
clarity are inseparable.
Immediate self-awareness is clear and present.
Even though activities exist, there is no awareness of an
agent who is the actor. Even though they are without any
inherent nature, experiences are actually experienced.
If you practice in this way, then everything will be liber-
ated.
With respect to your own sense faculties, everything will
be understood immediately without any intervening oper-
ations of the intellect.
Just as is the case with the sesame seed being the cause of
the oil and the milk being the cause of butter,
But where the oil is not obtained without pressing and the
butter is not obtained without churning,
So, all sentient beings, even though they possess the actual
essence of Buddhahood,
Will not realize Buddhahood without engaging in practice.
If he practices, then even a cowherd can realize liberation.
Even though he does not know the explanation, he can
systematically establish himself in the experience of it.
(For example) when one has had the experience of actually
tasting sugar in one's own mouth,
one does not need to have that taste explained by someone
else.
Not understanding this (intrinsic awareness), even
Panditas (Scholars of scriptures) can fall into error.
Even though they are exceedingly learned and knowl-
edgeable in explaining the nine vehicles, it will only be

*like spreading rumors of places, which they have not seen
personally.
And with respect to Buddhahood, they will not even
approach it for a moment.
If you understand (intrinsic awareness), all of your merits
and sins will be liberated into their own condition.
But if you do not understand it, any virtuous or vicious
deeds that you commit will accumulate as karma leading
to transmigration in heavenly rebirth or to rebirth in the
evil destinies respectively.
But if you understand this empty primal awareness, which
is your own mind, the consequences of merit and of sin
will never come to be realized, just as a spring cannot orig-
inate in the empty sky.
In the state of emptiness itself, the object of merit or of sin
is not even created.
Therefore, your own manifest self-awareness comes to see
everything nakedly.
This self-liberation through seeing with naked awareness
is of such great profundity, and this being so;
you should become intimately acquainted with self-awareness.
Profoundly sealed!*

-Padmasambhava

In these statements, Guru Rinpoche, as the Precious Guru is called in Tibet, relates how we should look at everything from the perspective of naked awareness. Self-awareness is a simile of self-knowledge for only when we know our own reality can we know what God is and then live in this world in love and harmony with all existence.

It is not an easy task to be instilled in this awareness and be mindful of the inner and outer movement of life without being attracted by the sense objects outside or to the senses of the inner body. This is where effort is needed to keep the mind honest and empty in that awareness. Guru Rinpoche is clearly pointing out, as do all other masters, that everything that appears, appears through the mind and whatever we get attached to takes us away from the state of awareness and therefore keeps us in bondage.

Christ also addressed this in the Gospel of Mary where he points out that the mind stays between the spirit and soul, therefore whatever we see or experience is done by the mind, and mind, as we have seen, is not personal, it is just mind. Adi Shankara also points out that whatever we imagine, see or experience is done through the mind.

> *In dreams, when there no actual contact with the external world, the mind alone creates the whole universe consisting of the experiencer and the like. Similarly, in the waking state also there is no difference. Therefore, all this phenomenal universe is just a projection of the mind.*
>
> -Adi Shankara

> *And she began to speak to them these words: she said, I saw the Lord in a vision, and I said to Him, Lord I saw you today in a vision. He answered and said to me,*
> *Blessed are you that you did not waver at the sight of Me.*
> *For where the mind is there is the treasure.*
> *I said to Him, Lord, how does he who sees the vision see it, through the soul or through the spirit?*
> *The Lord answered and said, He does not see through the soul nor through the spirit, but the mind that is between the two that is what sees the vision and it is [...]*
>
> -The Gospel of Mary

From the masters of all traditions, we see that the mind is a powerful thing indeed if one can keep it pure and not allow it to run after the senses. If the mind does not cling or reject anything, it is the beginning of resting in its natural state where one will find the treasure, as Christ has pointed out to Mary and as Guru Rinpoche points out also. This is also what Buddha pointed out regarding mindfulness or intrinsic awareness: this is a state of our true nature and only by being in that state do we see with the eye of wisdom and get to know ourselves and understand life by observing the mind.

In this state, we see that suffering is only a creation of our own mind; that loneliness and suffering are also a by-product of it, and all are just apparitions in the mind based on our conditioning and tendencies of our own mind and the attractions, attachments based on our memories. This is where any spiritual practice is helpful to get us closer to that state of awareness and slowly being able to stay in it, go deeper and deeper into understanding reality as it is, not as we may imagine it to be.

> *When the meditator (mind), the object of meditation (Brahma, the ultimate Self) and meditation itself become one, beyond the awareness of the knowledge of meditation, only then will there be a Void like awareness which is called Samadhi, or Atonement.*
>
> -Lahiri Mahasaya

Above, Lahiri Mahasaya points out the void-like awareness which is our natural state. We may call it Samadhi or Nirvikalpa Samadhi, which is when you are at one with God or have "Atonement." All yogas and spiritual practices are designed to take us back to our natural state of being. The brain is the seat of the mind and the mind, in its pure state, allows the naked awareness to be. This is when our personality has been exhausted and the mind is in its pure state where the absolute reality God can be then reflected in it and where intelligence operates.

> *The mind resting in the Self is its natural condition, but instead of that our minds are resting in outward objects.*
>
> -Sri Ramana Maharshi

Here, Ramana Maharshi points out that when the mind rests in the self, it is in our natural state which is the awareness of being. To attain this highest state is our natural intrinsic goal and everyone has to find out for themselves the road which is appropriate for them. When one is ready, a teacher will appear, either from within or from the world at large, to help in the process of letting go of the ego and in doing so, understanding the mind. In the process of understanding the mind, one will surrender fully to the awareness of the present moment where one will start to see reality as it is. Next, we should talk about the one energy which keeps us unaware of our own reality and that is Ignorance.

CHAPTER 20

IGNORANCE AND KNOWLEDGE

To be ignorant means to lack knowledge or understanding about a situation, a person or oneself. Ignorance can arise from a lack of exposure, confusion or even from deluded thinking. We are all somehow ignorant about our true reality and if we were not, the world would be a better place. The word ignorance has a very negative connotation, but in reality, is just a state of unawareness. In unawareness one can be ill informed or conditioned to false information, an idea, or concept which does not match with reality but is held as reality.

Most of our ignorance comes into being, from our way of thinking and narrow way of looking at things and understanding life. The more conditioning and more beliefs we have about the world and ourselves, the more ignorant we can be. Even the smartest person who has accumulated lots of knowledge about lots of things can still be unaware of their own reality and the knowledge which they have accumulated is just added to memory. This so-called knowledge can be a spoke in a wheel, of getting rid of ignorance if given too much value. If we become attached to worldly knowledge, it becomes pride.

This Zen saying is self-explanatory regarding ignorance, illusions, delusion:

*Ignorance /illusion/delusion are acting like a broken
mirror: It distorts facts of life.*

Furthermore, let's look at what the Isha Upanishad says relating ignorance and knowledge:

*They who worship ignorance enter into darkness. And they
who worship knowledge enter into greater darkness.*

-Isha Upanishad

This seems to be a contradictory statement but it is not. The ones in ignorance will enter into darkness for ignorance is by nature darkness: the darkness produced by ignorance when we think that what we know is reality. They who worship knowledge enter in greater darkness because when we are attached to the knowledge we have, we actually limit our knowledge to what we know, and therefore are bound by that knowledge and never free for all such knowledge is of the past. The right knowledge about ourselves will get rid of ignorance and will allow us to get out of the bondage of ignorance or of what we think we know.

Jiddu Krishnamurti and many other masters have stated that knowledge is of the past; is always memory. In the Chapter "Thus Spake the Master," Sri M's guru describes knowledge and the kinds of knowledge one can be assisted by.

Master: The moment you have listened to my words, they have vanished from the present and have become things of the past. They constitute memory, and memory is a thing of the past. Knowledge, as we know it is then something that you remember, whether it is from the recent past, a split second ago, or years ago. That is, it is memory. All knowledge is, therefore, memory – a thing of the past.

On the other hand, Brahman, the Ultimate Reality, is never a memory, never a thing of the past. It is the living present, the eternal, immediate present and, therefore, can never be comprehended by knowledge, which has only the past as reference.

M: If knowledge refers only to memory, what is it that can know Brahman?

Master: To understand it even conceptually, we may have to go into different kinds of knowledge. At the lowest end is ajnana, knowledge about the world obtained through our sense organs. Higher than ajnana is jnana or knowledge of the Self and other things acquired through the reasoning intellect, buddhi, and from scriptures and teachers. Still higher is vijnana, discriminative knowledge, that is able to differentiate the real from the apparent or relative. One who has reached the level of vijnana can hone it to perfection by trying to remain constantly at that level. If this is done, the intellectual understanding of jnana and the passion-arousing ajnana and even the earlier stage of the discriminative capability, vijnana, are overcome or transcended, thereby attaining the intuitive and unitive experience of Brahman (GOD). In this context, even the word 'experience' is a misnomer, a wrong term, because it implies an experience and, therefore, an object of experience. All that can be said about such a state is that it is a mental/ spiritual enlightenment where nothing but an all-pervasive knowledge exists without the duality of the knower and the known.

-Sri M

In this discussion, Sri M, a renowned Kriya Yoga master, and his guru discuss in a simple way the three types of knowledge that exist and state that if one establishes oneself in the discriminative knowledge *or* direct knowledge, which is seeing reality as it is without any judgements or prejudice, one will have insight. Christ has likewise discussed that knowledge when he stated:

> *"Know what is in front of your face, and what is hidden from you will be disclosed to you. For there is nothing hidden that won't be revealed."*

-Gospel of Thomas: 5

If one looks with no judgement, has insight and establishes oneself in the naked awareness of being then one will be able to know reality and there lies all knowledge. In order to get to the highest knowledge, one has to go through the lesser degrees of knowledge which will make one experience and understand life and how the process of life moves one slowly but surely towards that perfect knowledge as wisdom. This wisdom cuts through all illusions.

> *Just as the fire is the direct cause for cooking, so without true knowledge no emancipation can be had. Compared with all other forms of discipline knowledge of the Self is the one direct means for liberation. Action cannot destroy ignorance, for it is not in conflict with or opposed to ignorance. Knowledge does verily destroy ignorance as light destroys deep darkness.*

-Adi Shankara

Above, Adi Shankara points out that only with self-knowledge can one destroy the ignorance which has enveloped us from time immemorial and by doing so become liberated from the clutches of illusory existence.

He who subjects himself, nearly all will be subjected unto him. He who knows himself, the knowledge of all things will be given him. The word, know yourself means the accomplishment of all knowledge. As all is encompassed in your being, so in the knowledge of your being all knowledge is encompassed, and in the subjection of your being, the subjection of all the world.

-St Isaac the Syrian

Similarly to Christ, one of the early fathers of Christianity, Saint Isaac, reveals to us the same truths as Adi Shankara, the Upanishads and so on: that self-knowledge is the key to all knowledge and once we know ourselves all knowledge is revealed from our inner being.

And so that those endowed with knowledge may know that it is the truth from your Lord, and so believe in it, and their hearts soften to it. God guides those who believe to a straight path.
O ye who believe! When ye are told to make room in the assemblies, (spread out and) make room: (ample) room will Allah provide for you. And when ye are told to rise up, rise up Allah will rise up, to (suitable) ranks (and degrees), those of you who believe and who have been granted (mystic) Knowledge. And Allah is well-acquainted with all ye do.

-Quran 58–11

In the Quran, it states that the one who has faith and a pure heart will be given the inner knowledge which is the truth from the Allah.

The thoughts of liberation and bondage are present only during the state of ignorance. The Original Nature is self-evident. It is neither bound nor liberated.

-St Shri Samartha Ramdas

Dasbodh, a well-known Indian spiritual book, states as we can see above: for one who is in the natural state, neither liberation nor bondage exist.

> *Sutra 18: "Emancipation (Kaivalya) is obtained when one realizes the oneness of his Self with the Universal Self, the Supreme Reality."*
>
> *Sannyasi or Christ the anointed Savior. When all the developments of Ignorance are withdrawn, the heart, being perfectly clear and purified, no longer merely reflects the Spiritual Light but actively manifests the same, and thus being consecrated and anointed, man becomes Sannyasi, free, or Christ the Savior.*
>
> *See John 1:33. "Upon whom thou shalt see the Spirit descending, and remaining on him, the same is he which baptized with the Holy Ghost."*
>
> -Swami Sri Yukteswar

Swami Sri Yukteswar also points out that when all the developments of ignorance are uprooted then the union of the self with universal self is obtained, and all knowledge is obtained also.

It is not easy to arrive at the right knowledge for we have been conditioned to compete, to want, to be better than the other, to become this or that, and to succeed. An example of conditioning is as follows: a small boy with not much knowledge acquires some part of it through a book, a teacher, a father, a brother or sister then goes to school or is in company of friends and all of a sudden a discussion comes about on that very subject previously learned, then he is quick to add to the discussion about what he has learned and assert that he knows when in fact he only knows a small part. Most of us, if we care to look, have such or similar experiences and know the feeling of pride of believing we know. In our day-to-day life this happens all the time: we think we know better or more and this becomes competition. Such competition, not being healthy, always brings about conflict with others and likewise, people, families and nations are always in a state of conflict.

Worldly knowledge is needed at the practical level and should never become a platform where we think that we are better human beings than someone else. Worldly knowledge should be used for the betterment of humanity. Inner knowledge is needed for us to slowly be free of ignorance. To arrive at inner knowledge, we have to have an insight into how the mind works.

The ignorance is the belief that all creation is only the material manifest, and nothing lies beyond, and that belief makes us identify only with the body and mind and never be able to break through this limitation. Most people, even if spiritually inclined, are stuck with this belief. Because of this, we are prone to so much conflict. We think that we are a small entity that needs to be preserved and improved and we always work from a small center, the me. The real Self does not have a center. It is free and therefore in oneness and not in need of a center which is always limited regardless of its condition. The self does not need any improvements for it is perfect and has been since the beginning of time.

Education of humanity in any field plays an important role in giving strength to ignorance, thinking that by science alone we can acquire knowledge of God. Science may be knowledge of the physical level of existence, but it is restricted only to that level. The Vedas and other scriptures are slowly being looked at with different eyes for as the consciousness of humanity develops so too does understanding of these sacred scriptures which can reveal a reality beyond the seen and unseen if one cares to look and to listen with no judgement or prejudice.

Most people are stuck at the knowledge of the senses or somewhere between and the knowledge arrived at by the intellect, by reason. What is called wisdom is the ability to think and act, utilizing knowledge, experience, understanding, common sense and insight. Life cannot be learned in a classroom like specific subjects such as mathematics and so on. To be wise in life one needs a mind that has touched reality and has the ability to have insight into the complexity of life and the relationships we have to one another and with the environment around. But this is not something that can really be taught, it can only be pointed out. For example, drinking too much alcohol is bad for you, but how can you explain that to an alcoholic? One has to penetrate into the inner being of that individual in order to be able to help in seeing the problem at hand. All the masters who have touched reality have had that ability to help and guide others towards a broader thinking.

Worldly knowledge is necessary and so inner knowledge is necessary. Through them we arrive at true wisdom, which helps in becoming one with all and in doing so having all the knowledge at our disposal for that is our inherent nature. In order to get to that, a healthy body and mind are needed. Longchenpa in Chapter the Second Vajra Point: Magical Illusion.

> *Deluded mind and its habitual tendencies, phenomenal existence, the objects of the senses And the five poisons that fixate on them – All these occur because of ignorance. Devoid of real existence, they all appear unceasingly. They are like conjured apparitions. From now on be convinced That they are empty, false reflections.*
>
> -Longchenpa

In the above statement, Longchenpa states that the condition of the mind is one of ignorance, and because of that, awareness is distorted by the duality of the apprehender and the apprehended. It is thus that hallucinatory appearances, the universe and its animate contents, appear to be real.

Ajita's Questions
The Buddha was asked by his disciple Ajita, "What is it that smothers the world? What makes the world so hard to see? What would you say pollutes the world and what threatens it most?"
The Buddha answered, "It is ignorance which smothers, and it is carelessness, and greed that makes the world invisible. The hunger of desire pollutes the world, and the great source of fear is the pain of suffering."
"In every direction," said Ajita, "the rivers of desire are running. How can we dam them and what will hold them back? What can we use to close the floodgates?"
The Buddha, Answer "Any river can be stopped with the dam of mindfulness. I call it the flood stopper. And with wisdom you can close the floodgates."

-Buddha

Above, Buddha clearly points out that the Ignorance with the five poisons is what makes the world (reality) not seen and the hunger for desires pollutes it and therefore, produces great fear and suffering. In the second part he points out that mindfulness as naked awareness and wisdom as discriminative knowledge are the key in dispelling ignorance.

So, we see so far that ignorance, which is born of our desires, attachments and the passions which came through the senses, makes us create the habits we have, the patterns of thought we have acquired with the beliefs, ideas and concepts about life. This is what we call the ego, and this is the root of all evil. It is so because as long as we live a selfish life, we will always create division between the little center, me, and all others. So as long as we work not for the benefit of others and only for the benefit of ourselves, we will always be ignorant and unable to see the unity of all existence. This makes it very much impossible to touch love and compassion. As we mentioned before, when we are capable of bringing our passions in life into a single unitary movement, then we can say that we have compassion, which is the bringing of all passions into a single one and that is the compassion everyone has to touch.

So, we come back to the ego, which is the cause of all grief and suffering in the world because it is always afraid and sustaining itself through division. This division we see in our way of thinking – in families, in nations. It is all destructive and always breeds conflict. So, my dear friends, without understanding ourselves, our minds and how we act in the world, we never will find peace as individuals or the world, for everything starts with us and if one of us is able to see reality we can call him a noble one, one who has crossed the ocean of life.

The understanding of who we are does not come from suppressing or running away from anything. It is pure observation: when we observe, for example, that we are angry and see that angriness has not arrived by a foreign agency, but that anger is one with the one being angry. The spark which ignites the anger may have come from a situation or by someone, but the anger is and will be the individual. Where anger is love is not, where jealousy is, love is not, where greed is, love is not, where envy is, love is not, where selfishness is, love is not, where grumpiness is, love is not, where resistance is, love is not, where clinging is, love is not. If we are mindful, we will grasp that the only real feeling which does not come with thinking – does not come from the little center, the me – is the energy of love. It includes everything and everyone and does not discriminate a criminal from a saint. Just as the sun gives light to all, so God gives love to all and makes all in that love and of that love, even if in our ignorance we cannot see it.

We need full faith and to fully surrender to the present moment in order to be able to stay in that mindfulness, in that naked aware-ness, and it does require us to die of ourselves in order to find ourselves. This is not an easy task; everyone will do it at their own pace and in their own time. It takes time because we always run away from what it is and want to be somewhere else but not here.

A sanyasi in India once told the writer, "Just Listen, Observe and Wait." It took me years to grasp this statement, which even at that time, was only understood at an intellectual level. That statement in one word is mindfulness.

We all cling to something – to wife, to mother, to father, to teacher, to church or saint, to our traditions and so on and we are doing that because we want security, some kind of comfort, some kind of support. We do not want to feel lonely or abandoned. We want to be included, never excluded, and because we cling, we cannot let go and therefore can never surrender. We all do it because our lack of love makes us want to feel secure. But as we asked earlier, where can we find any security? Is it in your insurance, in money, in what one may find? Unfortunately, there is no security in anything because nothing that we see is real and how could false reality give security? When one finds real love, one has all the security here and now. The world can disappear in a flash and also appear in a flash. With the creator, everything is a possibility. Then, only when we enter back into oneness is there security in the hands of the Lord of Love.

We are all prisoners of our own making, and we all want to be free and do whatever we desire. We call that freedom. We only surrender to pleasure for that gives us satisfaction and makes us happy; we never surrender to pain for we always try to run from it. Most people think freedom lies in permissiveness to do what we want and enjoy life the way we want. We act in that state of mind and most of us never see the consequences of our actions. Some see them but are still too weak to change their course of actions and are taken only if the action fits in the comfort zone, selfish actions are detrimental to self and others. If we observe, we can see how we act and the wars and destruction we all produce to any level of existence. Then we say we love God, or life, or the nation and so on, but we have not really touched love for true love comes with its own actions without the me interfering and that is always the right action. We say we love our sons and daughters, but we send them to futile wars to die, and for what? It is sad that we are asleep unable to wake up from the deep conditioning of our own minds. We don't have the ability to see that we are all together, like apples in a single basket. Apples do not separate themselves: there is no need, but we are all divided into nations, groups, religions and so on. The world is a basket, and we are all apples which come from the same tree of life. We are not different. We are all of the same nature of reality. Why do we separate ourselves? Why hate one another? For what? An idea or concept, a flag or whatever it is? This separation is of our own making and will never bring peace and love into our hearts and the world will always be in a state of turmoil.

God loves all, nourishes all, does not discriminate in any way, shape or form. All the masters have followed the Lord of Love and have acted with Love. Why are we not capable of doing this and in the process, making heaven here and now? Christ said, "It is in your midst," but we are unable to see it. Ignorance makes us not see it. If we understand this then we will start to make an effort towards trying to uproot that ignorance and in the process get in touch with our true nature and unveil our true potential of love, including all in oneness. It is possible to act in that love and with that love, of course. Yes, we see glimpses of that love in action every day in hospitals, in acts of charity, in the help one gives to another person or animal. We see it in the smile of a person, in an act of kindness, in a gesture, or a poem, in music or art, in looking after nature. We see the mind have the power to act in selfish ways or for the benefit of all in unity, love and compassion are to be found in unselfish acts and we are the ones who choose how we act according to our conditioning.

Love always prevails because it is eternal where everything else is not, and we are a part of that love. Being fully aware of this, we then act in that love, then seeing and acting becomes one without thought interfering in the affairs of life.

The awareness or consciousness of the Lord of Love (God) is the same consciousness all masters have discovered, one by surrendering into the Krishna consciousness by the study of the *Bhagavad Gita*, one through the Sutrayana and therefore surrendering to the Buddha consciousness, one through the teachings of an awakened guru like Guru Nanak of Sikh tradition surrendering to his consciousness, one through the study of the Quran therefore, surrendering to the Muhammad and Allah consciousness, one through the teachings of Christ through the Bible surrendering to the Christ consciousness and so on with all traditions and non-traditions, for awakening can also happen without any religious belief, or support.

Now it is fair to state that all the awakened masters have entered God consciousness and so the disciples who follow them have also entered the God consciousness and become one with the father, oneness, naked awareness: call it whatever you want to call it, God, for the infinite answers to all names. So why do we make so much fuss about religion and fight with each other when we all enter through the same door anyway. The only difference is in the vehicle which takes us to that door. But the opening of the door is done by our hearts. Only in the openness of love we have for everyone and everything is there the key to opening the door of the unknown, the only reality.

We have to drop the personal idea of God for that is selfish and is not the real God. It is only a conditioning or an idea one thinks is God. Any attempt to describe God is foolish for we cannot describe something infinite with finite words or symbols. It is an impossibility and no matter how marvelous the description may be, it is not the truth for the real God cannot be described but only experienced when the experiencer is no more.

Ignorance, as we can see, is the great mother of all misery, and the fundamental ignorance is to think that the Infinite spirit in us is finite. This is the basis of all ignorance: that we, the immortal, the ever-pure, the perfect Spirit, think that we are little minds, that we are little bodies – and that thinking comes from selfishness. As soon as I think that I am a little body, I want to preserve it, to protect it, even at the expense of others and then you and I become separated. As soon as this idea of separation comes, it opens the door to all mischief and leads to all misery. If a scenario unfolded wherein a very small fractional part of human beings living today put aside the idea of selfishness and littleness, this earth would become a paradise tomorrow. Technical improvements of material knowledge alone will never lead to paradise. Without self-knowledge, all material knowledge is only adding fuel to the fire; only giving into the hands of selfish man one more instrument to take what belongs to all, instead of working for the benefit of all.

Truth does not pay homage to any society, ancient or modern. Society has to pay homage to Truth or die.

-Swami Vivekananda

Self-knowledge which leads to wisdom is a necessity in order for us to uproot all the ignorance and the poisons which have grown like weeds in society and in our own minds. Next, we should look at wisdom and see how all the teachings of all traditions are full of this wisdom.

CHAPTER 21

WISDOM

What is wisdom and who were the men and women of real wisdom? In English terms, wisdom is defined as: "the ability or result of an ability to think and act utilizing knowledge, experience, understanding, common sense, and insight."

Real wisdom can be exposed only by the awakened masters who do not look at life with any filter of conditioning and therefore have no ego involved. Wisdom in them springs up like a fountain and they drink from its waters whenever they need to share that wisdom for the benefit of humanity. If we observe in our own lives, we know that old people have lived and understood life and have acquired some wisdom in the process, but only flashes of it and very few live and act fully in that complete wisdom.

A Zen proverb says:

> *Knowledge is learning something new every day.*
> *Wisdom is letting go of something every day.*

This is the wisdom which sees without knowledge because knowledge is in observing and perceiving reality as it is without a knower and the known. To be in that wisdom, one has to really understand life in its totality: understand love and live like Christ, Buddha, Muhammad, Rama, Krishna and many others who transcended the limitations of nature. Wisdom is the ability to have an insight into everything; to see the truth at any point for truth is a living thing, a movement and nobody can say "I have it." We cannot possess it and put it in a box and use it whenever convenient. The one who walks step by step with wisdom is a free human being.

The wisdom of Indian Rishis of the past, of the Aztecs Indians or American Indians, of the Australian Aborigines, of the Greeks, of the Tibetan Tantric masters, of the Christians Monks, the Zen masters and so on is the same unifying wisdom which comes from the depths of our being. It is the same wisdom which Christ imparted, the same wisdom which Buddha or any other awakened master imparted. This wisdom is not mine or yours. It is ours and it can be seen by one who has the eye to see it, one who has a pure heart and a pure mind.

Tagore explains what Rishis were and what they stood for:

> *They were the rishis. What were the rishis? They who having attained the supreme soul in knowledge were filled with wisdom and having found him in union with the soul were in perfect harmony with the inner self; they having realized him in the heart were free from all selfish desires, and having experienced him in all the activities of the world, had attained calmness. The rishis were they who having reached the supreme God from all sides had found abiding peace, had become united with all, had entered into the life*

> *of the Universe. Thus, the state of realizing our relationship with all, of entering into everything through union with God, was considered in India to be the ultimate end and fulfillment of humanity.*

-Rabindranath Tagore

The same goal of the rishis was found to be viable in all spiritual traditions: old, contemporary and present day. All the statements imparted to us by all masters are full of wisdom and this wisdom touches every individual who is interested in finding out about reality and life, about love and God. Everyone at some time has been touched by wisdom in one way or another. This wisdom carries with it love, compassion, patience, simplicity and humility; it comes from the essence of all things. The more we are able to let go of our illusory state of mind – which is the ego with all the constructed images about the world – the more we tap into this pool of wisdom that never runs dry, that is always present and fresh.

So far, we have encountered many words of wisdom in this book from many masters and we shall continue to do so for the wisdom they impart to us will awaken the fountain of wisdom which lies in every sentient being. In wisdom there is laughter, there is joy. Laughter and joy come together, always supporting

each other and the one who lives with this wisdom and imparts it to others is a person of peace and of unreserved love.

This wisdom has been presented through the ages in a form particular of time and place, and according to the traditional language and knowledge of the particular society at the time of transmission. Christ transmitted this wisdom in a form familiar to the times and the place where he lived. Unfortunately, he was never understood because only a few had received it at that time, but he knew that the seeds which he planted would grow far and wide. Buddha did the same, as did Muhammad. Unfortunately, with time, because of weakness and selfishness, in all traditions this wisdom was used to serve some more than others. This wisdom is slowly and surely reviving in our present time with the advent of the internet and our technological progress which allows us to access these teachings far and wide. The problem is how these teachings are looked at and who is spreading them and what interest one can derive from them.

This wisdom can be used to impart truth or to keep others in bondage. This is why it is of vital importance that we study the teachings and in doing so start to live the teachings in everyday life and see for ourselves the impact they have. We have to observe every day the impact of the teachings if they are making us more peaceful, less selfish, less greedy, less angry and so on. We can test ourselves in our everyday relationship with the world around us. This is why it is important, if we have a teacher or a guru, not to give much importance to the form of the guru but to grasp the teachings. If we want to see more about the teacher, we have to observe the teacher for a time in his everyday life.

One of my teachers stated, "Do not look for a teacher. It will show up when the time is right, same as a fruit will fall from the tree when it is ripe." All teachings and practices, whatever they come from, should be seen and understood by us then we will know if they are suited for us or not. If we are blessed to find an awakened teacher, that teacher will advise the right person to the right practice.

Here is a story of a Kriya Yoga master who knew which kriya practice to impart to whom. One day a man full of pride who had been initiated in the practice of kriya yoga come to the master to ask for a higher initiation. The master kept silent and at the same time the postman arrived, who also had been recently initiated into a first kriya practice. The master asked the postman, "Would you like to have a second kriya initiation?" and the postman, bowing to the master, said, "No sir. I have had enough. So much bliss comes from the practice, I hardly can do my duties during the day." Then the pride in the man who asked to be initiated in higher kriyas dropped at the wisdom of the master and the humility of the postman who practiced and trusted the master with all his heart touching the divine with one practice full of love and humility.

From this story we see how the wisdom of the master works in many ways, impacting individuals according to their conditioning and state of mind, for an awakened master recognizes these states of mind in his disciples, and by his wisdom, he imparts the right medicine. Wisdom can also be gained from our ability to learn from our own experiences and have an insight to penetrate the root of every problem. One has to be somehow directed how to look at a problem. If we are able to look, with no judgements and look at what is exactly in front of us, we will see with direct perception what needs to be done about the problem and in that state, problems do not exist. A master is the one who can teach us how to look at life and if we have the wisdom imparted by the masters, we will know how to respond or not to respond at all.

Practical wisdom is easier to explain, it is the same as common sense. Before we do something which we have never done before, we must learn from one who has done it or at least observe it being done. For example, if we are trying to cross a big puddle of water on a road, a wise person will check its depth with a stick before crossing it, but the unwise will presume is ok, not deep at all, and will plunge in. Inner wisdom or spiritual wisdom is much more complex. It comes when the individual reaches a level of maturity in all levels of existence: physical, mental and spiritual. This maturity and growth come with experience and maybe life-times of experience; of inner learning where we expand the mind and heart little by little by discriminating against what is real and what is not. By doing so, we slowly enter into wisdom, until that wisdom envelops us, and we realize the reality of life, love and truth. Then all is known.

To arrive at the truth, we have to be always present in the moment. We have to see life with no judgement or prejudice, with no opinions. We have to drop all filters of conditioning and transcend the world of duality. To be wise is not only to say a few words you have learned from others or from books: it is much more profound than that.

Let's look into the profoundness of wisdom from a master's perspective:

> *The nature of the mind, the self-arisen primordial wisdom, is primordially pure and space-like. Within this state, which does not exist as anything at all, there move the five winds, of which the life-supporting wind is the root, this leads to the manifestation of the self-experience of awareness in the state of luminosity.*
>
> — Longchenpa

Above, Longchenpa describes what wisdom is and declares its purity and the self- arisen state which will lead one into the naked awareness or awareness in the state of luminosity. This is hard to grasp unless one touches this state of primordial wisdom. He continues to state the factors which impede wisdom.

> *The factors that run counter to wisdom are states whereby the mind is utterly obscured and which arise through perverse views and through clinging to the supremacy of one's beliefs.*
> *This is what appears to the minds of beings, The form of their habitual tendencies. When these are cleansed, there manifest spontaneously the triple kāya of the buddha-element, together with the self-experience of luminous primordial wisdom. It is as the Māyājāla says: There is the self-experience of the ordinary mind and then the self-experience of primordial wisdom.*
>
> — Longchenpa

Here he goes further and explains that primordial wisdom arrives with the cleansing of habitual tendencies where one experiences the self of ordinary mind and then the self of primordial self-arising wisdom. So, it is this wisdom that is and was imparted to us by all perfect masters of all times and places and we should have the intention to understand and practice this wisdom in order to liberate ourselves from the clutches of illusion.

> *Whatever mercy God unfolds for the people; none can withhold it. And if He withholds it, none can release it thereafter. He is the Exalted in Power and Full of Wisdom.*
>
> -Quran: 35–2

The Quran here clearly states that wisdom is power which the Lord unfolds upon people, and nobody can keep it, they can only be it.

Guru Nanak also in Japji Sahib expresses that in wisdom supreme we find beauty and bliss.

> *In the Realm of Wisdom, spiritual wisdom reigns supreme. The sound-current of the Naad vibrates there, amidst the sounds and the sights of bliss. In the Realm of Humility, the Word is beauty. Forms of incomparable beauty are fashioned there. These things cannot be described. One who tries to speak of these shall regret the attempt. The intuitive consciousness, intellect, and understanding of the mind are shaped there. The consciousness of the spiritual warriors and the Siddhas, the beings of spiritual perfection, are shaped there.*
>
> -Guru Nanak

He nicely points out that wisdom incorporates humility, bliss and beauty, and in that wisdom is intuitive consciousness as awareness, intellect, and pure mind. Everything is shaped into the highest wisdom where one reaches the perfect state.

By cleansing our minds of all habitual tendencies and any ideas which we hold about ourselves, we slowly get into the wisdom which will then help us cut through ignorance and allow us to find rest in our true self. It is all our conditioning with all the experiences, memories and habits which we need to uproot and understand, in order to allow the mind to rest in a primordial state of clear light, there we can then reflect the light of the Lord of Love. This is what most of us, if not all of us, consciously or unconsciously aspire to achieve: to find the everlasting love and peace supreme which is our true nature. If only one finds it, that one will influence millions of people to seek the kingdom as Christ stated, and in finding it, everything else will be added on to you.

The possibility of unveiling our true nature is there. It is inherent in us. It is our birthright from time immemorial. It is as Christ pointed out to the Pharisees:

> *Jesus answered them, "Is it not written in your Law, 'I have said you are gods'? If he called them 'gods,' to whom the word of God came – and the Scripture cannot be broken – what about the one whom the Father set apart as his very own and sent into the world? Why then do you accuse me of blasphemy because I said, 'I am God's Son'?"*

-John 10:34–36

He clearly points out that we are all Gods, but we are so unaware of our own divinity and so much steeped in ignorance of our own making that we cannot see the reality of which he speaks. Here is what Tagore had to say regarding this matter:

> *Though the West has accepted as its teacher him who boldly proclaimed his oneness with his Father, and who exhorted his followers to be perfect as God, it has never been reconciled to this idea of our unity with the infinite being. It condemns, as a piece of blasphemy, any implication of man's*

becoming God. This is certainly not the idea that Christ preached, nor perhaps the idea of the Christian mystics, but this seems to be the idea that has become popular in the Christian west.

-Rabindranath Tagore

It is the right idea that man must reach for the divinity within, and Christ has shown us the way. Unfortunately, Christianity after the meeting of Constantinople has put another spear in Christ's body by dividing the Church and choosing what they think was the direction the Church should take accordingly to their will, not God's will, and these divisions are still visible today.

From an early father of Christianity, Saint Isaac the Syrian:

When the impulses are immersed in delight, after (having tasted) the wisdom contained in the (divine) words, by means of the faculty that absorbs information from them, then every man will leave the body behind him. Forgetting the world and all that is in it, he will also banish from his soul all recollections on which are based the images of the material world. And often the soul in its thoughts during ecstasy will desist from the use of the wonted deliberations – natural practice – by reason of the novel (experiences) which reach it from the sea of their mysteries. Even when the mind is floating on its upper waters, without being able to make its impulses deep as the depth of the waters (so that it can see all the treasures in its abysses) – still meditation, by its (power of) love, will have sufficient force to bind the thoughts firmly together with thoughts of ecstasy so that they are checked from thinking of and running after the nature of the body. As one of those, who are clad with God says: "Because the heart is weak, it is not able to bear the evil influences that reach it from without, nor the struggle within. For you know, that the evil thoughts of the body are strong. And if the heart is not accustomed to teachings, it is not possible to bear the troubled thoughts of the body."

-St Isaac the Syrian

Above, the saint explains in yogic terms what wisdom does with the one who has attained it, through meditation and listening to the words coming from divine beings, showing how it will help one forget the world, and therefore be able to bathe in the bliss and ecstasy of the Lord.

God then is called Mind and Reason and Spirit and Wisdom and Power, as the cause of these, and as immaterial, and maker of all, and omnipotent. And these names are common to the whole Godhead, whether affirmative or negative. And they are also used of each of the subsistence of the Holy Trinity in the very same and identical way and with their full significance. For when I think of one of the subsistence, I recognize it to be perfect God and perfect essence: but when I combine and reckon the three together, I know one perfect God. For the Godhead is not compound but in three perfect subsistence, one perfect indivisible and uncompounded God. And when I think of the relation of the three subsistence to each other, I perceive that the Father is super-essential Sun, source of goodness, fathomless sea of essence, reason, wisdom, power, light, divinity: divinity: the generating and productive source of good hidden in it. He Himself then is mind, the depth of reason, begetter of the Word, and through the Word the Producer of the revealing Spirit.

-St John of Damascus

Here we have, in a nutshell, the teachings of Buddha and Christ and the Upanishads and of all traditions, written by a saint of early Christianity, John of Damascus or John Damascene, an Arab Christian monk, priest, hymnographer and apologist.

> *The disciple says: Which are the bonds captivating the mind [and withholding it] from running after evil things?*
> *The teacher says: The constant search after wisdom and desire for the teachings of life. For bonds stronger than these against the unruliness of mind do not exist.*
> *The disciple says: Where is the limit of the course of wisdom for those who seek it, and where does the course of teachings end?*
> *The teacher says: The way of this course is foreign to any limit, to such an extent that even the holy angels do not reach perfection. The course of wisdom is without end. It ascends to such a height that it mingles with God him that follows it. And even this is a sign of its unlimitedness, that its distinctions are without end; wisdom is God.*

-St Isaac the Syrian

Here, Saint Isaac points out that the seeking of wisdom and the teachings of truth are the two most valuable subjects in helping us not fall into ignorance, or as he calls ignorance, evil things. And he goes on in saying that wisdom has no limits: it is God himself, and all other masters have pointed out the same truth.

> *Just as firewood is turned to ashes in the flames of a fire, all actions are turned to ashes in wisdom's refining flames. Nothing in the world can purify as powerfully as wisdom; Resolute, restraining his senses, practiced in yoga, you will find this wisdom within yourself. the man of faith becomes wise; once he attains true wisdom, he soon attains perfect peace. Ignorant men without faith are easily mired in doubt; they can never be truly happy in this world or the world beyond.*

A man is not bound by action who renounces action through yoga, who concentrates on the Self, and whose doubt is cut off by wisdom. Therefore, with the sword of wisdom cut off this doubt in your heart; follow the path of selfless action; stand up, Arjuna!

-Lord Krishna

Just as all masters have imparted wisdom to us, Krishna imparted to Arjuna the way to wisdom by infusing faith in Arjuna that by the intention to know the truth and by practicing yoga, restraining the senses (no suppressing them making a point here) one will find the fountain of wisdom. Saint Isaac declares that wisdom, naked awareness, pure mind are just names of God. So, from the wisdom imparted to us by God through all masters, from all traditions we should see how God works through all for he is in all and in everything. When we also start to die of our own selfishness and stupidity then he will also be able to allow his will to manifest in us and through us for the benefit of all, in order to bring a state of love and bliss to this beautiful earth which is our home on this dimension of existence.

Let's look at two examples of wisdom at work from Ramdas:

Saying that oneself is "I" or "me," is ego. The sense that one is an individual is what is meant by ego. Ego is ignorance, which means having attachment to the sense of an independent "I." When attachment is given up, there is unity with That which is unattached. This is the authority of the attainment of That which is without imagination. When one does not know one's Self, it is called ignorance.

When ignorance is removed by Self-Knowledge, one realizes oneself as Parabrahman (God). Understand that body-identification is not important in Parabrahman (God). There, the sense of "I" has no place.
Brahman is said to natural, existing at all times, pure wisdom, beyond everything, permanent, and beyond words.

-St Shri Samartha Ramdas

The saint here explains that when we touch true wisdom, the realization of the ego or ignorance is dispelled and when attachment to the idea that we are the body is given up, then realization of the self is attained without any imagination. This allows us to enter into oneness, knowing that the body is just a vessel to help us realize our true reality and therefore allowing us to live life by the universal will of the Lord of Love with no worries about tomorrow.

Here we can state that, with the help of yoga practices, by intense faith, by being mindful of what we do and do not, by sincere prayer, by being aware of every step of the mind we slowly purify the mind. Then in that mind the Lord of Love will start to shine by his wisdom supreme. We have to be aware of our attachment, habits and tendencies, by the various feelings arising, by various sensations, by the fluctuations of our mind, by any conditioning of our mind, by any attractions to various objects that attract the senses, in doing all that watching like a hawk, with no judgement, only watching, then in that watching, wisdom will by itself dissolve the ego little by little and only the self which is love will remain.

So far, we have hopefully grasped wisdom, the awareness of being, the self-knowledge leading us in wisdom and helping us reduce the ego or dissolve it for good in the self of supreme reality. Next, we should look at the traps the ego can set for us, making us fall in such illusion and delusion.

CHAPTER 22

ILLUSION &
DELUSION

What is illusion and what is reality? How do we discern one from the other? We have explained so far that awareness is the key which takes us into wisdom, which then cuts through ignorance, allowing us to see reality. Before we can be established in awareness, most of us need to take it step by step like a baby who begins to walk and falls but still gets up and keeps going, with practice gaining stability and with stability coming to walking.

In the Upanishads there is a verse where one has to be attentive that yoga comes and goes.

> *When the five senses and the mind are still, and the reasoning intellect rests in silence, then begins the highest path. This calm steadiness of the senses is called yoga. Then one should become watchful, because yoga comes and goes.*
>
> -Katha Upanishad

Here, we see how we should always be aware for the mind's nature is to think and when we think, the mind is easily lost in the world of the senses and imagination therefore becoming deluded and lost in illusion. We have to be attentive not to fall into that state and to get out soon as attention warns us. Nevertheless, most people's attention spans these days are very limited or are there only when they are attracted by something. Just as the baby gets up from falling and continues endeavoring to walk again, so we need to always be aware when we are out of the state of awareness, in that attention we are back in awareness. We cannot force ourselves to be in a state of awareness because that is the ego's doing and it will fool us into believing that we are. We can only be attentive that we are not aware, which is the natural way and does not require effort.

This is not easy for most of us, unless we have had many lifetimes of practice after which watching becomes easier. To be watchful we have first and foremost to learn to concentrate on the task at hand without allowing the mind to take us away in different thoughts, therefore never being fully present in the moment. For example, we are at work and performing a task, but the mind is distracted by the thought of what the partner may be doing at home or maybe what the boss is thinking of us, or are we doing a good job? Anyone can observe that this happens numerous times during the day and the thinking never stops. This is what we call illusion: the abstract process of thinking and creating images which are illusions.

One who has the intention to reach peace, and love must put effort into observing this process every day. In doing so slowly, the thoughts will gradually reduce in number and in potency. This is why in yoga, concentration and meditation on an object helps us be attentive either on breath or, perhaps, a candle; these are means to keep the mind for longer periods in one spot. Buddha taught Vipassana meditation, where we always keep attention on the breath until we slowly reach the naked awareness.

All this is of no benefit if we do not keep the practice going throughout the day. The more involved we are in the world with lots of activities keeping us busy, the harder it is to make progress in silencing the mind. We understand an illusion, but delusion is a greater evil because it fools us into believing that we have reached awareness, love and wisdom but we still get upset; still have worries, frustrations, anxiety; still have likes and dislikes and so on. If one of the states described from duality are present, we cannot reach love. We may do charity, we may do spiritual work, be psychic and so on, but we are still in an illusory state of mind and from there some could fall deeper into delusion.

Illusion is when we are lost in abstract image making and the mind still works in duality, always living in that abstract way of thinking, all the time lost in thoughts. Delusion is when we fall into abstract thinking and believe it to be reality. The moment we construct ideas and images about ourselves, we are in illusion. The moment we believe them to be true, we fall into delusion. Delusion is a hard construct to come out of because it is an abstract construct which was turned into reality where the illusion is still abstract and can be discarded as soon as we are aware. In naked awareness, all illusion dissolves.

Some people are aware of how our minds operate, some not. Both groups are much in the world, and they are not ready to give up enjoyment of the senses and the attachments which come with it, thinking all is fine. Everyone will do this in their own time. We do not have to give up enjoyment forever, but until the attachment can be severed from mind and heart it is best to abstain. This is what Christ meant by saying one has to die of oneself, meaning cut all attachments for they are all illusory, as we have pointed out previously. This is why in days of old, monks and yogi retired to secluded places to have less sensory excitement for the senses, which made it easy to practice and detach from the senses.

Some went to the other side, giving up everything and in doing so became deluded as well. Here, Alan Watts points out how the ego can fool us into anything and how trying to dispel the ego with the ego is absurd.

> *You cannot teach an ego to be anything but egotistic, even though egos have the subtlest ways of pretending to be reformed. The basic thing is therefore to dispel, by experiment and experience, the illusion of oneself as a separate ego.*
>
> -Alan Watts

Illusion can be dispelled by meditation and awareness, but delusion needs experience in order to see that any idea or concept held as reality in fact is still an illusion: only experience in awareness can break delusion. The one who thinks that he is this or that and knows this or that does not realize that these are just states of mind and when one holds onto them for a while, one can become deluded. The universe and all of existence is energy in continuous movement, alive all the time, always fresh every moment. The ego is not. Ego is always memory, or an idea based on memory, an event that happened in the past. Ego is always walking step by step with death, for it is death. Awareness is always alive and in motion.

We can state that thinking is always of the past therefore death. Ego always relies on the past to sustain itself therefore all thinking regarding oneself, or another is illusion. We live like this every day, and it is very hard to get out of it because it has become natural: we do not know a different way. Our education systems all over the world enhance this thinking and enhance the ego; enhance the illusion of oneself. Therefore, it is important for one who desires to be free to begin to watch every day, every moment, how one thinks, where thinking takes one, and start some practice in order to always bring oneself back in the self, in the awareness of being.

Thought is responsible for the image-making process and one who becomes aware of this takes steps towards stopping this image making process. Here we look how Jiddu Krishnamurti explains how thought operates:

The human mind demands freedom. Freedom is essential, it is even demanded politically, but you don't demand freedom from all images. Thought has created these images for thought and the image various sociological, economic and cultural reasons. These images are measurable: the greater, the lesser. One asks: can thought observe without distortion? Obviously, it can't. There is a distorting factor in thought, because thought is the response of the past. Is there an observation without the interference of thought? – that means without the interference of any image. You can find this out; it's not a question of just accepting or believing. You can look at your wife or your husband, the tree, the cloud, or the person sitting next to you, without any image.

-Jiddu Krishnamurti

Above, Krishnamurti is pointing out what we have stated earlier in previous chapters and what all masters have also pointed out too: namely, that we can look at life and also function from the state of awareness where the image making process has stopped where there are no judgements or prejudices about anything, only pure observation. In pure observation reality is. Some small image making at a practical level of existence may still be necessary. Memory is also necessary, to function to remember where one lives, for example, but abstract images as talked about earlier are not necessary: they are destructive and always will create conflict between the image we created and what is real.

Thoughts are predispositions accumulated in innumerable former births. Their annihilation must be the aim. To be free from them is Purity. Man is deluded by the intermingling of conscious self with insentient body; this delusion

*must cease. The ever-present Self needs no efforts for reali-
zation, but delusion alone is to be removed. When camphor
burns no residue is left. The mind is the camphor: when it
has resolved itself into the Self without leaving the slightest
trace, it is realization. Mind is a bundle of thoughts, having
its origin in consciousness or Self. Thoughts are not real;
the only reality is the Self. The enduring background free
from thoughts, the expanse devoid of thoughts, is the Self.
Mind in its purity is the Self.*

-Sri Ramana Maharshi

Above, Ramana Maharshi points out clearly that all thoughts
are illusory and when we are free from them, we are residing
in our true reality. He also points out our greater delusion
being in believing our bodies to be our true reality for we have
seen in previous chapters that this is a wrong belief and has to
be uprooted. The mind in its purity is the self, pure awareness.
Every belief, idea or concept arises in the mind by thought and it
does not matter how real it may seem to be, it is still illusory. That
awareness does not come easily. Only a few come to this readily.
Most of us need effort to discern between the necessary practical
thoughts we need for practical living and abstract thoughts which
are not needed at all.

Here is where the practices of yoga, prayer, meditation and
fasting come to be of support. In the Patanjali yoga sutras, the
sage explains the eight limbs of yoga and the practices necessary
for subduing the mind. All come to the extinguishing of all energies but love. When ego is understood as being only memory and
thought, seeking ends, surrender then can happen and wisdom
will take care of the rest.

One has then to be observant of how the mind works and little by
little gain insight into the limitations of it, for the limited can never
touch the unlimited. This requires that in the end it surrenders
fully and in doing so purifies itself in the awareness of being. At
first when we start to practice, it is not an easy process to dissolve

the ego for it will do anything in its power to survive and keep us in ignorance because at first, we try to overcome it by thought which is still the ego and thus always ahead of us, knowing our next move.

This is where most seekers get stuck in a trap of an illusory state of mind. One has to first understand how the thoughts are taking the sensations which come from the senses and how feelings and emotions are produced in the mind. Sensations are nerve impulses working on the five energies which run through the body. Each sensation has its connection through an organ of sense. Light comes through the eyes, touch through the skin, taste through the mouth, hearing through the ears, smells through the nose. All of these sensory organs have a connection with the brain which processes the five energies accordingly.

If we touch a hot pot, the brain receives stimuli from the nerves which are in the muscle and soft tissues. Then the brain reacts through the nerves and the muscles. A child does not know that the fire burns and is attracted to it and wants to touch it; even if told not to, he will somehow attempt to do it. When he does, he will recognize by experience that it was hot and not pleasant, thereby learning from direct experience. That experience is then put into memory and next time he encounters fire he knows it is danger and deals with it accordingly. Sensory perception serves a purpose; it was given to help us function in this world and survive. We have distorted the purpose of the senses by indulging them in all sorts of mischief for the pleasures we can get through them and in doing so we are caught in a vicious process without end.

For example, we eat something nice, and the senses perceive the pleasure given by eating. Now, instead of just enjoying it, thought comes in and registers it in memory and wants to have more and in doing so gives birth to desire. Then the memory of eating it comes again which gives pleasure and satisfaction, then attach-ment is born, forming habit. If for some reason the desire is not fulfilled the opposite feeling is born, dissatisfaction, which can be transmuted to a depressed feeling or frustration which may transform into anger. This is an example of how, out of sensation, memory, desire, feeling and then emotions are born. This process is sustained by thought which is ego and repeats itself all day and for most of us even in the dream state. This process needs to be observed and understood for if not understood, it can play havoc in people's lives.

By carefully observing the process, we can point out that feelings and emotions are created by thought, by the ego they are not real; they are just like mirages appearing in the mind. Unfortunately, we take them to be real and by identifying with them, we give strength to the identification that I am the body and mind, giving birth to illusions and delusions. This process can be observed in everyday life. The objects of desire may be different, the way of perceiving them through one sense or a combination of them, but this is the way of getting into illusion which then gives birth to the five poisons: ignorance, attachment, aversion, pride, envy.

Of course, there is nothing wrong with eating or whatever one enjoys but the attachment should not be there. This is why, in the process, we should stop in the moment we create the attachment. If attachment is not there, then there is no problem if the desire is fulfilled or not and we can stay in a state of equanimity of mind and be at peace. This is where most of us fail: where the desires run with too many passions where we cannot stop the flood gates. Here a reminder of what Buddha had said to Ajita:

> *Ajita's Questions: The Buddha was asked by his disciple Ajita, "What is it that smothers the world? What makes the world so hard to see? What would you say pollutes the world and what threatens it most?"*
> *The Buddha answered, "It is ignorance which smothers, and it is careless ness, and greed that makes the world invisible. The hunger of desire pollutes the world, and the great source of fear is the pain of suffering."*

"In every direction," said Ajita, "the rivers of desire are running. How can we dam them and what will hold them back? What can we use to close the floodgates?"
The Buddha answered; "Any river can be stopped with the dam of mindfulness. I call it the flood stopper. And with wisdom you can close the floodgates."

-Buddha

As discussed previously, we see that it is imperative to understand how the mind works, how desires run riot, the process of making feelings and emotions and how to stop all the illusions of our own creations. Buddha has pointed out wisdom and mindfulness. By observing the process, by understanding it and by reading or listening to the wisdom of the masters we can overcome the illusory appearances of the world created by us and in doing so see the world as it is. By seeing clearly, we can rest more and more in the awareness of being and in doing so allow wisdom to cut the cords of attachments, ignorance, fears and inherent tendencies. Once all these are removed, we remain with our natural state of being and this state is the natural state of all sentient beings.

This process whereby the ego takes control of the mind gives rise to all sorts of evils in the world: rape, slavery, pedophilia, murders, theft, wars and so on. It does not matter how moral we may be, killing another is obviously the process of the ego creating havoc, thinking we have the right to do so for our morality dictates doing so, not realizing that that morality is illusory and deceiving and we are so much imprisoned by the five poisons.

Here, one great master describes sensation and its ramifications.

Sensation is always seeking further sensation, ever in wider and wider circles. There is no end to the pleasures of sensation; they multiply, but there is always dissatisfaction in their fulfillment; there is always the desire for more, and the demand for more is without end. Sensation and dissatisfaction are inseparable, for the desire for more binds them together. Sensation is the desire for more and also the desire for less. In the very act of the fulfillment or sensation, the demand for more is born. The more is ever in the future; it is the everlasting dissatisfaction with what has been. There is conflict between what has been and what will be. Sensation is always dissatisfaction. One may clothe sensation in religious garb, but it is still what it is: a thing of the mind and a source of conflict and apprehension. Physical sensations are always crying for more; and when they are thwarted, there is anger, jealousy, hatred. There is pleasure in hatred, and envy is satisfying; when one sensation is thwarted, satisfaction is found in the very antagonism that frustration has brought.

Mind can never find happiness. Happiness is not a thing to be pursued and found, as sensation. Sensation can be found again and again, for it is ever being lost; but happiness cannot be found. Remembered happiness is only a sensation, a reaction for or against the present. What is over is not happiness; the experience of happiness which is over is sensation, for remembrance is the past and the past is sensation. Happiness is not sensation.

-Jiddu Krishnamurti

Here we see how nicely he puts it: we are in that process, and there is never an end to it. True happiness is joy, as we have pointed out in previous chapters, and cannot be bought. It is our true nature. Only by finding our true nature can we bathe in the joy of the Lord of Love and call ourselves divine beings. We see how sensation leads to desire, to attachments, to habits, to a fragmented state of mind, to more and more disorder and conflict in us as individuals and in society at large.

This is where we have to look at life and the likes and dislikes we have. By looking, by giving up what we like and accepting also if given something which we don't like, we have one way of starting to cut through habits and attachments. We can start with something small and simple and see what happens, observe our reactions, feelings and the emotions which may arise when we do not have what we desire for a day. This is practical mindfulness, observing with no action or reaction. In that observation a miracle may happen if you are so blessed and that day you might get rid of one habit.

Next, we should see how Jiddu Krishnamurti invites us to observe and mindfully stay in the awareness of being. In that state ego has no place and cannot function.

To destroy sensation is to be insensitive, dead; not to see, not to smell, not to touch is to be dead, which is isolation. Our problem is entirely different, is it not? Thought can never bring happiness; it can only recall sensations, for thought is sensation. It cannot cultivate, produce, or progress towards happiness. Thought can only go towards that which it knows, but the known is not happiness; the known is sensation. Do what it will, thought cannot be or search out happiness. Thought can only be aware of its own structure, its own movement when thought makes an effort to put an end to itself, it is only seeking to be more successful, to reach a goal, an end which will be more gratifying. The more is knowledge, but not happiness.

Thought must be aware of its own ways, of its own cunning deceptions. In being aware of itself, without any desire to be or not to be, the mind comes to a state of inaction. Inaction is not death; it is a passive watchfulness in which thought is wholly inactive. It is the highest state of sensitivity. When the mind is completely inactive at all its levels, only then is there action. All the activities of the mind are mere sensations, reactions to stimulation, to influence, and so not action at all. When the mind is without activity, there is action; this action is without cause, and only then is there bliss.

-Jiddu Krishnamurti

The same as all masters, Krishnamurti describes the state of awareness where the ego cannot function, where reality is oneness, where love is oneness which cannot be fragmented by a little petty thought no matter how brave or big it may think itself to be or how moral.

Here, Guru Nanak points out that thought cannot touch reality as we have stated before:

> *By thinking, the True One cannot be reduced to thought,*
> *even by thinking hundreds of thousands of times.*
> *By remaining silent, inner silence is not obtained,*
> *even by remaining lovingly absorbed deep within.*
> *The hunger of the hungry is not appeased,*
> *even by piling up loads of worldly goods.*
> *There are hundreds of thousands of clever tricks,*
> *but not even one of them will go along with you in the end.*
> *So how can you become truthful,*
> *and how can the veil of illusion be torn away?*
> *O Nanak, it is written that you shall obey*
> *the Command of the True One,*
> *and walk in the way of the Divine Will.*
>
> -Guru Nanak

Guru Nanak not only points out that thought can never touch reality but also describes a way out of illusion. It is only found when one dies of the ego and aligns oneself to the universal will thereby following the right path and not the path given by the little ego with its own petty selfish will. It is imperative to observe being aware of all the movements of thought and how we fall prey to the tricks of the ego of the evil one. Evil does not mean being the evil you have been conditioned to know, that evil is only an illusion.

The God that can be told is not the real God and the same goes for the Evil that can be told, it is not the real Evil. It is just an image created by us or given to us by others to hold as true, which is an even deeper illusion; it is only a filter of our conditioning. We created filters of conditioning about everything we experience, and this is how we have been conditioned to function as robots.

As Christ and all the awakened masters have stressed, to die of oneself – which means to die of all the images we have created about the world – is imperative. In no other way can we touch love and therefore we remain in misery. This process whereby the ego hijacks us out of awareness and keeps us in all sorts of illusions happens so fast. This is why most of us cannot observe the moment when we are sucked into illusions. That is where spiritual practice is a necessity for most of us. We have to find a teacher, read spiritual books and by fasting, prayer, mediation, contemplation, chanting, mantra recitation or any other practice slowly silencing the mind to an extent that we can observe the ego at work, in that observation the ego will slowly lose all power over one who has touched the supreme wisdom.

Self-annihilation leads to eternal life in God the universal Noumenon, by whom all phenomena subsist.

-Rumi, Maulana Jalalu-'d-din Muhammad

A well-known Sufi master points out, as Christ did, that self-annihilation leads to eternal life. All awakened masters from all traditions have pointed to the same truth with different words, different traditions and different actions but nevertheless they point to the same door. Now the question arises as to why there is so much conflict between the religions. Next, we will explore a subject which is of a sensitive nature for many, but we have to look at it in order to understand why the conflicts and wars still exist in the world if all religions teach the same truth.

CHAPTER 23

RELIGION

Religion is defined in Wikipedia as:

> *Religion is a range of social, cultural systems, including designated behaviors and practices, morals, beliefs, worldviews, texts, sanctified places, prophecies, ethics, or organizations, that generally relate humanity to supernatural, transcendental, and spiritual elements although there is no scholarly consensus over what precisely constitutes a religion. Different religions may or may not contain various elements ranging from the divine, sacredness, faith, and a supernatural being or beings.*

Because it is hard to define exactly what religion means, it is equally difficult to reach a consensus whereby all individuals involved accept the other and love one another, even though love is the essential teaching of all religions, as we have seen in the teachings of awakened masters, today society has not reached a state where love is the primordial focus.

Wars have been fought because of religion from time immemorial to the present day. Many prophets and masters have come, walked the earth and taught love to no avail for wars are still going on; hate, greed, envy, ignorance and so on still run rampant in people's minds. If we carefully observe, humanity has not evolved much from the primitive state of mind, except perhaps at some level of consciousness observed only by the exalted ones who can understand reality.

If we observe, neither Christ nor any other awakened masters have left religions behind. They more or less have left teachings which point to a way of life whereby we find what is real (God) and in so doing live a life in love, without suffering and in harmony with all of existence. We may see religions like trains and the destination is God. Unfortunately, most people do not get off at the right station and are too attached to the trains, being afraid to take a leap of faith and get off at the right destination, for it is unknown and they are afraid of what they do not know.

Most religions have arisen after one or few awakened masters have left their bodies, and their teachings have been written down, forming the scriptures we have today, the Bible, Quran and so on. All the teachings intend to raise the consciousness of an individual to live life in harmony with others. Few are the ones who can do that and as we have observed in previous chapters the individual is the problem, not the religion. Religions may have contradictions between some of the teachings, but these exist only because of our ignorance and lack of understanding. Some teachings were already misunderstood to some extent by the disciples of the masters who did not have the capability at the time to fully grasp the energy behind the words, therefore falling into some errors.

We will not dwell on the structures of religions and write a thesis on religions for that would be a waste of time and would take lifetimes to complete, and who will have lifetimes to read when we barely can give some time to our spiritual practice? All spiritual hierarchical systems are doomed to failure for they have been constructed by thought and they suppress the true essence of the teachings which are meant to liberate individuals not to keep them in darkness where they are dependent on another for support. Some level of dependency may be needed for a short period as a child, for example, it needs to be helped to walk but once the child learns, it walks on its own. The same with religion: once we grasp the teachings and have touched the truth, we then do not need religion anymore; we have to drop it. This is a very sensitive subject for most people because most of us have been conditioned to the beliefs of a particular religion. Some have changed one religion for another, but they are merely changing one condition for another.

Unfortunately, most people rely on the traditions of religion and therefore miss the esoteric and mystic teachings of what religion has to offer. Most also distort the teachings for the ego is well versed in how thought works and is always a step ahead. This means we do not have a chance to understand religion with thought and this is the cause of all mischief between all traditions which fight for supremacy. The teachings point to an energy which can only be grasped by a pure

mind, and when the mind is pure then the heart can grasp the teachings, allowing that heart to connect with that energy to which the teachings point to and that is the love of the Lord of Love.

So, we observe that the individual is actually the problem, not the religion. If we understand and grasp the teachings of one particular religion, we will grasp all the teachings of all religions for all point to the same energy: to the omnipresent, omnipotent and omniscient God. God does not run the world from a hierarchical system. When we understand that God, intelligence runs all existence, we become one with God. For us it is imperative not to blame any religion or any teaching, but to only blame ourselves for misunderstanding the truth and therefore living in illusion and ignorance. Once we lift ignorance and illusion, religions will not give us any further trouble. When we say, "I do not know," from there we can move slowly towards the knowledge but if we came with any preconceived idea we obviously cannot move towards the truth.

Religion is not something separate. Like society, we make it, therefore it is part of us. As we change, we look at religion differently – with the eye of wisdom, the eye which can see through illusion. Now, some may want to include yoga as a religion, but yoga is just a system of science which helps an individual towards union with the divine. All yoga and practices can be taken up regardless of religious beliefs or traditions one has. All individuals, regardless of whether they are religious or not, can practice some kind of yoga. The highest form of yoga is that of self-knowledge, as we discussed previously. This yoga is not easy to take up therefore one must practice other forms beforehand to have some support. Below is a beautiful explanation of what we have presented so far in this chapter by an awakened soul, Ramana Maharshi.

> *All creeds are but preliminaries for the masses, leading up to the real truth of the Self. The religions are not necessarily the highest expression or the highest wisdom of their founders, who had to consider the times in which they lived and the mental capacities of the people. The highest wisdom is too subtle for most minds, and so a whole scheme of worlds, gods, bodies, evolution, etc. had to be given out because people seem to find it easier to believe all these things rather than believe the simple Truth of the one reality – Self. Thus, reincarnation, astral planes, survival after death, etc. are true but only from a lower standpoint. It is all a matter of standpoint. From the highest, that of the real Self, all else disappears as illusory and only the Reality remains. It is true that subtle astral bodies exist, because in order to function in the dream-world a body is necessary for that world, but it too is real only on its own plane whereas*

the One self is always real, always and eternally existent, whether we are aware of it or not. Hence it is better to seek that, because the other self-bodies are only conditionally real. An ordinary Christian is only satisfied when told God is in some far off heaven, not to be reached by us unaided, that Christ alone has known Him and he alone can save us. Hence when told the simple truth that the kingdom of heaven is within you, he is not satisfied and will read far-fetched meanings in the statement. Mature minds alone can grasp the simple truth in all its nakedness.

-Sri Ramana Maharshi

As we see, the truth preached by all awakened masters was indeed hard to grasp and not many have done it during the times the masters were alive. Some attained the truth long after the masters were gone by practicing and having the pure intent to find the truth. That intent, together with spiritual practices which lead to self-knowledge, is liberation. Before we go any further, we ought to understand how one perceives and uses intellect in order to have an insight into life, therefore let us look at perception, intelligence and insight.

CHAPTER 24

PERCEPTION, INTELLIGENCE AND INSIGHT

How we perceive information gathered from the environment and from our inner life – emotions, thoughts, feelings – is of great importance. Depending on perception which uses intelligence to perceive correctly and therefore to have an insight which penetrates is vital, if we desire to eradicate suffering from our daily existence.

Perception is the ability to perceive the inner and outer movement of life, and this perception comes through the five senses. If the perception is clear without interference from thought or ego, intelligence operates freely and in that process body, mind and heart are in harmony. On the other hand, if the ego hijacks the process for its benefit, then whatever action follows is a selfish action.

When physicists discovered atomic energy, they did so by perception coupled with intelligence and insight: they never intended to discover the atomic bomb. The thought of building an atomic bomb came later, because of the selfishness of the ego which is always destructive. We clearly see that without an ego there is a clear perception where intelligence operates, and insight is gained into any problem of life, for then problems do not exist. Perception is also listening to anything without the filter of our conditions.

If we perceive something we look at or listen to without any image of past knowledge, then we use clear perception, and this is not easy to do but is a must in order to live a life with no conflict, therefore no suffering. Clear perception is itself intelligence and if this process is not hijacked by the ego, then there is insight and wisdom followed by the right action. Intelligence then can gather information or knowledge and, if there is no intervention by the ego, will always use that knowledge in the right way.

We can say that one can be intelligent without having acquired knowledge for intelligence can use knowledge to further add to the knowledge, but knowledge does not use intelligence for knowledge is the past, is the ego, which works from memory. Intelligence is a quality of love which cannot be used by thought but which can use thought at any time. We can say that perception without any interference from thought is intelligence and leads to insight which then grounds us in awareness for there we can find wisdom and love. Perception, intelligence, insight equals awareness and in that awareness wisdom and love run supreme.

Jiddu Krishnamurti points to perception and intelligence:

> *When thought sees that it is incapable of discovering something new, that very perception is the seed of intelligence, isn't it? That is intelligence: 'I can not do'. I thought I could do a lot of things, and I can in a certain direction, but in a totally new direction I cannot do anything. The discovery*

of that is intelligence. Thought is of time; intelligence is not of time. Intelligence is immeasurable. Intelligence comes into being when the mind, the heart and the body are really harmonious.

-Jiddu Krishnamurti

He goes further in explaining insight:

No. I think it is fairly clear, Sir. You come upon it when you see the whole thing. So, insight is the perception of the whole. A fragment cannot see this, but the "I" sees the fragments, and the "I" seeing the fragments sees the whole, and the quality of a mind that sees the whole is not touched by thought; therefore, there is perception, there is insight.

-Jiddu Krishnamurti

A mind which has a clear perception also has intelligence and then insight is never divisible. It works as a whole and that mind is capable of touching love and wisdom.

Guru Nanak on intelligence:

*The faithful have intuitive awareness and intelligence. The faithful know about all worlds and realms.
The faithful shall never be struck across the face.
The faithful do not have to go with the Messenger of Death. Such is the Name of the Immaculate True One.
Only one who has faith comes to know such a state of mind.*

-Guru Nanak

Guru Nanak also says that perception, intelligence and insight are intuitive awareness and one who possesses has full faith, one with such faith comes to know the state of mind free of all troubles. But to get to that state of mind is not an easy task, for the ego is cunning and smart in using knowledge, and keeping us in ignorance and mischief, therefore will do anything to interrupt insight and our ability to see the whole. It will always interrupt and therefore divide, and always perceives anything from a fragmentary perspective, therefore promoting isolation, division, and conflict.

A Sufi master below describes how insight is seeing the whole, not fragmenting what is presented by the senses which are corrupted by the ego.

> *The ear and the nose cannot see beautiful objects, but only the eye, and similarly the sensual eye, blinded by lust, is impotent to behold spiritual truth. On the other hand, men of spiritual insight, whose vision is purged from lust, become as it were all eyes, and no longer see double, but only the One sole real Being.*

> -Rumi, Maulana Jalalu-'d-din Muhammad

Saint Isaac in the next quote, the same as Guru Nanak, points out that a light mind is not a burden. It has faith and that faith is the revelation of insight, for faith does not cling to any knowledge. It is free perception which is intelligence and insight. He states that faith with instruction – which is belief – does not free man of doubts but the faith which comes with insight with no doubts or presumptions will lead on to truth.

> *The light of the mind gives birth to faith. Faith gives birth to the consolation of hope. Hope makes the heart strong. Faith is the revelation of insight. When the mind is dark, faith is hidden, and fear reigns in us and cuts off our hope. Faith through instruction does not free a man from presumption and doubts; only that faith which dawns by insight. It is called the revelation of truth. As long as faith understands*

God as God, through the revelation of insight, fear will not approach unto the heart. When we are left in darkness and we lose this insight that we may become humble, fear assails us which brings us near to humility and repentance.

-St Isaac the Syrian

In *"The Way of the Bodhisattva"*, Santideva points out the effectiveness of insight in eradicating afflicted states of mind and recommended first searching for calm abiding, which is given when perception and intelligence are present. Then the mind is clear of thoughts trying to hijack insight.

Penetrative insight joined with calm abiding Utterly eradicates afflicted states. Knowing this, first search for calm abiding, found by people who are happy to be free from worldly ties.

-Śantideva

There are many more similar quotes from the awakened masters but by now we should have an idea how we are to look, listen and intellectualize information especially on the spiritual level whereby we do not allow thoughts, images and memory to interfere with listening and seeing, therefore being able to get an insight into things. Even scientists, in order to discover the new look with an empty mind, and after they have insight, then employ thought to do what needs to be done.

The intuitive mind is a sacred gift, and the rational mind is a faithful servant. We have created a society that honors the servant and has forgotten the gift. The true sign of intelligence is not knowledge but imagination.

-Albert Einstein

Einstein also points to the intuitive mind as naked awareness and that we are too much in the mind of the servant, which is the ego.

In the second quote he states that the sign of true intelligence is imagination which comes from that intuitive state of being. It is imperative for us to be aware at all times of how we perceive everything and everyone, for then with clear perception we get insight and therefore we always act with no ego, in a constructive way for the benefit of all. It is not easy to be observant but if we persevere, we will get better at catching the ego when it does interfere with perception or in the process of hijacking insight.

Every instance of resistance or clinging to anything is done by the ego and in both there is conflict. In relationships with one another, with nature, with all existence we have to be observant of the inner and the outer movement of life and this is what Jiddu Krishnamurti called true meditation: gathering all energy in watching this movement in everyday life. Few are the souls who can always stay rooted in awareness, they are great souls indeed. In order to get our true freedom and unveil our true reality, it is imperative that we achieve this: it cannot be done otherwise. The object of any spiritual practice is to come to the place where we do not allow the ego to intervene in our everyday existence and only use the ego when is necessary, in the practical side of things and even there it needs to be watched. For example: on the practical level one drives the car, does the job, does any mechanical activity; on the psychological level, for example, one driving the car starts thinking about something else and is drawn into that thinking. Thinking can be stopped only when we are in deep state of awareness, but we cannot get in that state while driving a car. To attempt to do so is absurd; we will have a crash. What we can do is just be a witness to the thoughts which come and go without rejecting or clinging to any and that is enough to stay with our driving in the present moment. In doing so all the time, we will observe that thoughts will be less and less disturbing. In the end, only the thoughts relevant to our daily activity will arise in the mind.

We cannot maintain silence. It comes and goes own its own. Neither you or I can maintain or retain it. The moment you try to retain it there is conflict. When it comes enjoy it live with it. When it goes live it. Don't try to hold it however miserable you feel about.

-Sri M

Above, Sri M points out that we should not try to maintain silence or get it for the one trying is the ego. The same applies to thoughts: just let them come and go. They will slow down on their own accord. When we have understood how the mind works, we will have fewer and fewer desires or worries and therefore less to think about.

We may want to go into silence – to not speak – but that is not real silence. That is suppression, done by the ego, and it will fool us into thinking that is a state of silence. Likewise, we cannot copy spiritual masters who have maintained silence because their silence was not forced; it came by its own accord. The moment we suppress anything we are in illusion. Thoughts, sensations, feelings, cannot be suppressed, for we may suppress them for a lifetime but at any given moment they can resurface, and we must face them again. Any suppression or running away is the ego and as we mentioned before, the ego will outsmart us for as long as we are fighting it, we fight a losing battle, giving more power to the ego. All spiritual practices are done in order to surrender to the present moment.

Ramana Maharshi sustains this by saying:

The realized one does not think or plan for the future. He lets the future take care of itself. For him the future is in the present.

-Sri Ramana Maharshi

In the realization that nothing in this world can make you fully happy and at peace comes disenchantment with the world and the intention to find everlasting happiness grows. We are being drawn by the divine magnet and when we start to clean off the rust of ignorance then we start to realize the union with the supreme reality which is our true nature. The rust is the separation created by ignorance and that is the ego. By living a simple life, we curb desires, slowly cutting through habits and tendencies and can follow our intuition based on the wisdom of the masters who have walked before us on the road to awakening. Next, we should look at the aids one may need in order to be able to walk the path of awakening.

CHAPTER 25

PRAYER, CONTEMPLATION, MEDITATION AND FASTING

Have faith that all these titles in this chapter can help us reach the goal and raise human consciousness to a divine consciousness where you will be able to find everlasting happiness which, translated, means to be self-realized. Some are indeed blessed that they do not need those aids, but they are few and they have done the work in previous lifetimes. Most of us certainly need these aids to curb the ego and put it in its place or dissolve it, either way is the same way.

These aids are similar to when we are handicapped or injured and need the help of props to return to the natural functions of the body. In order to help the mind find its natural state most of us need the use of one, a combination, or all of these aids. Sages of old and most of the past masters have used these aids in order to awaken to our true reality and gain self-realization. As we stated earlier, the mind always chatters; even if we go into a cave, we take this chatter along. This chatter is of the ego and by always engaging in it we are making our own prison. To stop this chatter, the yogis observe it and try various methods of slowing it and understanding how it comes about.

The Christian monks employed fasting, prayers, contemplating God, surrender, faith and devotion to overcome the mind. Hindu and Buddhist yogis have also used various aids as described in yoga; we discussed the branches of yoga in previous chapters. Every individual has to find what works for them best and stick with that practice on a regular basis at least once a day.

Let's start by fasting and see how we may benefit from it, if at all. As we discussed earlier, the five poisons come to us through the gates of the body: the senses. One sense is taste, and it is an important one indeed and many people are led by it into greed. The purpose of taste is for our survival as we have to eat in order to have energy throughout the day. Taste gathers information and passes it to the brain and the brain reacts accordingly. Obviously, if the taste is bad, we will be attentive in eating or not according to our conditioning. Through experience accumulated over time, we know what we can eat as humans and what we cannot. Also, in present times we have come to an elaborate food-making process in order to satisfy the many pleasures which came through the taste faculty.

Most of us fall prey to it and the ego will try to keep us in that state of wanting and getting satisfaction through the sensory perception of eating. This is problematic, as seen in obesity prob-lems and the many sicknesses which derive from eating based on the ego. This is because we are weak and try to get satisfac-tion through food. There is nothing wrong with enjoying a nice meal but when we no longer know how much to eat because we are greedy, suffering comes to us as individuals and to society at large.

Previous chapters discussed sensation as a trap, leading us to find more and more, better and better, sensations. This trap is not only the fact that we eat too much but has everything to do with our state of mind too, for what affects the body also affects mind and vice versa. It is imperative to look at fasting and how we can use it to get out of the trap. What we are talking here about is spiritual fasting, not any other forms of fasting. Meditation, prayer and contemplation are also needed to support it.

Someone who has not fasted before should start by simply skipping one meal a day. During this fast, try to be attentive to the thoughts arising in the mind and see how the ego will try to get you back into the trap of breaking the fast, and will try to keep us in the habit and we know that is just a pattern of thought enforced by the ego. In the course of fasting, the body will always respond for it is accustomed to get its energy and it will be asking for it. Hunger in the mind will grow; thoughts about food will creep up and maybe we will give in and eat. Breaking the fast is fine, it can happen, but we have to try again and again until we succeed with one meal less a day. We can supplement the meal with water, which is best in fasting for water is a cleanser.

By fasting we not only help the body but also the mind. It will become quieter and calmer and will learn to rest, to observe, to be attentive to what happens during the fast. Most traditions have employed fasting in spiritual practice because it is good for the body to recover, and the organs to have a chance to rest. In an individual who has never fasted, the organs never rest. Fasting has many benefits for the body and mind alike. After successfully fasting through a meal a day, we then should attempt one day a week with only water but, of course, consult a doctor if necessary or if there are medical conditions to consider. Fasting more regularly will make the body and mind feel lighter.

By fasting, we will realize we are just a bundle of habits and by observing, we see how hard it is to break them, to let go of them, to be free of their hold on us. When we can curb hunger for food, we can likewise curb any hunger, for hunger is not only for food but for any other objects which sustain pleasure: that hunger is greed. Greed is one of the afflictions and because of it some have too much and some very little and some nothing at all. Observe the violence and conflict greed produces in the world and then maybe we will understand why it is imperative to let it go. Greed for power, for control, for money, for property and so on is one of the causes of great misery in the world from time immemorial.

The ego will try to get you out of fasting in any way it can and if not, it will support you and make you feel proud of the achievement and get you to boast about it and in this way it has you in its trap again. One must be careful about that, for its cunning ways are endless.

So faith shows us as it were before our eyes the reality of that future perfection. By faith we are instructed about those unattainable things, not by investigation and the power of knowledge. All works of righteousness: fasting, alms, vigils, holiness and the others which are performed with the body; and unneighborly love, humility of heart, forgiveness of sins, meditation upon beautiful things, investigation of the mysteries hidden in the holy scriptures, the occupation of the mind with the practice of good works, the keeping of the affections of the soul within the borders, and the other virtues which are accomplished with the soul: all these need knowledge as their regulating power. But all these are still degrees along which the soul ascends unto the elevated height of faith, and they are called virtues.

-St Isaac the Syrian

Mental fast is the real aid. Fasting is not an end in itself. There must be spiritual development side by side. Complete fasting makes the mind too weak. You cannot derive sufficient strength for the spiritual quest. The spiritual quest must be kept up right through a fast, if it is to benefit spiritually.

-Sri Ramana Maharshi

The two saints here explain that spiritual fasting has its place in helping the mind when employed with other practices and used intelligently. Before doing any fasting, be sure that fasting will benefit you on the physical and mental levels. Try it and be attentive: the answer is in that attention.

We have looked at fasting and now let us look and talk about prayer. What is prayer? Is it just a petition? And to whom? To a God of our own making or to the real God? If it is to the God of our own making it will definitely never be heard but if it is to the real one, it will be heard but that does not mean that the prayer will be answered immediately.

In the Greek translation of the Syriac Homily 2245 two quotations from the Thoughts of Evagrius ('prayer is purity of the mind which alone, to the amazement of the human person, comes forth from the light of the Holy Trinity' and 'purity of the mind is the disappearance of that which is thought. It is likened to the heavenly flower, during prayer the light of the Holy Trinity shines forth within it').

-St Isaac the Syrian

This is how the early fathers described prayer: as an aid to keep the mind free of thought for the period we are in intense prayer from the heart.

Accordingly, when you rise for prayer and service, instead of meditating worldly things, scriptural thoughts will be pictured in the mind. And thereby the recollection of that which it saw and heard before, will be forgotten and effaced in it. So, your mind will reach purity. This is what has been said: the mind is made chaste by recitation when it comes to prayer, and by recitation it is enlightened during prayer. This means: the soul will find strength to interchange outward distraction with the habits of prayer, viz. essential understanding shining in the mind on account of the wondrous recollections of that world. How often at those times has the power of contemplation (stimulated! by the scriptures, made silent and stupefied (the solitary) during prayer and left him standing without impulses the same power, which cuts off prayer by delight as I have said.

-St Isaac the Syrian

Saint Isaac further explains the power of concentrated prayer to get the mind slowly into a contemplative state.

Support with your word the weak and the distressed in spirit whenever you can, then the hand that bears the universe will support you. Participate with those who are suffering in heart, in passionate prayer and mourning of the heart then before your demand a fountain of grace will be opened.

-St Isaac the Syrian

He stresses that prayer from the heart will open new dimensions of consciousness which are blessings for the one undertaking them.

Whether you pray with brethren or alone, try to pray not simply as a routine, but with conscious awareness of your prayer. Conscious awareness of prayer is concentration accompanied.

-Evagrius the Solitary

Evagrius also states that real prayer comes from a mind which is consciously aware, the same awareness which Padmasambhava pointed out. Prayer must come from the heart and not just be a mental routine.

Sage Patanjali, India's greatest exponent of yoga, describes God the Creator as Ishvara, the Cosmic Lord or Ruler. "His symbol is Pranava (the Holy Word or Sound, Aum). By prayerful, repeated chanting of Aum and meditation on its meaning, obstacles disappear, and the consciousness turns inward (away from external sensory identification)."

-Swami Yogananda

Sage Patanjali states that by prayerful chanting of OM, the mind is turned within, away from the senses and in doing so finds reality.

Most people never really love God because they little know how lovable the Lord is when He visits the heart of the meditating devotee. This actual contact of the transcendental presence of God is possible to determined devotees who persist in meditation and continuous soulful prayers.

-Swami Yogananda

Swami Yogananda, a Kriya yoga master, also points out that by meditation and prayer with the heart intent, we will touch divine love and be able to share that with all beings.

Fasting and prayers have helped the early Christian saints to overcome the world and get in touch with the divine essence which is in all of us. The prayers and practices should be done from the heart, for if they are done with heart they will be 'heard', the heart is our connection with our own reality. Fasting with prayer will help in starving the mind of thoughts, allowing the mind to rest in its natural pure state and thus sink us in awareness where true meditation starts and letting us stay in that state, enjoying life as it presents itself.

> *Question: Is it right to pray to God for all kinds of things?*
> *Mātājī: The most excellent prayer is for God Himself.*

-Sri Anandamayi Mayi

Anandamayi points out the highest prayer is to know God which lies in every heart in all beings and in all existence and non-existence.

> *In the Kaliyuga the best way is bhakti yoga, the path of devotion – singing the praises of the Lord, and prayer.*

-Sri Ramakrishna

Ramakrishna also stated that devotion and prayer, which is the yoga of devotion, is an easy path to touch divine grace. So, we see how prayer is essential for most traditions; even some Buddhists are using prayer in their practices.

> *Due to the power of prayers, the experiential instructions on the transitional processes Are revealed for the sake of disciples who are training their mind- streams. In this there are the preliminary practices, the main practice, and the conclusion.*

-Padmasambhava

Padmasambhava also points out the importance of prayers to deities and gurus which are described as gods in tantric practices. So, in Buddhism also prayers have their place in helping individuals connect with subtle states of consciousness.

From prayer we can now move to contemplation, for in most traditions contemplative prayer is a state which does help get into the awareness of being in our true reality. Contemplation can be of objects but mostly focusses on self or God as the aim of spiritual contemplation is to purify the mind of all obstructions. Here the contemplation described in the title of Padmasambhava's teachings is the last stage of meditation before samadhi, which is entering into a pure state of awareness.

> *With discrimination (viveka), Illusion disappears, and one comes to realize Parabrahman (God) through contemplative thoughtfulness and inquiry.*

-St Shri Samartha Ramdas

Also, Saint Sri Samartha Ramdas describes the contemplative state as thoughtfulness and enquiring into the nature of reality as God. Contemplation on self is spiritual contemplation. We can also contemplate a subject or object which can give us the true knowledge of the object being contemplated on.

> *True is the Divine One,*
> *True is the Name of the One,*
> *speak it with infinite love. People beg and pray,*
> *"Give to us, give to us,"*
> *and the Great Giver gives divine gifts.*
> *So what offering can we place before the One by*
> *which we might see the glory of the Divine?*
> *What words can we speak to evoke Divine Love?*
> *In the Amrit Vaylaa, the ambrosial hours*
> *before dawn, chant the True Name, and*
> *contemplate Divine Greatness.*
> *By the karma of past actions, the robe of this*
> *physical body is obtained, by Divine Grace, the*
> *Gate of Liberation is found.*
> *O Nanak, know this well:*
> *all the creation is within the True One.*

-Guru Nanak

Guru Nanak also points to contemplation on divine greatness in order to connect with the one reality and all existence. We all ask and pray for needy things but most important is contemplation on his name and his love.

> *Let excellence be reckoned by you as the body, contempla-*
> *tion as the soul. The two (form) one complete spiritual man,*
> *composed of sensible and intelligible parts. And as it is not*
> *possible that the soul reach existence and birth without the*
> *accomplished formation of the body, so it is not possible that*
> *contemplation, the second soul, the spirit of revelations, be*
> *formed in the womb of the intellect which receives the full-*
> *ness of spiritual seed, without the corporeal performance*
> *of excellence, the dwelling place of the knowledge which*
> *receives revelations. Contemplation is the apprehension of*
> *the divine mysteries which are hidden, in the things spoken.*

-St Isaac the Syrian

Saint Isaac says here that by contemplation one can get insight into the truth without the intervening intellect. As we have seen by what the sages of the past are stating, contemplation on the name of God – whatever name is chosen does not matter, he answers to all names – we can pierce the veil of ignorance and find reality entering into oneness of being. Next, we look at Meditation and the yoga practices which lead to meditation.

Meditation is a very misunderstood word in many ways. Yes, we have methods to get us into meditation, but they are just tools to help us reach that meditative stage. A meditative mind does not run out every second after various thoughts and desires and being everlasting in a state of turmoil.

Krishnamurti mentions what meditation is like:

You watch while eating, when you are listening to people, when somebody says something that hurts you, flatters you. That means, you have to be alert all the time – when you are exaggerating, when you are telling half-truths – you follow? To watch, you need a very quiet mind. That is meditation. The whole of that is meditation.

-Jiddu Krishnamurti

Being always in a state of attention, being witness to all that's happening within oneself and outside, the emotions, the thoughts, understanding the whole movement of life is real meditation but most of us cannot do that. The Sages of old have left numerous systems to help us get to this state where meditation can happen. To get to the kind of meditation which gives us self-knowledge is the real meditative mind and when we have realized self-knowledge then self-realization is there too, in the awareness of being pure as it always was.

The primary purpose of meditation is to become conscious of, and familiar with, our inner life. The ultimate purpose is to reach the source of life and consciousness.

-Sri Nisargadatta Maharaj

Here Nisargadatta Maharaj points out the real purpose of meditation, which is self-explanatory.

Second, about the Mahamudra of the meditation, a tantra says: Let your basic nature settle without clinging; That is the Mahamudra of the meditation state. In this way, the Mahamudra of the meditation is to allow your original nature to let be without holding anything whatsoever in mind. So, it is not the result of thought, not indicated, not something that is or is not; it is without conflict and mental doing and does not exclude anything whatsoever.

-Padmasambhava

Above, Padmasambhava describes meditation in the same way and explains the state of mahamudra, where we are in a state of watchfulness without clinging to any thoughts or rejecting any. This is the meditative state where one is the self.

Lady Tsogyal asked the master: How should one keep the mind during meditation? The master replied: While meditating, let your body and mind relax. Since there is nothing whatsoever to be analyzed, the stream of dualistic mind and the mental states arising from it are interrupted. You do not have to deliberately halt them. While neither keeping nor rejecting anything, let go of all mental activity. Don't think of anything, and don't imagine anything. Your nature is aware, just as it is. Without moving toward anything, let be in your natural state. When remaining in this way, the knower and the known are not seen as separate, so do not think of the object as being there or the knower as being here. Do not conceive of something other than those two. Since you neither pursue an object there nor try to stop a thought here, you can allow the mind itself to be pure, lucid, and awake, without needing to dwell on anything whatsoever.

-Padmasambhava

Above, Guru Padmasambhava points out to his consort Lady Tsogyal how one should meditate. To get to this meditative mind wherein we can sit and watch the mind, we have to utilize some yoga practices like mantras, breathing techniques, concentration and contemplations on objects to aid us.

Q. If the efforts at meditation are hindered through past karma what remedy can there be?

A. It is self-stultifying to drown oneself in such fanciful fears. Fate and past karma relate to the external world. Dive boldly within you. These will not hinder you. It is the thinking of hindrances that forms a serious hindrance. We have all to return to our source. Every human being is seeking its source and must one day come to it. We came from the Within; we have gone outward; now we must turn inward. What is meditation? It is our natural self. We have covered ourselves over with thoughts and passions. To throw them off we must concentrate on one thought – the Self.

-Sri Ramana Maharshi

Ramana Maharshi also describes meditation as being our natural self. That is real meditation and when realizing the self which is full awareness of being then we are oneness with all existence. We have now an understanding of the meaning of meditation, which is to be aware of the whole movement of life. Now we can move on to methods and how one can get to the meditative mind.

We are told to fast not only to mortify our body, but also to keep our intellect watchful, so that it will not be obscured because of the amount of food we have eaten and thus be unable to guard its thoughts. We must not therefore expend all our effort in bodily fasting; we must also give attention to our thoughts and to spiritual meditation, since otherwise we will not be able to advance to the heights of true purity and chastity. As our Lord has said, we should "cleanse first the inside of the cup and plate, so that their outside may also be clean" (Matt. 23:26).

-St John Cassian

Saint John Cassian points out that fasting, spiritual meditation and mindfulness are the tools that we must use to clean the inside of the cup which is our inner nature and by doing so the outside will follow suit.

In the Yoga chapter, we introduced yoga to a small extent. Now let's look at how Sage Patanjali, the first yogi to expound yoga into written form has expounded yoga. Patanjali's eight limbs of yoga as described in the yoga sutras are:

- Yama - Restraints
- Niyama - Rules
- Asana - Posture
- Pranayama - Breathing techniques
- Pratyahara - Withdrawal of the senses
- Dharana - Concentration
- Dhyana - Meditation
- Samadhi - Awareness of being or Pure Contemplation

1. YAMA (RESTRAINTS)

The restraints are five ethical precepts that outline a code of conduct that should be observed when interacting with the world around us. They offer guidance on how to act towards others, for you are the world and the world is you, therefore others are included in you. Every tradition has expounded restraints, for example, the Ten Commandments in Christianity, and so on. Without practicing these restraints one can never obtain union for they are the platform from which to take off, much like a plane without a runway can never take off.

So, the restraints and the rules are to be watched, and one has to be mindful of them for they play an important role in helping us get rid of everything that we are not.

The restraints are as follows:

Ahimsa (Non-Violence)

Non-violence towards humans and non-humans is a primary prerequisite in order to establish a platform where we can practice yoga or any spiritual discipline. It includes no killing. Violence is not just outward violence but also in our thinking for that is where it manifests first. We have to be watchful of the mental violence which is the silent killer. The mind is there where thought is and these thoughts determine our course of action, more or less.

Satya (Truthfulness)

Telling the truth is a moral baseline and, in this era, it is easy to fall out of truth in order to fulfill a desire. In fact, in the current age, society is more prone to white lies and the need-to-know basis. Truths are not told sometimes in order to protect the arrival of some benefits.

Asteya (Non-stealing)

In Patanjali's day, this was undoubtedly primarily an injunction against taking someone else's property. While that continues to be good advice (not to mention the law), there are now so many more ways to steal, some of which may not be as obvious. Intellectual property today is prone to risks. Greed is so entrenched in our society that stealing can become legal for some.

Brahmacharya (Celibacy)

Brahmacharya is probably the most misunderstood in today's society. Yes, it's highly likely that the original intent was a total prohibition on sexual activity but only for the yogis who had taken the vow of celibacy. Yoga certainly wouldn't be the first school of thought to promote celibacy for its practitioners but is only those who had taken the vow. Fidelity, respect and having honest open relationships with our partners work as alternatives for those who practice yoga today, keeping sex in its proper place.

Most of the past sages, even the Rishis – the founders of the Vedas, scriptural books – were normal people with families living a normal life. The 84 Mahassidass (great souls) largely lived a family life. The Saints have conquered the body in previous lives so for them celibacy becomes natural. Most of the realized masters were householders, as were the tantra practitioners. Therefore, the sexual act is not a greater problem than eating is. The problem of sex is in the mind, and the ego bending the act for its desires. Sexual acts are a bodily need, but we make it more into being love. Sex can never touch love and is not love. Love can touch sex and keep it in the proper place; to be used for the purpose it was given to us. Love is not desire; sex can become a desire and lead us into unhealthy habits which then can make us act in a wrong way. Real celibacy is in the mind because there is where all sins are born, the body only serves.

Nobody can point out better than Krishnamurti what real celibacy means.

> *Can the mind be completely chaste? Not being able to find out how to live a chaste life, one takes vows of celibacy and goes through tortures. That is not celibacy. Celibacy is something entirely different. It is to have a mind that is free from all images, from all knowledge, which means understanding the whole process of pleasure and fear.*
>
> -Jiddu Krishnamurti

> *Let chastity be as dear to you as the pupil of your eye, and then you will become a temple of God and His cherished dwelling place. For without self-restraint, you cannot live with God. Chastity and self-restraint are born of a longing for God combined with detachment and renunciation of the*

world; and they are conserved by humility, self-control, unbroken prayer, spiritual contemplation, freedom from anger and intense weeping. Without dispassion, however, you cannot achieve the beauty of discrimination.

-St Theognotos

Here, Saint Theognotos also points out real chastity, whereby the mind is free of attachment and is humble and free from the distractions of the world. Dispassion is the starting point of everyone seeking the kingdom of heaven.

Aparigraha (Non-coveting)

Now, here's one that really stands out. Desiring what other people have, jealousy, envy, and greed are all words for desire turning to envy, an affliction that has apparently been with us since the beginning. It's a tough one to get past. Desiring is a force which moves the whole world, and it is impossible to stop, but not getting attached to what you desire can be observed and looked at. In the naked awareness, desires have no more hold over us.

2. NIYAMA (RULES)

If the yamas are looking outward towards society, then the niyamas are inward practices to improve the self. They are as follows:

Saucha (Purification)

Purification of the body and mind are specified in the *"Yoga Sutras "* as a necessary step in detaching from the physical world in preparation for meditation. For us, this might mean identifying and releasing thought patterns that have the ability to distract us from our purposes. This purification is done with the eye of wisdom which destroys habits rooted in us since time immemorial. A pure body leads to a pure mind and a pure mind to a pure soul unbound.

Santosa (Contentment)

Contentment is a real challenge for many people so it's well worth examining why it's so hard to feel happy with ourselves. Our culture is conditioned to always wanting more and this constant striving to become and to have, it has been so entrenched in us that it actually takes a bit of effort to realize that it's not compulsory. To be content is to flow with what life gives and takes. Joy is not dependent on anything, and we have forgotten that we are a bundle of joy. We are always in a state of becoming and having which is contradictory with what we are and have, and rarely accept what it is.

Tapas (Asceticism)

One of the translations of tapas is heat, so it is often interpreted as encouraging practices that stoke our inner fire. Purification through self-discipline is described in Patanjali's work. In contemporary yoga, tapas might be observed through the daily practice of postures or meditation which require self-control to maintain a healthy body and mind.

Svadhyaya (Study)

Svadhyaya is sometimes translated as self-study, which implies that it means introspection. Study of the scriptures, memorization and repetition of sacred prayers and mantras – which was and continues to be a customary practice in Hinduism – was the first step to lead to the second in getting to the self-knowledge which includes all knowledge.

Ishvara Pranidhana (Dedication to God/Master–teacher)

It could have meant a master, a teacher, or an unspecified god. Submission to a teacher is in line with the guru–student relationship that was an established tradition within yoga in India. For our purposes, we can perhaps think of it as a necessity to acknowledge that yoga is spiritual practice. It affects the whole person, whose constituent parts are mind, body and spirit. A teacher or teachers who walked the path is a necessity in any field and the spiritual path is no exception. Until we are established on the path, we need a teacher. Afterward, we can walk it alone, for the master can only show the way, they cannot walk it for us.

Without watching the rules and abiding by the restraints in everyday life, which is meditation, one cannot move on and decondition the mind in order to penetrate into the deeper layers of our consciousness and therefore gain the true freedom we are all looking for.

3. ASANA (POSTURE)

Hatha Yoga which was introduced in the West was not mentioned in original works by the Sage Patanjali. What he meant by posture was simply a comfortable seat. Patanjali's work has no other asana instruction other than the necessity of finding a posture in which to engage in the practices of pranayama and meditation. Hatha yoga was practiced in the caves by the yogis to keep the body healthy for they did not have much space for other exercises.

4. PRANAYAMA (BREATH CONTROL)

On the subject of breath control, Patanjali instructs that the practitioner should regulate the inhalations, exhalations and retentions of the breath. Since the eight limbs are concerned with preparing for meditation, any breath that is calming and brings us in contact with the present moment helps ready the body and mind to turn the focus inward. Breath is also the only sense which has not been corrupted by afflictions, therefore by breathing right we can bring subtle energies into the body and calm the mind thereby reducing thoughts. If we just take one breath and hold it for a bit, at the same time observing the mind, we will notice a sense of calm arising.

5. PRATYAHARA (WITHDRAWAL OF THE SENSES)

Isolating consciousness from the distractions offered by engagement with the senses is the final physical preparation for the meditation practices outlined in the final three limbs. This can be in itself a form of what we would call mindfulness in which sensory input – sounds, sights, smells – are noticed as external and then allowed to pass without capturing our attention. Here the restraints and the rules needed to be watched.

He who has succeeded in attaching or detaching his mind to or from the centers at will has succeeded in Pratyahara, which means, "gathering towards," checking the outgoing powers of the mind, freeing it from the thralldom of the senses. When we can do this, we shall really possess character; then alone we shall have taken a long step towards freedom; before that we are mere machines.

-Swami Vivekananda

Here, Swami Vivekananda points out that withdrawing the mind from the senses is not an easy task, but if one has the intention to free oneself from the senses one has made a big leap towards freedom. This withdrawl is not shutting down the senses or suppressing them; it is just watching when they capture our attention and making us react and drown in the pleasures they provide and if we are in any of them with much attachment to the pleasures they have to offer then, we are a slave to them, a machine as Swami points out. It is ok to indulge if a need arises but not as a habitual tendency towards them and therefore in them.

6. DHARANA (CONCENTRATION)

Dharana is the first stage of the inner journey towards freedom from suffering. During this type of meditation, practitioners concentrate all their attention on a single point of focus, such as the navel, or on an image in their mind or on a candle. Concentration is easier when one focuses on something pleasant so start there and then move to the body and the centers of energy within the body.

7. DHYANA (STAGE OF MEDITATION)

In this stage, the practitioner meditates on a single object of their attention to the exclusion of all others. The mind tries to think of one object, to hold itself to one particular spot, as the top of the head, the heart, etc., and if the mind succeeds in receiving the sensations only through that part of the body, and through no other part, that would be Dharana, and when the mind succeeds in keeping itself in that state for some time, it is called Dhyana (meditation).

8. SAMADHI (PURE CONTEMPLATION)

When dhyana is achieved, the practitioner enters a state of samadhi in which they merge with the object of their meditation. Although this has been interpreted to mean union with the divine or with the entire universe, Patanjali's explanation does not go this far.

> *People often misunderstand samadhi [absorption]. He [Bhagavan] told the story of the yogi who spent hundreds of years in trance on the Ganges and on awakening his first thought was for some water he had asked for before entering trance. The thoughts had resumed their sway. The trance was useless. Maharshi said real attainment was to be*

FULLY CONSCIOUS, to be aware of your surroundings and the people around, to move among them be aware of your surroundings and the people around, to move among them all, but not to merge your consciousness in the environment. Remain in your inner independent awareness of It. That is the highest – not to sit in trance which merely halts the mind. The mind must be destroyed entirely, not merely arrested.

-Sri Ramana Maharshi

Ramana Maharshi explains the state of samadhi as when we are aware of all the happenings but flow along with them unaffected; when we are immersed in the naked awareness where we are in our true nature as Padmasambhava has stated in this samadhi, we find eternal peace. Like the ocean which is never affected by its waves, or the sky, which is never affected by what flies through it, so we are also unaffected by the play of duality in the state of samadhi.

These eight limbs of yoga are just a system to help us get to a state of freedom and of course, they are, as we have discussed earlier, present in every tradition in one form or another. All are designed to make the mind arrive at a pure state wherein the heart can manifest our true reality of love eternal. Pure divine contemplation of the self on God is the divine state, which is our natural state of being, it needs to be unveiled in order to manifest its glory. So, meditation includes all these steps which help us to slowly detach from all conditioning and in so doing so grounds us in the awareness of being where meditation is the whole movement of life, eternal.

Germanos then asked: "How does it happen that even against our will many ideas and wicked thoughts trouble us, entering by stealth and undetected to steal our attention? Not only are we unable to prevent them from entering, but it is extremely difficult even to recognize them. Is it possible for the mind to be completely free of them and not be troubled by them at all?"

Abba Moses replied: "It is impossible for the mind not to be troubled by these thoughts. But if we exert ourselves, it is within our power either to accept them and give them our attention, or to expel them. Their coming is not within our power to control, but their expulsion is. The amending of our mind is also within the power of our choice and effort. When we meditate wisely and: continually on the law of God, study psalms and canticles, engage in fasting and vigils, and always bear in mind what is to come – the kingdom of heaven, the Gehenna of fire and all God's works – our wicked thoughts diminish and find no place. But when we devote our time to worldly concerns and to matters of the flesh, to pointless and useless conversation, then these base thoughts multiply in us."

-St John Cassian

The **Philokalia** – (love of the beautiful), from *philia* "love" and *kallos* "beauty") is "a collection of texts written between the 3rd and 15th centuries by spiritual masters" of the mystical hesychast tradition of the Eastern Orthodox Church.

The early fathers of Christianity point out that meditation and contemplation will help overcome the wicked mind and find the state of peace and love we all seek. The Church today should put more emphasis on those teachings. If we read **Philokalia**, we will definitely find the wisdom and the knowledge to overcome the conditioning of the mind, just as the early fathers did by practicing the most profound teachings of Christ which we can call the yoga of Christ. Meditation is a way of life. It is a movement to be acknowledged and followed with faith in everyday life. That intelligence which runs through and maintains the whole of existence seen and unseen knows what we need, when, and how much, and if we surrender to it, we will live a life of freedom regardless of what adversities life may have on offer.

Prayer, meditation, and contemplation bring us into silence and peace. This silence and peace are the same: where there is peace there is always silence and where there is silence there is always peace. It is the same energy. Silence is not an induced state with no noise; it is far from that. Silence is when the mind has emptied itself from all conditioning, all judgements, all desires and in doing so comes to a natural state of rest and peace, which is silence.

> *Intelligence is the servant of the intellect: whatever the intellect wills, the intelligence conceives and expresses.*
> *The intellect sees all things, including the celestial. Nothing darkens it except sin.*
> *To the pure intellect nothing is incomprehensible, just as for the intelligence nothing is beyond expression.*
> *By virtue of his body man is mortal; and by virtue of his intellect and intelligence he is immortal. Through silence you come to understanding; having understood, you give expression. It is in silence that the intellect gives birth to the intelligence; and the thankful intelligence offered to God is man's salvation.*
>
> -St Anthony the Great

Saint Antony the Great points out that intelligence is the energy which, when the mind is pure without any conditioning, allows us to see the reality of life and understand its mysteries. In the silent mind, intelligence works its wonders and by that intelligence we can slowly establish ourself in Christ (God) consciousness and find our salvation, then everything has its own place in the scheme of things where life and love dance with joy.

A soul that disdains everything unspiritual and that is wholly wounded by love for God undergoes a strange divine ecstasy. Having clearly grasped the inner nature and essence of created beings, as well as the upshot of matters human, it cannot bear to be imprisoned or circumscribed by anything. On the contrary, surpassing its own limitations, rebelling against the fetters of the senses and transcending all creatureliness, it penetrates the divine darkness of theology in unutterable silence and to the degree that grace permits it perceives in the intellective light of inexpressible wisdom the beauty of Him who truly is. Reverentially entering ever more deeply into intellective contemplation of that beauty, it savors, in loving awe, the fruits of immortality – the visionary intellections of the Divine. Never withdrawing from these back into itself, it is able to express perfectly their magnificence and glory. Activated, as it were, in a strange way by the Spirit, it experiences this admirable passion in unspeakable joy and silence; yet how it is activated, or what it is that impels it, and is seen by it, and secretly communicates to it unutterable mysteries, it cannot explain.

-Nikitas Stithatos

Nikitas Stithatos points out nicely how a soul finds reality in silence where lies beauty joy and love, by eradicating all that is not spiritual and therefore grasping the inner nature and the essence of all existence which is God. Silence such as this comes to one who, by spiritual practices and by inner knowing comes to understand the inner world of the soul and goes beyond the mind and the body but still uses the body and the mind for the goal of life, which is inherent in us all.

Krishnamurti on thought:

Then the question arises: can thought be completely silent and only function when necessary – when one has to use technical knowledge, in the office, when one is talking and so on – and the rest of the time be absolutely quiet? The more there is space and silence, the more it can function logically, sanely, healthily with knowledge. Otherwise, knowledge becomes an end in itself and brings about chaos. Do not agree with me, see it for yourself? Thought, which is the response of memory, of knowledge, experience and time, is the content of consciousness; thought must function with knowledge, but it can only function with the highest intelligence when there is space and silence – when it functions from there. There must be vast space and silence, because when there is that space and silence, beauty comes, there is love. Not the beauty put together by man, architecture, tapestries, porcelain, paintings, or poems, but that sense of beauty, of vast space and silence. And yet thought must act, must function. There is no living there, and then coming down. So that is our problem – I am making it a problem so that we can investigate together, so that both you and I discover something in this which is totally new. Because each time one investigates without knowing, one discovers something. But if you investigate with knowing, then you will never discover anything. So that is what we are doing. Can thought become silent? Can that thought, which must function in the field of knowledge totally, completely, objectively and sanely, can that thought end itself? That is, can thought which is the past, which is memory, which is a thousand yesterdays, can all that past, all that conditioning come totally to an end? – so that there is silence, there is space, there is a sense of extraordinary dimension.

-Jiddu Krishnamurti

The same as other masters, Krishnamurti is inviting us to look and find for ourselves if there is a way to be silent in ourselves and acknowledge that thought is as useful as it may be. Likely, it will never give us space and silence, therefore the question is, can thought be used in knowledge and be left there to be only used when needed? If we do not use memory except, when need be, then, of course, it is possible to be silent and observe from that silence. Each of us has to find that out for ourselves, merely accepting something as truth does not bring about silence, peace, beauty and love.

> *Thought is of time, intelligence is not of time. Intelligence is immeasurable – not the scientific intelligence, not the intelligence of a technician, or of a housewife, or of a man who knows a great deal. Those are all within the field of thought and knowledge. It is only when the mind is completely still – and it can be still, you don't have to practice or control, it can be completely still – then there is harmony, there is vast space and silence. And only then the Immeasurable is.*

-Jiddu Krishnamurti

Krishnamurti goes on to point out that when one looks with intelligence, which comes from a state of awareness with no intervening thoughts, then one can have space and stillness. As Christ stated: we are movement and rest:

> *Jesus said, "If they say to you, 'Where did you come from?', say to them, 'We came from the light, the place where the light came into being on its own accord and established itself and became manifest through their image.' If they say to you, 'Is it you?', say, 'We are its children, we are the elect of the living father.' If they ask you, 'What is the sign of your father in you?', say to them, 'It is movement and repose.'"*

-Gospel of Thomas: 50

Christ not only shows where we came from and who we are, but also what signs are in us that prove that. He is also saying that we are the manifestation which comes from that stillness, for from silence everything comes and into silence everything returns. That light is the intelligible energy as love and wisdom from whence all existence and non-existence manifest eternally.

Krishnamurti goes on in explaining further on silence:

> *We only know one thing: that thought is perpetually in operation. And when thought is in operation there is no silence, there is no awareness, as we pointed out. Awareness, or perception, implies a state of seeing in which there is no image whatsoever. Until I find out that it is possible to see without any image, I can't state anything else. I can't state that there is an awareness, there is a silence. Is it possible for me, in daily life, to observe my wife, my child, everything around me, without the shadow of an image? Find out. Then out of that attention there is silence. That attention is silence. And it is not the result of practice, which is again thought.*

> -Jiddu Krishnamurti

> *Expel from yourself the spirit of talkativeness. For in it lurk the most dreadful passions: lying, loose speech, absurd chatter, buffoonery, obscenity. To put the matter succinctly, "through talkativeness you will not escape sin" (Prov. 10:19. LXX), whereas a silent man "is a throne of perceptiveness" (Prov. 12:23. LXX). Moreover, the Lord has said that we shall have to give an account of every idle word (cf. Matt. 12:36). Thus silence is most necessary and profitable.*

> -St Theodoros the Great Ascetic

Saint Theodoros the Great Ascetic stated that idle talk is not necessary, and we should talk less – only when in need if possible.

Otherwise, we should watch what you say for as Buddha also pointed out, we become what we think, and talk is thinking. By being silent, we do not stir up passions and therefore silence is a necessity and is profitable because it allows us to be attentive.

> *The Sabbath (cf. Exod. 16:23; 20:10) signifies rest from the passions, and from the intellect's gravitation towards the nature of created beings. It signifies the total quiescence of the passions, a complete cessation of the intellect's gravitation towards created things, and its total entry into the divine. He who has attained this state – so far as God permits – by means of virtue and spiritual knowledge, must not ponder on any material thing at all for, like sticks (cf. Num. 15:32), such things excite the passions; and he must not call to mind any natural principle whatsoever. Otherwise, like the pagans, we will be affirming that God delights in the passions or is commensurate with nature. Perfect silence alone proclaims Him, and total and transcendent unknowing brings us into His presence.*

-St Maximos the Confessor

Saint Maximos here explains that the meaning of the Sabbath is the full rest from the passions, and of the intellect's gravitation towards the objects of the senses, thus one should be fully established in awareness of being. In the silence that follows is the reality of our being, the presence of God. The Jews at that time did not understand the significance of the Sabbath. That is why they accused Christ of doing work on the day of Sabbath not realizing that Christ was fully in Sabbath all the time; he did not need to practice tradition. This does not mean that he was above the law, but that he was in the law and of it.

There are three virtues connected with stillness which we must guard scrupulously, examining ourselves every hour to make sure that we possess them, in case through un-mindfulness we are robbed of them and wander far away from them. These virtues are self-control, silence and self-reproach, which is the same thing as humility. They are all-embracing and support one another; and from them prayer is born and through them it burgeons.

-St Gregory of Sinai

Saint Gregory explains that one who is immersed in stillness and practices self-control, silence and introspection is already entrenched in mindfulness which is the platform from where one can take off into the inner life of the spirit and start to understand the mysteries of life.

M: Before you can accept God, you must accept yourself, which is even more frightening. The first steps in self-acceptance are not at all pleasant, for what one sees is not a happy sight. One needs all the courage to go further. What helps is silence. Look at yourself in total silence, do not describe yourself. Look at the being you believe you are and remember — you are not what you see. "This I am not — what am I?" is the movement of self-enquiry. There are no other means to liberation, all means delay. Resolutely reject what you are not, till the real Self emerges in its glorious nothingness, its "not-a-thingness."

-Nisargadatta Maharaj

Nisargadatta Maharaj points out the way of self-enquiry, and the process of silence is a way into that. To listen, look with silence and in silence is to look with no judgements at all, no conditioning. It is only to observe and see. To have total insight into your own being is a way of self-enquiry and in the process, all that is not real drops away, without any effort.

When we understand the limitations of the mind, we realize that the mind by itself cannot do anything about going beyond itself! At this stage we fall silent. This means we are not restless, there is no conflict, no fighting against anything, we are silent. In this silence we ask, "Maybe there is a possibility of something happening which is other than the mind?" This is something that cannot be theoretically conceived, it can only be experienced.

-Sri M

Sri M points out that a silent mind cannot come about by induced thought. Silence comes when one surrenders and acknowledges that the thought cannot take us into silence for the one trying to bring about silence is still thinking. Thus, silence comes when one understands and really surrenders to what it is, to life, with no clinging, no rejection, with no conflicts inner or outer, with no judgements. When one looks and observes without any filter of conditioning, free from this or that, then comes a silence where even in the middle of a busy street with its noises, people, cars, and so on one is not disturbed, one is silent observing the coming and going of life with all the thoughts that come and go undisturbed by them. This then is stillness, silence, a mind which is healthy. In such a mind there is insight, awareness, and love can manifest freely.

To get to the inner silence and peace one has to deny oneself, but this denial has to be done by the eye of wisdom; by the intelligence which comes spontaneously in a state of full attention without past or any memory, without projecting the past into the future and making images about how life should be, or one wants it to be. True silence does not come by waiting or with signs. It is there as it has always been. It is one of our natural states. It cannot be cultivated by thinking; it can only be discovered by a mind which is fully aware, living in the moment, and where there is intelligence, love and compassion as they have always been, our true nature unveiled by letting go of all attachments, ideas, desires, and conditioning which is not of us.

> *It is the notion of "you" and "I" by which your mind has been held captive all along; you should understand that the combination of sounds which has the power to free you from this bondage is the one to be used. Verily, it is through sound that one penetrates into Silence; for He is manifest in all forms without exception. Indeed, everything is possible in the state that is beyond knowledge and ignorance. So long as you are not finally established in that supreme knowledge, you all dwell in the realm of waves and sound. There are sounds that cause the mind to turn outwards, and others that draw it within. But the sounds that tend outwards are also connected with those that lead inwards. Therefore, because of their interrelation, there may, at some auspicious moment, occur that perfect union, which is followed by the great Illumination, the revelation of what is. Why should not this be possible, since He is ever Self-revealed?*

> -Sri Anandamayi Mayi

Anandamayi points out that through sound one can penetrate into silence and when the outer sounds of life are merging with the inner ones, there then is illumination, is the perfect union with the self which is always self-revealed. When the inner movement and the outer movement of life become one then we have transmuted the world of duality, living always with what it is and therein is our freedom. All the masters point to the inner silence, not to the silence induced by thought where one does not speak. That is not real silence.

It is a product of the ego. There will be little benefit if someone practices that unspeaking silence, and we must be careful not to fall into delusion and be tricked by the ego.

Every tradition invites us to find our own self and by finding it we gain our true freedom in every action. We may next talk about freedom and see what real freedom entails too.

CHAPTER 26

FREEDOM

Is freedom a state of being whereby one does whatever one pleases, when one desires whatever, therefore falling into permissiveness as a selfish movement, only to fulfill one's own desires? If we observe, that is the present conditioning of the human mind related to freedom: a made-up bubble which one lives in with the comforts one has, with the relationships one has, based on the desires one has, with when and how one wants to enjoy and with whom.

Freedom has nothing whatsoever to do with selfishness. Real freedom is of a mind which has understood its limitations and has surrendered control to life eternal and, in that surrender, finds freedom if so blessed.

"What is important is not controlling thought, but understanding it, understanding the origin, the beginning of thought, which is in yourself. That is, the brain stores up memories — you can observe this yourself; you don't have to read books about it. If it had not stored up memories it would not be able to think at all. That memory is the result

of experience, of knowledge – yours, or of the community, of the family, of the race and so on. Thought springs from that storehouse of memory. So thought is never free, it is always old, there is no such thing as freedom of thought. Thought can never be free in itself, it can talk about freedom, but in itself it is the result of past memories, experiences and knowledge; therefore, it is old. Yet one must have this accumulation of knowledge, otherwise one could not function, one could not speak to another, could not go home, and so on. Knowledge is essential. In meditation one has to find out whether there is an end to knowledge and so to freedom from the known. If meditation is a continuation of knowledge, is the continuation of everything that man has accumulated, then there is no freedom. There is freedom only when there is an understanding of the function of knowledge and therefore freedom from the known.

-Jiddu Krishnamurti

Here, Krishnamurti explains how thought – however powerful it may be – can never give us freedom. On the contrary, it will always keep us in darkness and the whole essence of all spiritual practices is to free us from the bond of thought. This means finding freedom from our conditioning, which is wrong knowledge about us and our true nature. In true freedom, we find love and nothing else. It is not physical freedom but a psychological freedom which, when discovered, means being in prison or at home or in whatever physical circumstances we may find ourselves, would make no difference. When we have discovered that freedom, we are blessed indeed for nothing, and nobody can take away that freedom. It is boundless and timeless and cannot be expressed but only lived.

Money and possessions of any kind cannot give us that freedom. They may give us a sense of freedom, induced by our conditioning which matches our projections and desires, giving us full satisfaction if all our desires are fulfilled. Likewise, it may give flexibility to move on the physical plane and enjoy what money can offer but that is not freedom either; that is real bondage. This is why Christ said:

> *It is easier for a camel to go through the eye of a needle than for someone who is rich to enter the kingdom of God.*
>
> -Mark 10:25

What Christ meant is that for a rich man who has many possessions and worries regarding them, it is very hard to surrender his mind to the absolute reality which is God. Such people are too attached to their possessions and are unable to detach easily from what they possess, physical or otherwise. It is not to say that a rich person cannot do it, but it takes a bigger effort to give in to the universal will, to the love supreme. In contrast, a poor person does not have as much to let go of and might find it easier to surrender, but even the poor are still too much in bondage of the little they have. It does not mean we have to give away what we have: that does not secure freedom. It is true that living a simple life with only the possessions we need will aid in walking towards freedom. What we need to give away is the ego with all hopes, fears, desire and so on. If we have to give something up, that is what must be given up first.

When we gain that freedom, relationships with people, things and places are like a cool breeze on a sweltering day. The right relationship with all existence comes naturally in a loving way where we do not exclude anything, we do not cling or resist, not hate, not get angry, not possess or control another, not hurting anyone. In this state, we are a light onto ourselves. Exceedingly rare indeed are such souls and if we are blessed with their presence a change will happen in us naturally.

Blessedness, eternal peace, arising from perfect freedom, is the highest concept of religion underlying all the ideas of God in Vedanta – absolutely free Existence, not bound by anything, no change, no nature, nothing that can produce a change in Him. This same freedom is in you and in me and is the only real freedom. God is still, established upon His own majestic changeless Self. You and I try to be one with Him, but plant ourselves upon nature, upon the trifles of daily life, upon money, on fame, on human love, and all these changing forms in nature which make for bondage. When nature shines, upon what depends the shining? Upon God and not upon the sun, nor the moon, nor the stars. Wherever anything shines, whether it is the light in the sun or in our own consciousness, it is He. He shining, all shines after Him.

-Swami Vivekananda

Swami Vivekananda points to this freedom – which is God absolute – it cannot be found unless we stop identifying with nature, with money, with fame and human love. We can never know real freedom until we find our true nature.

The doctrine of deliverance that Buddha preached was the freedom from the thraldom of Avidyā. Avidyā is the ignorance that darkens our consciousness and tends to limit it within the boundaries of our personal self. It is this Avidyā, this ignorance, this limiting of consciousness that creates the hard separateness of the ego, and thus becomes the source of all pride and greed and cruelty incidental to self-seeking. When a man sleeps, he is shut up within the narrow activities of his physical life. He lives, but he knows not the varied relations of his life to his surroundings, therefore he knows not himself. So when a man lives the life of Avidyā he is confined within his self. It is a spiritual sleep; his consciousness is not fully awake to the highest reality that surrounds him, therefore he knows not the reality of his own soul. When he attains Bodhi, i.e. the awakenment from the sleep of self to the perfection of consciousness, he becomes Buddha.

-Rabindranath Tagore

Rabindranath Tagore exposes beautifully how when we awaken to our own reality we are no longer confined to the prison of our own making. All the teachings of the great masters have taught, in essence, deliverance from this bondage, the shedding of all conditioning which keeps the mind from expanding into the infinite consciousness of the absolute reality of being. In this awakening is freedom from all ideas we have, from all attachments, from all possessiveness and control, from all hopes and fears, from all subjects and objects. In that freedom we act in love with the wisdom which springs from the supreme love; a love which does not have a center, rather which flows undisturbed and is free to touch all existence and no existence. This freedom is inherent in us all; it is our true nature; it is as space, is infinite.

So, if we think we are free and have the means to do anything we like at any time, we must think again, for that is not freedom but is the greatest prison imaginable. Becoming free from the world and its attractions, free from our own ignorance, is a tremendous task, and this is why only a few can walk that path towards freedom supreme. Without finding our own path and walking on it and at every step dropping our baggage of accumulations – material and mental – we can never get out of suffering, and we can never touch love.

You cannot be or become spiritually intelligent in the way that is natural to man in his pre-fallen state unless you first attain purity and freedom from corruption. For our purity has been overlaid by a state of sense-dominated mindlessness, and our original in-corruption by the corruption of the flesh.

-St Gregory of Sinai

Saint Gregory of Sinai points to our natural state and that in order to regain it we need to purify ourselves from the corruption of our own egos from where springs all the ignorance and the five poisons.

So, we see that real freedom comes when the mind is in its pure state without the entanglements of the ego, without attachments, fears and conflicts. Then there is inner peace, tranquility and we are free to act at every moment the right way, to relate to another in a loving way. When the inner and outer life are in unison, there is no inner war of conflicts, guilt and so on. Whatever external situation we are in, we are not affected. We know when and how to react, for in that state of mind intelligence operates with no thought intervening, and that is the right way to act towards oneself and others. Then compassion is there for all sentient beings and love can flow undisturbed like a river that flows to the sea. One who acts that way does not ask anything, does not want anything: whatever is offered, he will accept; whatever is taken, he will gladly give. Our true freedom lies in our minds when the ego has surrendered all control and has realized its limitations. Then the self and the ego merge into oneness and work in harmony. For centuries, countries waged war against one another and these wars are destructive but they also represent the impurity of our minds which are so corrupted by greed, by power, by envy, by jealousy, by hatred, by anger, by our inability to break free and gain our inner freedom from these poisons which run havoc in our minds which have been conditioned since time immemorial, for the mind is not mine or yours. It is the universal mind; it is one mind not many, but we have divided everything, and in this division, there is always conflict therefore love's flow is restricted. When we purify our own mind, we also purify the universal mind, and that effect is felt by others. Thoughts cannot be stopped by force, for it is in the nature of the mind to think. Still, we can stop clinging to destructive thoughts; we can discern and by doing so, we do not react in a selfish way, in a destructive way. All the spiritual teachings point to a mind which is free from the shackles of ego, of selfishness, and this freedom cannot be bought at the altar of demand. This freedom comes when the mind becomes purified by fasting, prayer, meditation, mindfulness, observing oneself every moment in every act. We have to be our own judge, prosecutor and executioner in order to bring about the qualities of a pure mind and this is the hardest of all things to do. We are advancing at the material level in all areas of science, for we have been given intelligence, but that intelligence needs to operate at all levels of consciousness not only for the betterment of the body and its comforts.

The more we have in comforts and physical freedom to do as one pleases, the more detrimental it is. We become dull, lazy, enclosed in our comfort zone. The mind being conditioned to knowledge becomes full of pride over achievements. Everyone lives in a bubble of their own making, never being free so we only accept people and things according to our ideas, concepts, traditions and so on. How then can we have a true relationship based on love with another? As long as we are conditioned, a relationship with another is only superficial; it is just a business transaction. When two people drop all conditioning, all conflicts disappear, only then they can meet heart to heart, and therefore have a relationship based on love, but few are these souls who can do that.

Because we have been educated in this manner – to compete, to compare, to always judge another according to what we know – our conditioning directs the mind to think this way; it is a habit. It does not matter how smart we are in words or deeds; we are still confined in the bubble of our own making. We may have the capacity to acquire knowledge and use that knowledge in a selfish way: this is not intelligence. To act with intelligence which has not been corrupted by thought is to always act in the right way. We can observe this in everyday life and see how the ego takes advantage of intelligence and acts accordingly to selfish desires. Without selfish desires the ego would not have any power to act.

We can see that it is imperative for us to seek to know ourselves and in that knowing slowly, the self will reveal its own glory, its love for all beings. Only in this way can humanity unveil heaven on earth as the Lord has stated:

> *When asked by the Pharisees when the kingdom of God would come, Jesus replied, "The kingdom of God will not come with observable signs. Nor will people say, 'Look, here it is,' or 'There it is.' For you see, the kingdom of God is in your midst."*
>
> -Luke 17:20

> *"I took my stand in the midst of the world, and in flesh I appeared to them. I found them all drunk, and I did not find any of them thirsty. My soul ached for the children of humanity, because they are blind in their hearts and do not see, for they came into the world empty, and they also seek to depart from the world empty. But meanwhile they are drunk. When they shake off their wine, then they will change their ways."*
>
> -Gospel of Thomas: 28

Christ is clearly telling us that heaven is among us, but we are too drunk to see it. Drunk here means being too immersed in what the world has to offer which is nothing compared with the kingdom if only we could see it. When we become dispassionate and see our drunkenness, we may become thirsty for the truth and by shaking our wine, which is the veil of illusion, then by opening our hearts to the truth it may be possible to see the heaven he speaks of. In doing so we will no longer live empty, from this world because we do not have to go anywhere. Heaven then is here and now, and death has no power over us.

It is really so simple but at the same time so complex. We have created the complexity and until we become simple and live a life of simplicity and humility with patience for one another we will never see the heaven Christ is pointing at. This is why it is so important to gain our freedom from the clutches of ignorance and the poisons which have affected humanity for millennia. That freedom is here and now. If only we have the courage to look, to observe our everyday life and how we react to circumstances and conditions which arise in our lives, then maybe a change in consciousness may occur.

When we are free, we do not need a gun for we will have love as the greatest gun of all and if we are threatened with death, we will not care much for the body for we know we do not die if the body dies. We are free as Christ was on the cross; free from anything that corrupts love. That is a mind and a heart which are free because they have shaken the wine (ignorance) and awakened to the absolute supreme being of light and then we will love as Christ says:

> *Love your brother like your life!*
> *Protect him like the apple of your eye!*
>
> -Gospel of Thomas: 25

This love Christ speaks of cannot be cultivated by any morality or ethics. This love is eternal and does not need anything to be added onto it. When we uncover this love in our hearts we are at home, we are holy, we are in union with the absolute reality of being and that is real freedom.

> *Freedom is a state of mind. It's not to be free from something, but to be free to doubt and question everything so that you can throw away every form of dependence, slavery, conformity, and acceptance. To be free is to be alone. Solitude is an inward state of mind that's not dependent on any stimulus, knowledge, or experience. When you experience this solitude, you'll understand the necessity of living with yourself as you are, not as you think you should be.*
> *Freedom can only come about naturally, not through wishing, wanting, or longing. Nor will you find it by creating an image of what you think it is. To find freedom, you must learn to look at life without the bondage of time, for freedom lies beyond the field of consciousness.*

-Jiddu Krishnamurti

Krishnamurti describes the true freedom which comes naturally when we have rid ourselves of all attachments and dependence and inwardly face ourselves, getting to know who we are as we are, not as we wish to be. When we go inward with no dependence on anything or anyone then one can go beyond time, space, and the known for there we will find true freedom and not the imaginary freedom the mind has produced by thought and time, which are always limited.

> *Self-mastered, with mind unattached at all times, beyond desire, one attains through renunciation the supreme freedom from action. Learn from me briefly, Arjuna, that when a man gains success, he also gains perfect freedom, the ultimate state of knowledge.*
> *With a purified understanding, fully mastering himself, relinquishing all sense objects, released from aversion and craving, solitary eating lightly, controlling speech, mind*

and body, absorbed in deep mediation at all times, calm impartial free from the I, and mine, free from aggression, arrogance, greed, desire and anger he is fit for the state of absolute freedom.

-Lord Krishna

In the *Bhagavad Gita*, Krishna describes how a person can attain the state of absolute freedom, and like all other awakened masters, points out that after releasing desires, unattached, and with a mind absorbed in awareness free from the poisons, we are then fit for the absolute freedom and that is the only way.

Thoughts rule the life. Freedom from thoughts is one's true nature – Bliss. Death is a thought and nothing else. He who thinks raises troubles. Let the thinker say what happens to him in death. The real "I" is silent. One should not think, "I am this," "I am not that." To say "this" or "that" is wrong. They are also limitations. "I am" alone is true. Silence is "I."

-Sri Ramana Maharshi

Ramana Maharshi points out that our true nature is unveiled when we gain understanding of ourselves and realize that all thoughts are limited and can never give freedom; only silence can.

The intellect does many good and bad things without the body, whereas the body can do neither good nor evil without the intellect. This is because the law of freedom applies to what happens before we act.

-St Mark the Ascetic

Saint Mark the Ascetic also points out that all happenings in the world are because of our intellect and that determines how we act. If the mind is free and pure, then freedom follows everywhere. A mind free is a mind that does not cling and does not resist anything; it is in a state of equanimity where the right action follows.

> *Freedom and happiness of soul consist in genuine purity and detachment from transitory things. Keep in mind that you must always be setting an example through your moral life and your actions. For the sick find and recognize good doctors, not just through their words, but through their actions.*
>
> *Holiness and intelligence of soul are to be recognized from a man's eye, walk, voice, laugh, the way he spends his time and the company he keeps. Everything is transformed and reflects an inner beauty. For the intellect which enjoys the love of God is a watchful gate-keeper and bars entry to evil and defiling thoughts.*

-St Antony the Great

Saint Antony the Great here points out that a free heart is pure, detached from all transitory things. Mindfulness of intellect is a prerequisite of keeping mind and heart pure.

> *As long as we are in ignorance, we are seemingly free in minor matters only. Our weaknesses, our inadequacies bind us. We are the slaves of our moods, cravings, and impulses. Ānandamayī Mā likens the average man's freedom to that of a cow which is tied by a rope to a post. Within the limits of the rope, she has freedom. But, of course, were the cow able to break loose from the rope, she would gain complete freedom. Similarly, the person who makes the right spiritual effort can cut thereby the rope of delusion that binds him to the finite world of pseudo-happiness and attain freedom.*

-Sri Anandamayi Mayi

Anandamayi points out that we are always slaves to our moods, cravings and reactions to things and thus we are bound by the rope of illusion and in order to cut it, spiritual effort is necessary. This freedom comes in exchange for our denial of everything that we are not, what we think and know what we are, direct observation and experience is necessary. We can only know what we are when we have discovered what we are not, and by denying all of that, we will remain with what we are. Nobody can give us this freedom; only we can free ourselves if we have the intent to do so but here lies the impossibility for most.

It is the fear of losing the identity of what we have been conditioned to believe we are. To know what we are with knowledge of time and thought is not true knowing for it is limited. Self-knowledge comes only by direct perception and insight, by direct experience and after realizing what we are not we will remain with what we truly are: truth, existence, and bliss.

We have just seen that the Self cannot see Itself. Our knowledge is within the network of Mâyâ (unreality), and beyond that is freedom. Within the network there is slavery, it is all under law; beyond that there is no law. So far as the universe is concerned, existence is ruled by law, and beyond that is freedom. As long as you are in the network of time, space, and causation, to say you are free is nonsense, because in that network all is under rigorous law, sequence, and consequence. Every thought that you think is caused, every feeling has been caused; to say that the will is free is sheer nonsense. It is only when the infinite existence comes, as it were, into this network of Maya that it takes the form of will. Will is a portion of that being, caught in the network of Maya, and therefore "free will" is a misnomer. It means nothing – sheer nonsense. So is all this talk about freedom. There is no freedom in Maya. Everyone is as much bound in thought, word, deed, and mind, as a piece of stone or this table. That I talk to you now is as rigorous in causation as that you listen to me. There is no freedom until you go beyond Maya. That is the real freedom of the soul. Men, however sharp and intellectual, however clearly, they see the force of the logic that nothing here can be free, are all compelled to think they are free; they cannot help it. No work can go on until we begin to say we are free. It means that the freedom we talk about is the glimpse of the blue sky through the clouds and that the real freedom – the blue sky itself – is behind. True freedom cannot exist in the midst of this delusion, this hallucination, this nonsense of the world, this universe of the senses, body, and mind.

-Swami Vivekananda

Here, Swami Vivekananda also states that freedom is beyond time and space, behind the mind and the intellect. When we see the limitation of the intellect, then we surrender fully to the present moment and there we find freedom. For that surrender to happen effort is necessary for a time because the intellect – the ego – will find ways to trick us with a man-made freedom. We are free since the beginning time, as Christ has stated where the beginning is, so is the end.

The disciples said to Jesus: Tell us how our end will be. Jesus said: Since you have discovered the beginning, why do you seek the end? For where the beginning is, there will the end be. Blessed is he who shall stand at the beginning (in the beginning), and he shall know the end, and shall not taste death.

-Gospel of Thomas: 18

Here, Christ is pointing to the present moment for if one makes a stand at the beginning and does not allow the ego to bring time by judgements then one will see life as it is and in that seeing is living with no death.

I am not the mind, the intellect, the ego or the memory,
I am not the ears, the skin, the nose or the eyes,
I am not space, not earth, not fire, water or wind,
I am the form of consciousness and bliss,
I am the eternal Shiva.
I am not the breath, nor the five elements,
I am not matter, nor the five sheaths of consciousness
Nor am I the speech, the hands, or the feet,
I am the form of consciousness and bliss,
I am the eternal Shiva.
There is no like or dislike in me, no greed or delusion,
I know not pride or jealousy,
I have no duty, no desire for wealth, lust or liberation,
I am the form of consciousness and bliss,
I am the eternal Shiva.
No virtue or vice, no pleasure or pain,
I need no mantras, no pilgrimage, no scriptures or rituals,
I am not the experienced, nor the experience itself,
I am the form of consciousness and bliss,
I am the eternal Shiva.
I have no fear of death, no caste or creed,
I have no father, no mother, for I was never born,
I am not a relative, nor a friend, nor a teacher nor a
student,
I am the form of consciousness and bliss,
I am the eternal Shiva.
I am devoid of duality, my form is formlessness,
I exist everywhere, pervading all senses,
I am neither attached, neither free nor captive,
I am the form of consciousness and bliss,
I am the eternal Shiva.

-Adi Shankara

The above lines are taken from *Nirvana Shatakam* by Adi Shankara. Adi Shankara describes what he is not and in doing so unveils his true reality. But saying these words is not enough to gain true knowledge; one must put in effort and in doing so with steady practice all will be revealed by the grace of the supreme, for one who has the heart intent to find the truth will find it. We could talk forever about this freedom, but from what we have presented so far, we should have an understanding that this freedom is already inherent in us, just waiting to be unveiled. How to discover it, in the end, is through self-knowledge.

In this freedom there is love – they go together – and with that love we move through life without a hitch, without a worry, about anything. We are unmoved by action and have compassion and affection for all creatures. We will act in love with love and become free from all conditioning of past or future.

> *One has to find out for oneself what it means to die; then there is no fear, therefore every day is a new day – and I really mean this, one can do this – so that your mind and your eyes see life as something totally new. That is eternity. That is the quality of the mind that has come upon this timeless state, because it has known what it means to die every day to everything it has collected during the day. Surely, in that there is love. Love is something totally new every day, but pleasure is not, pleasure has continuity. Love is always new and therefore it is its own eternity.*

> -Jiddu Krishnamurti

Krishnamurti describes this love as a new moment in time, always fresh, alive and with immense energy. If we live with this love and in this love, we can relate to people with ease. We should next, talk about life and relationships for life is relationships and how we relate and interact with each other is of the utmost importance for there, love has its play.

CHAPTER 27

LIFE & RELATIONSHIPS

Life itself is relationships. It is just a matrix of intertwined relationships with people, the environment, the world at large and the inner relationship we have with ourselves. We have been in relationships since our birth: with mother, father, siblings, friends, and so on, but very few can have an open relationship based on love, for we are all ridden by our conditioning and by our problems. We have all made life a prison and we all battle to escape from it in the same way, replacing one prison with another which gives us more satisfaction. We are in an endless pursuit to find that perfect prison – which in fact does not exist.

Life is a living energy in a continuous transformation as our bodies are billions of organisms living together in one movement. So, it is with the whole of creation: it is God in movement. If we can just flow with the movement of life, then we have a chance to be free of all troubles. Life knows what we need, how much, and when, and it will provide if we surrender fully to it. Unfortunately, few are those who can do that. Most of us are flowing against life and against nature in a way that is destructive. We are not separate from nature; we are a part of it. Life is all-inclusive, never excluding, but we are creatures of exclusion and include only what gives us satisfaction and pleasure. People who dance to our tunes in life, we include, the rest we exclude and avoid.

Relationships today are just business transactions and when we stop giving, the relationship is in trouble. We find some true relationships: a mother with an infant, for example, is the closest relationship to the love which should sustain all relationships but only some have found that love uncorrupted in any way for it can never be corrupted by anything whatsoever. Life is love and love is life. The goal of life is described in the *Philokalia*, from which so far, we have looked at many masters and their teachings:

> *What first determined the choice of texts made by St Nikodimos and St Makarios, and gives them their cohesion? "Philokalia" itself means love of the beautiful, the exalted, the excellent, understood as the transcendent source of life and the revelation of Truth. It is through such love that, as the subtitle of the original edition puts it, 'the intellect is purified, illumined and made perfect'. The texts were collected with a view to this purification, illumination and perfection. They show the way to awaken and develop attention and consciousness, to attain that state of watchfulness which is the hallmark of sanctity. They describe the conditions most effective for learning what their authors call the art of arts and the science of sciences, a learning which is not a matter of information or agility of mind but of a radical change of will and heart leading man towards the highest possibilities open to him, shaping and nourishing the unseen part of his being, and helping him to spiritual fulfillment and union with God. The Philokalia is an itinerary through the labyrinth of time, a silent way of love and gnosis through the deserts and emptiness's of life, especially of modem life, a vivifying and fadeless presence. It*

is an active force revealing a spiritual path and inducing man to follow it. It is a summons to him to overcome his ignorance, to uncover the knowledge that lies within, to rid himself of illusion.

-G.E.H. Palmer, Philip Sherrard,
Archimandrite Kallistos Ware
(Bussock Mayne)

It is beautifully said that the state of watchfulness needs to be found in order to get to self-knowledge, which is not a mental activity by acquiring information but the intrinsic awareness of being, which will unveil the reality of who we are with the help of love and stillness, without the reactions and impulses of the intellect. Life is the ground where everything happens. It is an energy alive in love and includes all beings and non-beings in the fold.

Physics would stop when it would be able to fulfill its services in discovering one energy of which all others are but manifestations, and the science of religion become perfect when it would discover Him who is the one life in a universe of death, Him who is the constant basis of an everchanging world. One who is the only Soul of which all souls are but delusive manifestations. Thus, is it, through multiplicity and duality, that the ultimate unity is reached. Religion can go no farther. This is the goal of all science.

-Swami Vivekananda

Swami Vivekananda describes that life as all existence is the existential energy, the basis of all life, and in the end, science will discover the truth of this existential energy from which all energies manifest. He also states that when one has found the one who is the life supreme, then one has reached the peak of perfection of religion.

There are two kinds of pilgrims on life's journey: the one, like a tourist, is keen on sightseeing, wandering from place to place, flitting from one experience to another for the fun of it. The other treads the path that is consistent with man's true being and leads to his real home, to Self-knowledge.

-Sri Anandamayi Mayi

Anandamayi also points out the real goal of life is the life which leads to self-knowledge whereas most of us are attracted to a life of experiences for fun and pleasure.

The spirit is wrongly identifying itself with the gross body. The body has been projected by the mind; the mind itself has originated from the spirit. If the wrong identification ceases, there will be peace and permanent unbroken bliss. Life is existence which is your Self. That is life eternal. Otherwise, can you imagine a time when you are not? That life is not conditioned by the body and you wrongly identify your existence with that of the body. You are life unconditioned. These bodies attach themselves to you as mental projections and you are afflicted by "I-am-the-body" idea. If this idea ceases, you are your Self.

-Sri Ramana Maharshi

Ramana Maharshi also points out that we ourselves are life; we are existence which is the very self in all beings. Only with the advent of self-knowledge can the realization of what life is be understood. Until then, most of us will look at our lives from a narrow viewpoint of our own conditioning with all the pettiness that we produce. Life is the greatest gift that God has given for he has given himself in a multitude of forms in order for us to experience his greatness, it is life and love supreme. Life is a unitary movement in love, for life and love cannot be separated: they are one energy dancing the dance of life.

317

Life is everything – personal or not – as in it we encounter circumstances and conditions which arise and challenge us; it is the university of life. Most of these circumstances and conditions are not in our control or whatever control we may have, is minimal. The one thing which is in our control is how we react to what is presented in front of us. The one who is free will undoubtedly react in the right way but the one under the influence of the ego with all its conditioning will react in accordance with the filters of this conditioning, fears, desires and so on. For example, a person undergoing a breakup in marriage, if they are deeply attached and living in a web of images of how life should be, always projecting through the images, then that person will go through a lot of strife in that separation. On the other hand, someone established in awareness will not be affected by the news of separation and may have the wisdom to repair the relationship if it is at all possible and if not can fully accept the outcome and will separate in love but still by maintaining a relationship with the other party. Love should still be there, only the relationship changes, love never changes. Where true love is, problems do not exist.

On the practical side of life – the outer life so to speak – problems do not exist for the one who is unattached and free. Circumstances and conditions arise and if they can be changed, act on them, but if they cannot be changed, accept what it is. Even if they could be changed, act on them only if it is for the benefit of many, not only for the benefit of a few. The majority of us act only if there is something for us in that action.

The mind is conditioned along these lines of thinking and is selfish as the ego is.

> *Forgetfulness of your real nature is the real death; remembrance of it is the true birth, it puts an end to successive births. Yours is then eternal life. How does the desire for eternal life arise? Because the present state is unbearable.*

Why? Because it is not your true nature. Had it been your real nature, there would be no desire to agitate you. How does the present state differ from your real nature? You are Spirit in truth.

-Sri Ramana Maharshi

Ramana Maharshi shows how life is eternal – does not have a beginning or an end – and is our true nature. Because we are dead to the recognition of this truth unless we awaken, life can be a string of miseries and sorrows. As we have presented in earlier chapters, suffering is of our own making and if we suffer then, we suffer only because we go against the flow of life. The flow of life is the manifestation of the supreme God which is love. Everything in the universe flows with life, only we are going against the flow of life and the natural way. We try to conquer nature, but the true conqueror is the one who has transmuted the inner nature and in doing so, goes beyond time and space.

Life is multitudes of relationships – direct or indirect. We are in a relationship with all existence, from the smallest atom to the biggest of planets. How we relate to one another and to the environment has an impact on all things because we are all interrelated and what affects one will affect the other. Unfortunately, not everyone is aware of this fact. To become aware, we have to observe nature and people and see how one action has a ripple effect on many.

Here where most of us act in selfish ways, we become destructive towards nature and other creatures by acting only for our own benefit and satisfaction.

There is one who governs the world, and it is His look-out to look after the world. He who has given life to the world, knows how to look after it also. If we progress, the world progresses. As you are, so is the world. Without under-

standing the Self, what is the use of understanding the world? Without Self-knowledge the knowledge of the world is of no use. See the world through the eyes of your supreme Self.

-Sri Ramana Maharshi

Ramana Maharshi reminds us that the world progresses in accordance with our progress towards self-realization. A self-realized person flows with life and never goes against it. If we have not realized the truth, life will be in accordance with how much we are established in awareness and how pure our minds and hearts are.

"I am the self, Arjuna,
seated in the hearts of all beings:
I am the beginning and the life span,
of beings and their end as well."

-Lord Krishna

In the *Bhagavad Gita*, Krishna tells Arjuna that he is the life seated in all beings, and this is the truth that all masters have uttered from the beginning of time. We are just ignorant of this truth and treat life as a thing which just happens. If we allow ourselves to be molded by love, our lives will be blessed.

From childhood, we encounter life and go through many experiences from which we learn a great deal. However, that learning – if through the filter of a conditioned mind – is not true learning. True learning only occurs through true knowledge – in the now, not a memory brought in a present to be changed in the future. True learning happens by direct knowledge, with no judgements or presumptions. Seeing is together with understanding and acting; it is one movement in the present moment.

In practical ways, new scientific discoveries happen this way. Yes, we need to add to knowledge and use memory to function – to drive a car, for example, or to learn a skill or perform any practical action. That kind of learning is essential in order to function in society. All the progress made in technological fields is based on that kind of learning. Life on a practical level is one thing but the physiological level is another. At school we learned to become doctors and so on, but nobody taught us how to deal with the inner life, how to react and not react, how not to hate, and how not to be jealous. All these are taught in the same way one teaches arithmetic, but those inner workings cannot be grasped in the same way. The real teaching on this aspect needs to be by direct learning without any conditioning. We need to have the ability to pay attention to the inner aspects of our being, to observe the inner movement of emotions and feelings, where they are coming from, who is creating them, how they occur and why we respond in such destructive ways towards ourselves and others because of them; even how to deal with depression or anxiety which affects the heart and mind, creating so much suffering for ourselves and others.

Therefore, if we are serious about moving towards the spiritual goal and meditating, then we should act and live in this world as best as we can. We should try our best to be kind, both when it is easy and when it is tough. This will be different for different people, so you have to watch yourself carefully. Observing oneself in a relationship with others is a very important part of spiritual sadhana. I'll end with an example. I have said this before. If I go and sit in a cave in the Himalayas and meditate for thirteen years and at the end of it I say, "Now I am really free of anger, free of sorrow, free of jealousy, and so on," it actually makes no sense, because in the cave there is nobody to get angry with. I cannot get angry with the cave. I cannot get jealous of anything there, because there is nothing to be jealous of. It's only when I come out of the cave and into the world, when I board a bus from Rishikesh to go to Haridwar and somebody steps on my toe in the bus, that is when I know if I am really free of anger, jealousy, etc. Therefore, perhaps one of the most important markers of spiritual progress, of progress in our meditation, is how soft our heart is, whether we feel the pain of others, our care for others, not just our family but for everyone.

-Sri M

Sri M, one of the spiritual masters of today, points out also that spiritual life is embedded in worldly life and vice versa. It is not by running from the world but only by staying with our practice in our daily life that we have an idea as to how we are progressing in spirit, by how we react and respond to what life has to offer. Our masters have pointed out that only by gaining self-knowledge – by understanding the workings of the mind, the thoughts and the ego – can we go beyond the body and the mind for in doing so we touch love supreme, becoming one with life and having a right relationship with one another and nature. The ways to self-knowledge must be integrated into the education of the young for they are the future of humanity. The young today have lost their way; they are most confused. Wisdom and love are needed to awaken others, and it can be received only from the awakened masters of yesterday, today and tomorrow. They all answer if they are asked to help with an open heart, for they are not dead, they are alive in everything. This is why Christ has stated:

"I am the light that is overall. I am the All. The All came forth out of me. And to me the All has come. Split a piece of wood – I am there. Lift the stone, and you will find me there."

-Gospel of Thomas: 77

Christ is life and his light is everywhere. He is the love supreme. It is only for us to seek the kingdom, and everything will be added onto us. Life knows what we need and when, also how much.

All awakened masters share the same qualities, the same wisdom and love. It is the same consciousness which responds through Christ, Buddha and so on.

Why man suffers. So long, however, as man identifies himself with his material body and fails to find repose in his true Self, he feels his wants according as his heart's desires remain unsatisfied. To satisfy them he has to appear often in flesh and blood on the stage of life, subject to the influence of Darkness, Maya, and has to suffer all the troubles of life and death not only in the present but in the future as well.

-Swami Sri Yukteswar

Sri Yukteswar reminds us that as long as we think we are the body and we do not find rest in the self, we will always be stuck in the cycle of birth and death, coming back to the university of life to learn how to love and let go.

This complex struggle between something inside and the external world is what we call life. So, it is clear that when this struggle ceases, there will be an end of life. What is meant by ideal happiness is the cessation of this struggle. But then life will cease, for the struggle can only cease when life itself has ceased. We have seen already that in helping the world we help ourselves. The main effect of work done for others is to purify ourselves. By means of the constant effort to do good to others we are trying to forget ourselves; this forgetfulness of self is the one great lesson we have to learn in life. Man thinks foolishly that he can make himself happy, and after years of struggle finds out at last that true happiness consists in killing selfishness and that no one can make him happy except himself.

-Swami Vivekananda

Swami Vivekananda points out that the struggle between the self and the world is called life and unless we get rid of our selfishness, we are not going to be happy. If we can achieve this, life is only bliss. There are no more struggles, and even if struggles are there, we are not affected by them. So, we can live the life of the senses with the desires life has to offer, or we can rise above and in doing so live a life of love and bliss without any struggle. Life does not change. It is there, but how we react to life is a choice and depending on how we react therein lies our happiness or sorrow. We have been educated wrongly in where to look for happiness, and that conditioning brought up by education is hard to eradicate for habits are instilled in our psyches. Spiritual education is essential for us to transform ourselves and the world. Without it, we will not be able to get out of the rat race and we will struggle and suffer at our own hands.

> *First, take care of the duties of worldly life, then take up the spiritual life using the power of discrimination. The wise will not be lazy about taking care of both aspects of life. If you neglect the worldly life and only follow the spiritual life, you will create suffering for yourself. If you take care of the worldly life along with the spiritual life, then you can be said to be wise.*
>
> *If one completely gives up the worldly life for spiritual life, then he cannot even get food for his meals. How can such a destitute person have any success in spiritual life?*
>
> *If spiritual life is forsaken and one only pursues worldly life, then there will suffering at the time of death. With no spiritual life you will be extremely miserable at the end of your life when death comes.*
>
> *If one does not carry out the work assigned by the boss but only sits lazily at home, the boss will punish him, and this will be seen by others.*
>
> *In such a situation one loses his reputation and people cruelly make fun of him. In this way, the living being*

creates great suffering and sorrow during one's life.

The same principle applies with regard to what happens at the end of one's life. Therefore, you must have devotion to God and gain actual experience of your own divine True Form (Swaroopa).

Understand that one who is liberated while still leading a worldly life is a true yogi. He continuously sees clearly and gives thought to what is proper and what is inappropriate.

One who is alert in worldly life can easily understand what will make the spiritual life successful. One who has no capacity to function appropriately in worldly life will also not be successful in spiritual life.

Therefore, take care, and be alert in both worldly life and in spiritual life. If you fail to do this, you will suffer many sorrows.

Even worms and insects look carefully when stepping from one leaf to another. All living beings in the world move about using some sense of discernment and discrimination. What then can be said about human beings who live their lives wandering about in delusion?

-Saint Shri Samartha Ramdas

Saint Shri Samartha Ramdas above points out that worldly life and spiritual life have to go hand in hand in order for us to achieve the goal supreme which lies in us all. He also states that the one who finds freedom while leading a worldly life is a true yogi. For true liberation is to be found in the midst of the world, not by escaping from it. There are times when we have to withdraw for a period in order to become established in awareness, but once done, we can then return and live a moral life and follow the morality of the heart.

Again, some pleasures are true, others false. And the exclusively intellectual pleasures consist in knowledge and contemplation, while the pleasures of the body depend upon sensation. Further, of bodily pleasures, some are both

*natural and necessary, in the absence of which life is impos-
sible, for example the pleasures of food which replenishes
waste, and the pleasures of necessary clothing. Others
are natural but not necessary, as the pleasures of natural
and lawful intercourse. For though the function that these
perform is to secure the permanence of the race as a whole,
it is still possible to live a virgin life apart from them.
Others, however, are neither natural nor necessary, such
as drunkenness, lust, and surfeiting to excess. For these
contribute neither to the maintenance of our own lives nor
to the succession of the race, but on the contrary, are rather
even a hindrance. He therefore that would live a life accept-
able to God must follow after those pleasures which are both
natural and necessary: and must give a secondary place to
those which are natural but not necessary, and enjoy them
only in fitting season, and manner, and measure; while the
others must be altogether renounced.*

-St John of Damascus

In the above, Saint John of Damascus points out that the pleasures needed for sustaining life are not a problem as long as one
gives them the appropriate attention and uses them only when
needed, not forming a habit out of them. Living a life only taking
what is needed is right living in that everyone is included, and all
humanity will have the necessary things to live life in goodness.

*To live in perfect goodness is to realize one's life in the
infinitive. This is the most comprehensive view of life which
we can have by our inherent power of the moral vision
of the wholeness of life. And the teaching of Buddha is to
cultivate this moral power to the highest extent, to know
that our field of activities is not bound to the plane of our
narrow self. This is the vision of the heavenly kingdom of
Christ. When we attain to that universal life, which is the
moral life, we become freed from the bonds of pleasure and
pain, and the place vacated by our self becomes filled with*

an unspeakable joy which springs from measureless love. In this state the soul's activity is all the more heightened, only its motive power is not from desires, but in its own joy. This is the Karma-yoga of the Gita, the way to become one with the infinite activity by the exercise of the activity of disinterested goodness. When Buddha mentioned upon the way of realizing mankind from the grip of misery he came to this truth: that when man attains his highest end by merging the individual in the universal, he becomes free from the thralldom of pain.

-Rabindranath Tagore

Tagore uses the master's teachings on life to point out that our life should be spent in perfect goodness by merging our lives in the universal life, and by doing so we become free from the bonds of pleasure and pain, manifesting joy which springs from love supreme our natural state of being. If one gives up one's personal will and aligns to the universal will, then freedom is there, for the universal will know the direction we have to take and will keep on the right path to freedom.

Life is a web of relationships and how we relate is of the utmost importance because it determines how we live our lives. If the relationships that we have are not made in love they will lead to suffering; it all depends on who is relating: the ego or the self. The ego with all its selfishness, judgements and so on or the self which is free and able to connect with anyone through love.

I think one has to understand, not as a theory, not as a speculative, entertaining concept, but rather as an actual fact – that we are the world and the world is us. The world is each one of us; to feel that, to be really committed to it and to nothing else, brings about a feeling of great responsibility and an action that must not be fragmentary, but whole. I think we are apt to forget that our society, the culture in which we live, which has conditioned us, is the result of human endeavor, conflict, human misery and suffering. Each one of us is that culture; the community is each one of us — we are not separate from it. To feel this, not as an intellectual idea or a concept, but to actually feel the reality of this, one has to go into the question of what relationship is; because our life, our existence, is based on relationship. Life is a movement in relationship. If we do not understand what is implied in relationship, we inevitably not only isolate ourselves, but create a society in which human beings are divided, not only nationally, religiously, but also in themselves and therefore they project what they are into the outer world. I do not know if you have gone into this question deeply for yourself, to find out if one can live with another in total harmony, in complete accord, so that there is no barrier, no division, but a feeling of complete unity. Because relationship means to be related — not in action, not in some project, not in an ideology — but to be totally united in the sense that the division, the fragmentation between individuals, between two human beings, does not exist at all at any level. Unless one finds this relationship, it seems to me that when we try to bring order in the world, theoretically or technologically, we are bound to create not only deep divisions between man and man, but also, we shall be unable to prevent corruption. Corruption begins in the lack of relationship; I think that is the root of corruption. If we examine our present relationship with each other closely, be it intimate or superficial, deep or passing, we see it is fragmented. Wife or husband, boy or girl, each lives in his own ambition, in personal and egotistic pursuits, in his own cocoon. All these contribute to the factor of bringing about an image in himself and therefore his relationship with another is through that image, therefore there is no actual relationship. Each person is doing this all the time, and how can there be a relationship with another, if there is that personal drive, envy, competition, greed and all the rest of those things which are sustained and exaggerated in modern society? How can there be relationship with another, if each one of us is pursuing his own personal achievement, his own personal success? I do not know if one is at all aware of this. We are so conditioned that we accept it as the norm, as the pattern of life, that each one must pursue his own particular idiosyncrasy or tendency, and yet try to establish a relationship with another in spite of this. Isn't that what we are all doing? You may be married, and you go to the office or to the factory; whatever you are doing during the whole of the day, you pursue that.

-Jiddu Krishnamurti

Nobody can explain this better than a master who has done it, who has penetrated into truth and gained deep insight into the very workings of the mind. Krishnamurti points out as all masters have done, that when we are relating through the little narrow self, the relationships we have with one another are very superficial, are at the level of ego, and only a few can go deep into the self to find love, which always relates in perfect harmony. That love is not divisible; it is only unity, an energy which cannot be divided and cannot be given to one more than another, not to a son or a daughter, a mother or father. It has the same intensity, whoever this love is directed to, a daughter or a stranger, it makes no difference to love. The difference is the role we play with each other: one is a son; one is a stranger and so on. Then we should play any role in love and there lies the true relationship with one another. Humanity still must touch that love and it cannot be touched unless we stop working through a narrow ego which creates conditioning and keeps us in a bubble of comforts and illusions.

Only when each one of us sees the reality of what is happening in the world – namely that most of our relationships are based on pleasures, satisfaction, success comparison, judgements and so on, about ourselves and others – only then, in pure observation, we may, if so blessed, come upon love which can never be touched by thought. Only through love will we have a true relationship. When all conditioning has been eradicated then in that awareness of being, love flows unimpeded, and relationships are harmonized by the love supreme.

In relationships, we can understand how our mind works. In intimate relationships, where unconscious conditioning comes to the surface, we have to watch and observe how it plays and what kind of reactions and responses we have. By observing and being fully attentive, we come to understand what is real and what is not, what are the images we build and project and what pursuit they have in everyday life. Only in worldly life do we see our own faults as they are without trying to change them, for in pure awareness of it there is the change. A wife/husband has the capacity to help the partner uncover this conditioning through the love they share with one another, if the image-making process in the mind has stopped on both sides. In an intimate relationship, the love shared is the closest to the love of God. This is why the love of God can be reached through the intimate relationship, if both have the intention to understand themselves. In merging worldly life with spiritual life, we can slowly but surely pluck the feathers of illusion from the mind, if one has the intention to do it, of course.

Many of us separate, so to speak, the spiritual and the practical creating an inner conflict with what spiritual life demands and with what the practical gives. These conflicts will never cease, making us live in fear and hope, therefore creating suffering for ourselves and others.

> *The woman loves her father; she loves her mother; she loves her child; she loves her friend. But she cannot express herself all to the father, nor to the mother, nor to the child, nor to the friend. There is only one person from whom she does not hide anything. So, with the man. The [husband–]wife relationship is the all-rounded relationship. The relationship of the sexes [has] all the other loves concentrated into one. In*

the husband, the woman has the father, the friend, the child. In the wife, the husband has mother, daughter, and something else. That tremendous complete love of the sexes must come [for God] — that same love with which a woman opens herself to a man without any bond of blood — perfectly, fearlessly, and shamelessly. No darkness! She would no more hide anything from her lover than she would from her own self. That very love must come [for God]. These things are hard and difficult to understand. You will begin to understand by and by, and all idea of sex will fall away. "Like the water drop on the sand of the riverbank on a summer day, even so is this life and all its relations."

-Swami Vivekananda

Above, Swami Vivekananda confirms what we have stated earlier: that love in an intimate relationship is all-inclusive; we have the other's love included in oneness. If two people have the intention to touch together divine love, they are blessed. If the love for the husband or wife is pure, then that love will melt all conditioning. Unless we get established in the naked awareness, we cannot do it right for we will always be influenced by the ego with all its conditioning, desires and so on. We have to come to an understanding that thought cannot give that freedom, thought can only sugarcoat what we wish it to be, but this is the same wolf in sheep's clothing.

Krishnamurti describes further:

We want security, both outwardly and inwardly; therefore we depend on people, whether it is the priest, or the leader, or the guru who says: "I have experienced, that is why I know." One has to stand completely alone — not isolated. There is a vast difference between isolation and being completely alone, integral. Isolation is a state of mind in which relationship ceases, when in your daily life and activity you have actually built a wall around yourself, consciously or unconsciously, so as not to be hurt. That isolation obviously prevents every form of relationship. Aloneness implies a mind that does not depend on another psychologically, is not attached to any person, which does not mean that there is no love – love is not attachment. Alone-ness implies a mind that is deeply, inwardly without any sense of fear and therefore without any sense of conflict.

-Jiddu Krishnamurti

Most of us isolate ourselves more or less in our own world, the bubble the mind creates with its ideas, comforts and desires. We come out to relate with others only if that bubble is not at risk, perpetuating a state of mind which can never relate fully, but can only relate through images and the filters of our conditioning, this is not relationship at all and sadly this is how we relate to each other in today's world. Krishnamurti further points out that in the awareness of being we are the world and not apart from it. In that awareness relationships are natural as the five elements are in nature, dancing and relating to each other forever in harmony of love.

Why, if I may ask, do you use the word privilege? What is there sacred or privileged about being aware? That's a natural thing, isn't it, to be aware? If you are aware of your own conditioning, of the turmoil, the dirt, the squalor, the war, the hatred, if you are aware of all that, you will establish a relationship with another so complete, that you are related to every other human being in the world. You understand this? If I am related to somebody completely, totally – not as an idea or an image – then I am related to every human being in the world. Then I will see I will not hurt another – they are hurting themselves. Then go, preach, talk about it – not with the desire to help another, you understand? – that's the most terrible thing to say, "I want to help another." Who are you to help another? – including the speaker. Sir, look, the beauty of the tree or the flower doesn't want to help you, it is there; it is for you to look at the squalor or at the beauty, and if you are incapable of looking at it, then find out why you have become so indifferent, so callous, so shallow and empty. If you find out that, then you are in a state where the waters of life flow, you don't have to do anything.

-Jiddu Krishnamurti

The text, "The kingdom of heaven has drawn near" (Matt. 3:2; 4:17), does not in my judgement imply any temporal limitation. For the kingdom "does not come in a way that can be observed: one cannot say, "Look, it is here" or "Look, it is there" (Luke 17:20–21). The phrase has reference to the relationship which the saints have with the kingdom, each according to his or her inner state. For "the kingdom of God," says Scripture, "is within you" (Luke 17:21). The kingdom of God the Father is present in all believers in potentiality; it is present in actuality in those who, after totally expelling all-natural life of soul and body from their inner state, have attained the life of the Spirit alone and are able to say, "I no longer live, but Christ lives in me" (Gal. 2:20)

-St Maximos the Confessor

Saint Maximos the confessor shows us a different angle. The relationship becomes a true relationship when we have gone beyond nature and attained the life of the spirit. In that person the ego is no more, and one becomes one with the world having then a true open relationship with all and there is the kingdom of heaven the oneness of God in love.

An eternal relationship exists between God and man. But in His play it is sometimes there and sometimes severed, or rather appears to be severed; it is not really so, for the relationship is eternal. Again, seen from another side, there is no such thing as relationship. Someone who came to meet this body, said: "I am a newcomer to you." He got the reply: "Ever new and ever old indeed!" The light of the world comes and goes, it is unstable. The light that is eternal can never be extinguished. By this light you behold the outer light and everything in the universe; it is only because It shines ever within you that you can perceive the outer light.

-Sri Anandamayi Mayi

If the relationship which is eternal is seen, then as Anadamayi states, there is no relating; it is only union in a state of mind which is free, and the only bond is love eternal, the true relation with all existence and non-existence.

If you keep the minds of others pleased, there is naturally a mutual relationship and sense of unity with others. If you hurt the minds of another, then the relationship becomes spoiled.
For this reason, one who keeps the minds of others pleased is truly a great spiritual leader (Mahanta). Many people are naturally attracted to such a person.
Outwardly the nature of a relationship is of a man with a woman, but the subtle relationship is only of the Self with itself.

-St Shri Samartha Ramdas

Ramdas points out one who has established a true relationship with the self will be able to act properly in all relationships and that person is a great soul.

One can assume other attitudes toward God as well – the attitude in which the devotee serenely contemplates God as the Creator, the attitude of service to Him, the attitude of friendship, the attitude of motherly affection, or the attitude of conjugal love. The conjugal relationship, the attitude of a woman to her husband or sweetheart, contains all the rest – serenity, service, friendship, and motherly affection. (To M.) "Which one of these appeals to your mind?" M: "I like them all." MASTER: "When one attains perfection one takes delight in all these relationships."

-Sri Ramakrishna

From all the teachings so far in this chapter, we see the necessity of the right relationship with the self and the world. This includes all relationships, for all of them are a part of life and nothing is apart from life. Some may dispute this, for they may be prompted to be only looking from a small angle of their own personal lives. It was pointed out that the relationship which is closest to the divine relationship, and which helps the most is the intimate relationship between the wife and husband. It is in this relationship where all the loves are concentrated into one and harmonizing this relationship in love will get us closer to our own reality. In tantras, the love between the woman and man is to unite the two energies of male and female into a single one, as a male is no longer male, and a female is no longer female. The tantric union of mother-female energy/father-male energy becomes:

- the union of compassion (male) and wisdom (female)
- skillful means (male) and insight (female)
- relative truth (male) and ultimate truth (female)

In this union, the two energies become one, transmuting the world of duality and placing us in the clear light of wisdom, in the naked awareness as Padmasambhava mentions in his teachings.

Christ also made a reference to this in his teachings:

Jesus said to them, "When you make the two into one, and when you make the inner like the outer and the outer like the inner, and the upper like the lower, and when you make male and female into a single one, so that the male will not

*be male nor the female be female, when you make eyes in
place of an eye, a hand in place of a hand, a foot in place of
a foot, an image in place of an image, then you will enter
[the kingdom].*

-Gospel of Thomas: 22

Christ also describes this union in perfect love which transmutes the duality and makes the two energies become one. In that oneness, minds become empty of any conditioning and there we do not feel any hurt, any emotion. Nothing can enter apart from love. With this practice, the two can take the awareness of love found in the union and establish themselves in everyday life. The two have to be prepared with prayer, meditation and contemplation before they can enter such practices, otherwise they can fall under the spell of lust and pleasure. In the same way that one needs a teacher to learn a skill so here one needs a teacher who has done this. A master will know which practice is better for each individual. If an individual has the intention to find the truth, a teacher will appear, and a path will be open. The path may be to do it alone or with a partner but in the end one will know.

In this kali era, the simple path is the path of faith and devotion to God. Then comes the path of self-knowledge, but this path needs intellectual vitality in order to enter it. The path of yoga and retreat from this world is still in practice today, but it is not an easy path. Spiritual practice, along with living a normal life, is what is needed where we observe in everyday living, our reactions, our emotions and feelings, and in that pure observation we see the hurts, the insults, and we recognize the impermanence of everything. The play of life happens first in the intellect. If we purify the intellect by observing all the ins and outs of life, then slowly, by that observation coupled with spiritual practice, we will establish ourselves in the awareness of being, in the state beyond time and space where whatever life offers, we accept without any resistance or clinging. From there we will always act rightly.

So, it is in the relationship we have with our inner self that the inner war is won, and the ego eradicated. We will see the self in others; will recognize God in every living being. Then we will not hurt each other but rather have compassion, affection, and love for all beings. This is the highest teaching of all masters and all traditions: to come to relate with one another in love.

Q: Is introspection an important aspect in understanding the mind?

M: Introspection is the most important part. In Shankaracharya's Vivekachudamani, both vichara (discrimination) and viveka (discern), are considered to be very important parts of understanding life. The word "introspect" means to look carefully at all that is happening in oneself, to look at our interactions with the world. It is not to look for anything in particular. To introspect is to examine the relationship between you and I, the world and I. How do I react in different situations? If there is a reaction, why do I react this way? This is called introspection. This happens along with watching the mind carefully, watching how it gets caught up by various desires or how it cannot do without a certain thing because the mind gets so habituated to something that it cannot leave it. Introspection also means, Am I seriously looking for freedom from all of this? Or am I only looking at a minor, cosmetic alteration of my being? Am I happy with a couple of "feel-good" medicines and placebos? Or am I trying to find the root cause of the disease? Am I ready to bring in drastic changes that may be required for a total cure?

-Sri M

Sri M Guru here describes introspection as an inner observation, and we have been introduced to it throughout the book from all different teachers and teachings. Without introspection, we cannot get true insight into the truths of life. So, one has to be watchful how we are at the pleasure of the world of the senses and in opening the doors for the poisons to enter our minds, corrupting the mind and imprisoning our hearts. When working, driving a car or whatever activity we undertake, if we are attentive to our inattention, then we can bring the mind back in attention by not letting it be carried away too far. We can still enjoy life but not interfere much with it, just allowing life to unfold beautifully by the will of supreme intelligence. So, the early fathers of Christianity, the Rishis of India, the Buddhist masters and all other traditions point to self-knowledge and to the need to look within for there lies the treasure supreme, the love which is the essence of all existence and non-existence.

Next, Nisagarata Maharaj expresses nicely what we just stated:

For him the right procedure is to adhere to the thought that he is the ground of all knowledge, the immutable and perennial awareness of all that happens to the senses and the mind. If he keeps it in mind all the time, aware and alert, he is bound to break the bounds of non-awareness and emerge into pure life, light and love. The idea – "I am the witness only" will purify the body and the mind and open the eye of wisdom. Then man goes beyond illusion and his heart is free of all desires. Just like ice turns to water, and water to vapor, and vapor dissolves in air and disappears in space, so does the body dissolve into pure awareness (chidakash), then into pure being (paramakash), which is beyond all existence and non-existence.

-Nisargadatta Maharaj

"To develop the feeling "I" in reference to one's True Nature is what called the mind. It is only Ignorance to identify different bodies as "I," my wife, etc. The relationship of "wife" does not exist in the beginning. It develops later, but one gets carried away with it. This is Ignorance. This happens because we identify Brahman with many

different bodies, although it is a single entity. This entire world appearance is delusion. Give it up. Go about it step by step. First, get over the feelings "This is my house," "This is my village," etc.

-Shri Siddharameshwar Maharaj

Above in *"Amrut Laya"* the master is telling us not to identify ourselves with anything and to practice detachment from me and mine whenever possible, bringing the focus of attention back to the self as soon as we are being aware of being inattentive.

M: What is wrong with its seeking the pleasant and shirking the unpleasant? Between the banks of pain and pleasure the river of life flows. It is only when the mind refuses to flow with life, and gets stuck at the banks, that it becomes a problem. By flowing with life I mean acceptance – letting come what comes and go what goes. Desire not, fear not, observe the actual, as and when it happens, for you are not what happens, you are to whom it happens. Ultimately even the observer you are not. You are the ultimate potentiality of which the all-embracing consciousness is the manifestation and expression.

-Nisargadatta Maharaj

As all other masters have stated that we have to flow with life, Nisargadatta Maharaj points out the same truth: do not cling, do not resist, allow whatever comes and goes and enjoy life as it presents without any attachment and in that flow of life one will find freedom in love and love in freedom.

Q: How does one go beyond the need of help? And can one help another to do so?
M: When you have understood that all existence, in separation and limitation, is painful, and when you are willing and able to live integrally, in oneness with all life, as pure

being, you have gone beyond all need of help. You can help another by precept and example and, above all, by your being. You cannot give what you do not have and you don't have what you are not. You can only give what you are – and of that you can give limitlessly."

-Nisargadatta Maharaj

In this teaching, Nisargadatta Maharaj points out nicely how one goes beyond help to find one reality and live an integral life in oneness. Then we can help others by just being a living example of freedom. Next, in the answer to a question, he describes how we should relate to each other and how words are just needed for exchange of information but cannot really describe reality.

Q: Words are needed for communication.
M: For exchange of information – yes. But real communication between people is not verbal. For establishing and maintaining relationship affectionate awareness expressed in direct action is required. Not what you say, but what you do is that matters. Words are made by the mind and are meaningful only on the level of the mind. The word "bread": neither can you eat nor live by it; it merely conveys an idea. It acquires meaning only with the actual eating. In the same sense am I telling you that the Normal State is not verbal. I may say it is wise love expressed in action, but these words convey little, unless you experience them in their fulness and beauty.

-Nisargadatta Maharaj

In awareness, we know what we need, how we feel, and we act in compassion towards all beings, knowing what action is required. One who lives in that awareness which the sages have presented to us has a conscience which is highly developed and sensitive, and that sensitivity allows us to know what the other's feelings and emotions are and to act in a way that is helpful to others. In that awareness, love manifests and healing of the heart and mind occurs. Our minds and hearts have been wounded for millennia by our conditioning. In our narrow and selfish way of thinking where love does not have a place to manifest, and healing is also absent.

We always want to control nature, control the child, the wife/husband, and so on. In families today there is no peace; always conflict: father with son, mother with daughter, and so on, these conflicts are due to our dullness of mind for we always know better, and one should do as the expert says. Unfortunately, today experts are machines always based on the knowledge of yesterday, shaped in the present and presented in the future. People in power always want to control and shape others in a way they think is best and the laws of today are made in order to divide society. It is sad but it is the truth. Unless humanity brings spiritual life in line with the material life, we will destroy ourselves and much suffering will come upon us at our own hands. The life of the spiritual human being is merged into oneness, spirit and the matter of working together. The spiritual human being will only take from life what is needed and no more, therefore living in harmony with nature and all beings. All of us need to act in that way, otherwise we will never have a peaceful life.

We see from all the teachings of awakened masters how our life and relationships should be in order for us to live in love, in harmony with all creatures and with nature itself. What is the point progressing in the technological field, we may conquer and find life in the universe, prolong the life of a human, cure most diseases. To what avail, if we have not changed our hearts a bit towards goodness and have not conquered ourselves? If we do not bring about a revolution in our inner being, all efforts in any other direction will be for nothing.

In everyday relationships, we need to act in an unselfish way and with simplicity, humility and patience, always thinking of what the other does. Is it just a different way? Do not judge anyone, for the moment we judge or compare, we are working from the ego, giving it strength. We need to diminish the ego in our everyday relationships, especially in the ones where more conflict is prevalent. When we are being humble and simple, the ego does not like it for then the ego losses all power, all control and will fight back attacking us with all sorts of thoughts especially the ones where we are more prone to fail. We have to be watchful and try to not react to any thoughts, not to cling to them, for the moment we cling to one thought, another hundred will appear keeping us in a turmoil of thinking. Most people do not have a five-second rest from thoughts, even on holiday. Is that a holiday or suffering?

If we want to find a little peace in the mind, we have to put some effort into coming to a state of peace. We have to give up some things in exchange for that peace; some practical habits or mental habits need to be eradicated. Not many people in western society pray, for they have lost touch with the practice of prayer. Still, as we have seen in the teachings of our masters, many saints have risen with the humble prayer of the heart in sainthood. If one prays from the heart not for oneself but for the benefit of all beings, the prayer will be heard, for the one who hears it is in us, closer than our breath. The self, the supreme God, which is absolute love, lives in the hearts of all beings, therefore nothing can be hidden from an omniscient God who knows all our thoughts, all our worries and all our pains and if we take a step towards him, he will take three towards us.

So, when we relate to other beings, know this truth and keep it in the heart: he lies in the hearts of all beings, from the criminal to the saint all are in his grasp. In our hearts he awaits us to unite with him through love which, in fact, is our true nature. When we have unveiled our true reality, we will be immersed in that blissful love and peace wherever we are or in whatever situation. Nothing will disturb the love and peace supreme.

In children up to the age of six, there are hardly any judgements. The filter of conditioning has not set in on the mind and the mind is not yet corrupted. Small tendencies may exist but nothing too drastic. The tendencies and conditioning from past lives have not surfaced yet from the unconscious. Such a child looks with a free intellect, the intelligence working. Such a child still has the capacity to learn from direct insight – which is called direct learning – but in order for a child to learn in this way, the parents have to give the child space and time to learn by themselves and not hijack the process with what they know, with their conditioned lives full of norms and so on. If parents are conditioned, then the child will be conditioned. In addition, our schools and institutions are designed to condition the mind. This is a great problem today where a child is in a classroom all day listening to and assimilating information, 70% of which will never be used by many. This is a fact; we can observe and see, and it is something which needs to change in order for us to decondition the mind from all psychological authority.

The less we condition the children, the more likely they are to be able to deal with life and understand life better, and in doing so allow themselves to flow with it and live a life in love. Today most children are lost and because of technological progress, relations are made on the phone with emojis and so on, they have few true relationships at all. When they are confronted with true relationships, with the likes of the fives poisons which can trouble them at the core level, most do not know how to handle the situation, going into further conditioning, running away from what needs to be faced, relying more on psychiatrists and medication which is not true healing. If we look at the suicide rates of children in present times compared with the past, we will see the terrifying numbers all over the world but especially in western societies where pressures have increased. This is why direct contact in relationships is necessary, where one can act with affection, in awareness which springs from the heart and which knows how to act in the moment and the right way. The phone and the iPad cannot give you that interaction even if Artificial Intelligence becomes perfect.

That is why it is important for us all to look within, for there are the answers we are seeking. Without turning inward and continuing to escape our inner life through all sorts of experiences which keep us busy, we will never be able to have a healthy mind, which can work effortlessly and have a true insight into life bringing about a full understanding of life. The inner life needs to be in order and the outer life will follow suit. The children need to be taught how to observe, how to not react in a selfish way, how to bring goodness from their being and act with it. Yes, they are the ones who have to learn to act in the right way, who have to look within and find the treasure of love, for they are the future, and the future is projected by how one acts in the present.

We all need to start looking within in order to find reality. When this is achieved, our relationships will become transparent, and everything will flow with no effort. When one genuinely loves that love comes spontaneously from our core, from our essence of being and non-being. When the mind is purified, and one has unveiled our true self then one can relate to all, this is the truth that all masters from all traditions have taught. In the end it only comes to one word: Love. And if we grasp that energy, ignoring the world, then we are home at peace in silence, a silence and stillness which cannot be described, only lived. By self-knowledge we can come to a state of mind which is free, where love can manifest in that freedom and where we act always with love. Next, we should look at self-knowledge, for it is imperative to understand who we are, and this is the direct way to freedom.

CHAPTER 28

SELF-KNOWLEDGE

In earlier chapters, we have already looked at how self-knowledge impacts our world and needs to be an integral part of our life. Because it plays such a key role in our lives, we ought to look further into it.

Knowing who we really are is not like going to school and learning in class. Self-knowledge does not become clearer by adding information about oneself. On the contrary: by subtracting what we *are not*, we remain with what we really are. What cannot be added to or taken from it is our true nature. The self is covered by lots of conditioning, ideas, concepts, habits, tendencies, desires, likes and dislikes, attachments, aversions, identifications and so on. All of these interfere with knowing or realizing our true nature.

Knowledge, that is to say, is of two kinds. The first resides in the intelligence and its divine intellections, and does not include, in terms of actual vision, a perception of what is known. The second consists solely in the actual enjoyment of divine realities through direct vision, without the help of the intelligence and its intellections. But the intelligence is capable of giving us an intimation of what can be known through true knowledge and so of arousing in us a longing for such knowledge.

-St Maximos the Confessor

Saint Maximos explains the two types of knowledge we have: one is through intelligence and pure intellect and the other is experimental and lies in the joy of experiencing the divine realities with direct insight. The divine knowledge can be understood by intelligence, but it cannot be expressed: intelligence can only point to such knowledge. Self-knowledge falls in the second type of knowledge, which is divine.

Self-knowledge can dawn on us through self-enquiry, through faith and devotion, through fully surrendering to God. It can come by providence and grace, but in the end, whatever avenues it comes from, in that realization of who we are there is self-knowledge also. Self-knowledge is a process of getting rid of what we are not by pure observation, mindfulness and spiritual practices. It is an experimental process of elimination of what is not real.

Nearly all mankind are more or less unhappy because nearly all do not know the true Self. Real happiness abides in Self-Knowledge alone. All else is fleeting. To know one's Self is to be blissful always.
Q. Is the world progressing now?
A. There is one who governs the world, and it is His look-out to look after the world. He who has given life to the world, knows how to look after it also. If we progress, the world progresses. As you are, so is the world. Without understanding the Self, what is the use of understanding the world? Without Self-knowledge the knowledge of the world is of no use. See the world through the eyes of your supreme Self.

-Sri Ramana Maharshi

Ramana Maharshi points out that real happiness lies in self-knowledge alone and there is where we find the blissful state: all else is fleeting and temporary.

> *Only when you know yourself as entirely alien to and different from the body, will you find respite from the mixture of fear and craving inseparable from 'I-am-the-body' idea. Merely assuaging fears and satisfying desires will not remove this sense of emptiness you are trying to escape from; only self-knowledge can help you. By self-knowledge I mean full knowledge of what you are not. Such knowledge is attainable and final.*
>
> -Nisargadatta Maharaj

Nisargadatta Maharaj, as we have seen in previous chapters, refers to self-knowledge as the process of fully knowing what we are not. By that we arrive at self-knowledge, the realization of the self which cannot be put into words or be described by thought for thought can only describe what we are not and is limited in describing the infinite.

> *There are many teachings, but without Self-Knowledge all of them are meaningless. On this subject there is one statement made by Lord Krishna: "Many people read many scriptures, and worship many deities, but without Self-Knowledge, everything is meaningless. The opinion of the shaivas, shaktas (devotees of Shiva and Shakti), or others, are many. There are many faulty doctrines of individuals in illusion who are confused. There is nothing which purifies like Self-Knowledge.*
> *There is nothing that can be found that is as pure as Self-Knowledge. Therefore, one must first acquire Self-Knowledge.*
> *Of all teachings, the teachings about Self-Knowledge are*

special. This has been said by God in many places.
The greatness of Self-Knowledge is not known to even the
four-faced Brahma, what can mere individuals understand?
The value and status of Self-Knowledge is billions of times
greater than the benefit of all pilgrimages, the results of all
sacred baths, or the merit of giving in charity.

-St Shri Samartha Ramdas

The master explains to the students that, without self-knowledge, one is like a bird with no wings and that self-knowledge is the purifier of the mind which then leads to purification of the heart.

In order to get self-knowledge, we have to have an intellect with the power to discern and a clean conscience in working order. Self-knowledge is a process of discovery. It is like unearthing, an archaeological site where a lot of patience and effort is put into unveiling the objects found. This unveiling is done by our spiritual practice, by observing ourselves in everyday life, by having faith in the unknown and the conscience which directs us from within, by prayer, meditation and contemplation on the discoveries of our habits and tendencies, and then carefully discarding them in the awareness of being. It is not an easy task to uproot all our ideas, concepts, identifications, and attachments. It takes lots of effort at the beginning. As we slowly become established more and more in the awareness, the effort becomes less strenuous and a moment will come when we fall into a state of equanimity of mind where we have penetrated through duality, and where bliss and love start to flow like a spring of water coming out of the ground of being which is our true essence.

Each of us will find different spiritual practices depending on what we are attracted to, but the one tool we all have to use in any spiritual practice is our pure observation. It takes time to become purified and here we have to watch how the ego interferes, with judgements, with the know-how mechanism of thought which creates all our feelings and emotions. All those attributes need careful observation and mindfulness, in order to be understood and grasped as illusory. Just to say, "all is illusion, and everything is love and oneness" and in the next minute hurt another, is just empty talk. We have to find a soul who has done it in order to be guided in the right way. It is like having a seed and planting it in the ground. It needs lots of care and protection till it can stand alone as a plant. Just so, the one who has decided to unveil our reality needs some guidance on where to start and what to look for. As already mentioned, the ego knows our every move in the field of thought. How can we outsmart that? We cannot. We must starve the ego slowly by reducing what it feeds on – thoughts, emotions, feelings, and so on – till the day comes that we can surrender fully to what is, to the present moment.

One who has given up the pride of family name, has put to shame the "public shame" of the public's eye (doesn't care for social status), and who nourishes spirituality by the strength of his detachment, is called an aspirant.

The aspirant is one who breaks the connection with ignorance, escapes from the bondage of family entanglements, and quickly slips out of the hands of greed.

The aspirant is one who is not concerned about greatness or wealth and is uninterested in personal importance because of the strength of his detachment.

The aspirant is one who has broken duality, given up and thrown away the ego, and smashed the enemy named doubt.

The aspirant is one who kills the imagination of alternative arguments, who with a mighty blow destroys the ocean of mundane worldly life, and who cuts off and throws away any opposition from all of the five elements.

The aspirant scorches the fear of worldly bonds, breaks the legs of time, and beats and breaks the head off of the cycle of birth and death.

The aspirant is one who attacks being haunted by bodily identification, annihilates desires, and quickly kills the deception of imagination.

The aspirant beats up all inner fear, wins over the subtle body (mind, intellect, thoughts, etc.), and overpowers heretical talk with the power of discrimination.

The aspirant has beaten down pride, destroyed selfishness, and has put to destruction the immoral life and shown it to be meaningless by living a virtuous life and upholding justice and morality.

The aspirant tears apart temptations, cuts away pain, and throws away sorrows. The aspirant banishes envy, casts away non-devotional feelings, and makes illogical thoughts and behavior flee.

For the one who is an aspirant, Self-Knowledge is strengthened by discrimination, conviction becomes firm, and vices are destroyed with the power of detachment.

For the one who is an aspirant, the lack of any true religion is wiped out by one's own "Self-Religion," (Swadharma) and one's Self Nature. Wrongful deeds are replaced by good deeds, and thoughtlessness is replaced by right thinking.

The aspirant enthusiastically crushes hatred, carves out and discards envy, and always remains happy by smashing down sorrows.

The aspirant has thrashed down anger, pounded out the scheming from within, and is considered a friend to all of the people of the world. The aspirant has renounced outwardly oriented activities, given up the association of worldly friends, and achieved "Union through Knowledge" (Jnana Yoga) on the path of turning away from worldly concerns.

-St Shri Samartha Ramdas

Saint Shri Samartha points out some of the aspirant work to be done in order to be established in the awareness of the self and become free from all illusions. As we have seen in earlier chapters when we talked about the five poisons which need to be annihilated so here the master points out beautifully how we have to destroy with the power of discrimination and detachment all that we think we are in order to unveil what we really are. All is the process of self-knowledge, unfolding as we go and eradicating the five poisons and detaching from all desires, even the desire for liberation. He goes further in pointing out how by finding reality in the self with the help of the sadguru which lives in all of us, we gain our true freedom by following the instructions of an awakened teacher, which helps us find the greater teacher who lies in our hearts.

> *First there is listening to spiritual discourses, then comes serving at the feet of the Sadguru (following his instructions), and finally there is "Identification with the Self" through the blessings of Sadguru.*
>
> *Beyond this "Identification with the Self" there is only the eternal Absolute Reality. This is the inner understanding that the Self always has of itself.*
>
> *With that Self-Realization of Brahman, the sorrow of the worldly life goes away and the fate of the body is effortlessly given up to follow out it's due course.*
>
> *This is called Self-Knowledge. With this Self-Knowledge one obtains complete satisfaction. The devotee is inseparable from the Absolute Reality, Parabrahman.*
>
> -St Shri Samartha Ramdas

Sadguru refers to an accomplished master and also to God which resides in all beings and who guides us to find reality from within. A guru is an outside being, so to speak, who has walked the path and can point out how to find the sadguru within. The wisdom which the guru and sadguru impart is the same wisdom which is dormant in all; it only needs a spark from a master to awaken in us the wisdom supreme.

So, in everyday life, we have to observe and see how we react and respond to life. If we react and respond with wisdom which does not involve the ego, then we are acting rightly and can live and flow with life and love. In the observance of ourselves every day, something will be discarded and depending on our intention, one day there will be nothing to be discarded for we will find the essence of the self and the reality of being.

As mentioned, discarding illusionary appearances can be done in many ways but in the end, regardless of the avenue taken, we will arrive at self-knowledge. We may walk many paths and encounter many teachers or only have one path and one teacher. It does not matter as long as we have pure intention and follow the wisdom, we will arrive at the light of all lights.

> *Let us sit still and keep our attention fixed within ourselves, so that we advance in holiness and resist vice more strongly. Awakened in this way to spiritual knowledge, we shall acquire contemplative insight into many things; and ascending still higher, we shall receive a clearer vision of the light of our Savior.*
>
> -Evagrius the Solitary

Saint Evagrius points out that in order to get spiritual knowledge, which is self-knowledge, we need to keep our focus on ourselves in mindfulness. Without it, we cannot break through the illusory states of mind which the ego produces.

> *He who has attained spiritual knowledge and has enjoyed the delight that comes from it will no longer succumb to the demon of self-esteem, even when he offers him all the delights of the world; for what could the demon promise him that is greater than spiritual contemplation? But so long as we have not tasted this knowledge, let us devote ourselves eagerly to the practice of the virtues, showing God that our aim in everything is to attain knowledge of Him.*
>
> -Evagrius the Solitary

Evagrius again points out that once spiritual knowledge is attained, then we are home and in union with the supreme reality God.

If someone asks, "Who are you?" The response is usually automatic. "I am Joe Blogs, live in such and such, I do such and such" and so on. The response will be of a conditioned mind, and it will spit out information according to the content of the consciousness of the individual answering the question. If we look and observe that, we are only a response – a moment in time of who we think we are – but in fact every moment we are different. The body changes, ideas and concepts and conditioning changes in every moment so, every moment we are not the same as we were a moment ago in every aspect. We are in a continuous transformation. We are a process in time and there is nothing that we know that is permanent in any of us. Thought may do what it will, but it can never come upon anything permanent.

All the awakened masters have stated the same truth: the self is the only permanent entity, we can call it such for the sake of expressing it, but God which can be told is not the real God. The real one can only be in all and of all. The goal of self-knowledge or spiritual knowledge is not to gain anything or to accrue anything but only to discard everything till what remains is the awareness of being. This is why Christ said, "You are all Gods." The only thing for us left to do is to unveil the God in ourselves. It's like peeling an onion. When we peel an onion, only emptiness is at the center. In that emptiness we will see reality which cannot be expressed but only lived.

This is why it is so extremely hard for us to peel away our conditioning. We fear that in discarding and peeling our conditioning, we will be left with nothing, and in that process, become exterminated. Still there is a pull towards the truth. Regardless of our fears, something deep inside ourselves is urging us on. If someone asks an awakened person, "Who are you?" the response would be either silence or "I am you in a different form." Enlightenment or awakening to our true reality is not a goal to be achieved, for the moment we think along those lines we fall into the world of duality and the ego has the better of us. We are it already; we do not have to become. Buddha repeatedly mentioned to his disciples to stop becoming, as did Christ, Krishna and all the awakened masters.

So, it is very important for us to understand why self-knowledge was taught by all masters, for in spiritual knowledge something is dropped every day where in practical knowledge something is added. This is the only way to liberation, and it does not matter what spiritual practice we have chosen, we have to drop something every day.

> *If you keep to the thought of the Self, and be intently watching for it then even that one thought which is used as a focus in concentration will disappear and you will BE, the true Self. Meditation on Self is our natural state. Only because we find it hard do we imagine it to be an arbitrary and extraordinary state. We are all unnatural. The mind resting in the Self is its natural condition, but instead of that our minds are resting in outward objects. After the expulsion of name and form (nama-rupa) which compose the external world, and by dwelling on existence-knowledge-bliss (sat-chit-ananda), take care to prevent the re-entry into the mind of the expelled name and form.*

> -Sri Ramana Maharshi

Ramana Maharshi points out that the self is our natural state of being. When we stop identifying with names and forms, then we revert to our natural state which the Hindus call *existence-knowledge-bliss (Sat-Chit-Ananda)*. Self-knowledge will allow us to manifest love and live a life of a natural order where there is not a shadow of conflict, internal or external, for there is no duality: the inner life and the outer life have merged into oneness. When we live with love and flow with the beat of life, we do not need to be dependent on anything; no religion is needed, no nation and so on. We are free. In that freedom, we are not affected by the ups and downs of life, the miseries which humanity creates and the ignorance which causes havoc in the world. When Buddha was asked, "What is the one thing that smothers the world?" he told his disciples "It is Ignorance." It is ignorance of the reality of who we are. When ignorance is lifted then we live in accord with the natural laws which were written by the pen of love, and that natural law resides in our hearts.

For anyone who is serious and desires a life of peace where there are no conflicts, no frustrations, no stress, they must come to that state of mind which fulfills and allows us to live and flow with life. We have to start to look, to observe, to listen to all the movements of life in the inner life and outer life. We have to observe our reactions to people and things, see to our emotions and feelings – anger, jealousy, envy – the control we have over others. In pure observation, if we see that we are angry, then just stay with it without a movement to change, to become non-angry, for any movement is the movement of thought wanting to change what it is into what it wants it to be, which keeps us in the world of duality and therefore still in illusion. In watching with naked awareness, not responding or reacting, anger or whatever it is will dissolve on its own because there is nothing to keep it going. Just as fire dies if you do not feed it with fuel, so thoughts, emotions, tendencies will dissolve in stillness, in awareness. We have to try it and in doing so not dissipate energy but become energized, alert with enough energy to keep the watching going and when we are out of it, bring ourselves back in that awareness.

Krishnamurti shows us this in the next quote:

> *I want to find out whether the mind can be quiet and only function when necessary. Control, because it implies conflict, is a great waste of energy; that is important to understand, because I feel meditation must be a releasing of energy in which there is not the slightest friction. How is a mind to do this? How is it to have such energy in which every form of friction comes to an end? In enquiring into that, one must understand oneself completely, there must be total self-knowing – not according to any psycholo-*

*gist, philosopher or teacher, or the pattern set by a partic-
ular culture – but to know oneself right through, both at
the conscious level as well as at the deeper levels, is that
possible? When there is complete understanding of oneself,
then there is the ending of conflict – and that is meditation.*

-Jiddu Krishnamurti

Krishnamurti points out that total self-knowing is necessary for one to be established in meditation which comes by pure observation. All are interlinked and all will bring about a state of mind where we can function rightly; where there is no friction and conflicts, as he states.

This is the most important practice. By it, self-knowledge will dawn on those who are serious about getting out from suffering and eliminating all the vagaries of the ego. Before we start on this journey, we have to be simple, to have patience, and learn to be humble: these are our three treasures to keep. In being simple there are fewer desires to deal with and by having patience we become calmer with a clearer mind. Humility will lower our pride and that is an important factor in impoverishing the ego. With steady practice and faith, we will dissolve the shell of the ego which covers the self, and the self alone will shine, transforming our inner and outer life on the journey into a life of peace, bliss, and love. When we have done that, all beings will benefit. Life then will have a different meaning, and we will be able to really enjoy a sunset, or a walk, or a smile from a child and so on. Without the ego interfering, life is full of light and Love.

We have looked at awareness, at what freedom is and what meditation is, what contemplation is. We have understood where suffering is coming from, how we perceive life, how intelligence works. We have seen the illusions created by us. We understand attachment to be a key element in our suffering. We grasp the wisdom of the awakened masters which all points to the same truth.

We look at the mind and see how all that we experience and all that we observe is seen and experienced through the mind. We know how relationships should be in order to transform life into heaven on earth. We looked at religions and the contradictions they produce by not putting into reality the teachings of the masters and only allowing ourselves to be in the ego which can never touch reality. We looked at the loneliness which rips our heart apart; at the temporary happiness we take from the senses instead of aligning with the joy of our being. We looked at how we cling to objects of the senses, to all sorts of things, and resist whatever we do not like. We looked at God and understood that we are a part of it, not apart from it, and God cannot be seen by thought, only by a heart and mind which are pure. We need to watch like a hawk the whole movement of life. Then we will come to learn the mysteries of life, love and God.

We have made references to love but before we can look in more depth into what love is, we may want to talk about spirit and soul.

CHAPTER 29

SPIRIT & SOUL

Spirit and soul. We often talk about them but are we aware of what we are talking about or are we just repeating what we have learned from others and placing a little flavor of ours on top?

The soul is the self alone, and it does not identify with anything, only with the universal soul, if we can call it that. The moment we make the soul personal, it is not the soul; it is the ego trying to survive through the so-called soul. Everything in this universe is energy; the soul is just a subtle form of energy which cannot be distinguished by the five senses. We can talk about it but when only talking about it we do not come to know it, the same as we can talk about the ocean without seeing it. The word soul points to an energy we also call the heart, or the self, for they all point to the same energy, nevertheless.

> *Isvara, a personal God or Supreme creator of the Universe, does exist. (This is true only from the relative standpoint for those who have not realized ultimate truth and who believe in reality of individual souls.) From the Absolute stand-point the sage cannot accept any other existence, other than*

the impersonal Self, one and formless. Isvara has a physical body, a form and name, but it is not so gross as this material body. It can be seen in visions, in the form created by the devotee. The form and name of God are many and various, changing with the religions. His essence is same as ours, the real Self being only one and without form. Hence the forms he assumes are only creations or appearances.

-Sri Ramana Maharshi

Ramana Maharshi points out that a soul exists as long as the individual has not realized the ultimate truth. When we realize the truth about what the soul is, there is only love which bonds us with the divine realizing oneness. Then the soul, as we call it, merges with the universal, being in oneness with all. Identification with anything is not needed for we are all oneness.

Evil is a passion found in matter, and so it is not possible for a body to come into being free from evil. The intelligent soul, grasping this, strives to free itself from the evil burden of matter; and when it is free from this burden, it comes to know the God of all, and keeps watch on the body as being an enemy and does not yield to it. Then the soul is crowned by God for having conquered the passions of evil and of matter.

-St Antony the Great

Saint Anthony refers to the soul as not matter. To the intelligent soul which has grasped this truth through experiences undergone in the body and the mind, there is no more separation from God. We can claim that the self as the soul is both an intelligible entity or still the one part of God which appears to be separated through the illusion, which gives the impression that we are only a soul or a self, when in reality the separation exists only in the illusory state of mind.

> *Impurity of soul lies in its not functioning in accordance
> with nature. It is because of this that impassioned thoughts
> are produced in the intellect. The soul functions in accor-
> dance with nature when its passible aspects - that is, its
> incessive power and its desire - remain dispassionate in the
> face of provocations both from things and from the concep-
> tual images of these things.*

-St Maximos the Confessor

Saint Maximos refers to the soul as pure when it does not desire things or images, and this is also in accordance with what Ramana Maharshi refers to as the impersonal self which is free and so is the soul which has been risen in God.

> *Without proper investigation, many people say that the
> soul of man and the soul of woman are different. However,
> the Self of all is only one. This subtle secret must be experi-
> entially understood.*

-St Shri Samartha Ramdas

Saint Ramdas also discards any differences in a soul of a woman or a man and states that the self, which is the soul, are the same. We will only know when we are realized. As God cannot be described, so realization also cannot; a pointer to it may be given but these are limited in describing the infinite.

> *That in whom reside all beings and who resides in all
> beings, who is the giver of grace to all, the Supreme Soul of
> the universe, the limitless being – I am that.*

-The Amritabindu Upanishad

The Amritabindu Upanishad states that the supreme soul is not different from our soul, it is only our ignorance which sees the separation. Christ also has stated the same. When he said, "I and the father are one," he referred to the same supreme reality in the father. Therefore, the soul is not existent by itself: it exists in all beings. The soul exists only in relation to the body and after the dropping of the body, if realization was not attained, a subtle body is needed to continue the journey towards full realization.

> *Existence, consciousness, and bliss are the three longings (of the human heart). Ananda, bliss, is the contentment of heart attained by the ways and means suggested by the Savior, the Sat-Guru. Chit, true consciousness, brings about the complete destruction of all troubles and the rise of all virtues. Sat, existence, is attained by realization of the permanency of the soul. These three qualities constitute the real nature of man. All desires being fulfilled, and all miseries removed, the achievement of Paramartha (the highest goal) is made.*
>
> -Swami Sri Yukteswar

Swami Sri Yukteswar points out that by realizing the three longings of the human heart inherent in us all (Sat – Truth, Chit – Existence, Ananda – Bliss), we come to realize the permeance of the soul. Without realizing the soul, we may have faith in its existence and flashes of light and wisdom, but we must have a pure mind and heart in order for the three qualities to manifest fully in us and for us to understand and see what our intellect cannot comprehend.

With the intention to find the truth, doing our spiritual practice, being established in the awareness of being, we will, with the grace of God, come to realize the self or soul and by the spirit supreme come to realize the unity of all souls in oneness of God. Spirit is the consciousness or awareness which is the essence of all manifestations, and the mind is the middle agent between the soul and spirit. This is why in Christianity it is called the Holy Spirit for its purity cannot be corrupted by anything: it is pure awareness. Thought can stain the mind and the heart, but it cannot touch the essence of all existence which is the only reality God.

Christ points out to Mary that the mind is the one which see it is the medium between the two. We bring here some quotes from other chapters for, as we have mentioned, the spiritual teachings are multidimensional and give insight in any context.

And she began to speak to them these words: she said, I saw the Lord in a vision, and I said to Him, Lord I saw you today in a vision. He answered and said to me,
Blessed are you that you did not waver at the sight of Me.
For where the mind is there is the treasure.
I said to Him, Lord, how does he who sees the vision see it, through the soul or through the spirit?
The Lord answered and said, He does not see through the soul nor through the spirit, but the mind that is between the two that is what sees the vision and it is [...]

-The Gospel of Mary

The Upanishads also states that a pure mind and heart can see, and reality is not beyond then as long as they have been purified.

Beyond the reach of the senses is he, but not beyond the reach of a mind stilled Through the practice of deep medi-tation. Beyond the reach of words and works is he, But not beyond the reach of a pure heart Freed from the sway of the senses.

-The Upanishads

The true sight of the angels is emotion by spiritual under-standing concerning their domain. But it is impossible for us to see the nature of spiritual forces without the mind. When man is deemed worthy of seeing them in their nature and in their place and as they are in their spiritual creation, grace moves his mind by the revelation of spiritual insight concerning them. When the soul has been purified and is worthy of seeing its fellows, their sight is perceived with these eyes. They are not objects and they cannot be seen as they are, without alteration, but by psychic sight which is true contemplation. This means without deterioration of their nature by sight. This sight cannot be acquired by any man without the second purification of the mind.

-St Isaac the Syrian

Saint Isaac also states that it is impossible to see without the mind and when the mind is purified by spiritual practice and grace then we can see the spiritual dimensions with the psychic eye, which by purification, opens to see reality. So, spirit, awareness, or consciousness can have content, but they are not affected by the content, just as space is not affected by what passes through it. One can see the spirit or holy spirit is the essence: it is God for God can take any form and he answers to all names without any discrimination.

Conscious spirit and unconscious matter Both have existed since the dawn of time, With maya appearing to connect them, Misrepresenting joy as outside us. When all these three are seen as one, the Self Reveals his universal form and serves As an instrument of the divine will.

-The Shvetashvatara Upanishad

In the Upanishads we can find reference by the sages that Spirit is Conscious and when the illusion of thinking that joy is outside, falls, then the self can serve as an instrument of the divine will.

When man thus entering into the spiritual world becomes a Son of God, he comprehends the universal Light – the Holy Ghost – as a perfect whole, and his Self as nothing but a mere idea resting on a fragment of the Om Light. When he sacrifices himself to the Holy Ghost, the altar of God; that is, abandons the vain idea of his separate existence, and becomes one integral whole. Kaivalya, the unification.

Thus, being one with the universal Holy Spirit of God the Father, he becomes unified with the Real Substance, God. This unification of Self with the Eternal Substance, God, is called Kaiualya.

See Revelation 3:21. "To him that overcometh will I grant to sit with me in my throne, even as I also overcame, and am set down with my Father in his throne."

-Swami Sri Yukteswar

Swami Sri Yukteswar points out that the Holy Spirit is God and when we become one with the essence, the Holy Spirit of God, the self will appear as merely an idea. He gives an example from the Bible in Revelation 3:21 of Jesus pointing to this unification. So, it is the same with the soul, which is the self, it is only used as an idea until we realize our own divinity and reunite with God.

We could go on and talk about it but until we realize and grasp reality with the mind, body and soul, we will still struggle with the confusions which the ego will produce. When the mind and heart are pure, the soul will unite with one God and realize its own (*existence, consciousness, bliss*). When God is realized while we are still in the body, then we must change from a human being to a divine being, which is the inherent reality in all beings. Realization is not a goal to be achieved by becoming, it only needs to be realized, for we are perfect in every way. We looked at awareness and have pointed out the substratum and the essence of all existence and here we come to see that spirit is just another word for the same essence and every tradition uses different words to express it. When we are established in the spirit, or awareness, all words and concepts have no meaning. They are burned by the clear light of wisdom where love is recognized as one energy from which all manifested and unmanifested come and go. Love is the one energy which embodies all qualities of goodness and cannot be explained as being this or that. It can only be lived by sharing it with all beings, as a relationship of love with all. It is all inclusive and can never be extinguished by anything for it is everything. So, we talked so far of Love throughout this book. Now it is time to look at love and what constitutes love from the perspective of the realized masters of past, present and future. We mention the future also, for they are beyond space and time.

365

CHAPTER 30

LOVE

In these four letters reside so much energy that the whole universe can be burned in a flash by this supreme energy we call Love, though most of us have no real grasp of its reality. We may have encountered flashes of it, but that is it.

All spiritual disciplines, founded from time immemorial are to bring an individual into that love and make manifest that love fully in everyday life. If we are adamant to grasp this energy and unveil it, we are blessed indeed, for eternity lies in it. We all use this word extensively in our daily existence and very rare are the moments when we are one with it. This love is God and the love which can be described is not the real one like God, it cannot be described, only realized. The masters and sages of old have mentioned how to come upon this splendor and only by going within will we find the treasure in our own hearts. When we discover it, we are free. It is total freedom in love, dancing with love, being in love with being, total bliss. One who has touched the supreme love will become a magnet of love attracting all towards oneness, the same as a powerful magnet attracts all objects of metal. Christ, Buddha, Krishna Rama and so on have been like a magnet of love for the ones who have not yet been fully enveloped by the rust of the ego and are still able to be attracted by their love.

Christ says in Gospel of Thomas:

> *Love your brother like your life!*
> *Protect him like the apple of your eye!*
>
> -Gospel of Thomas: 25

Christ has pointed to this supreme love and urged us to find it within ourselves, we cannot come upon the Love which Christ taught us in any other way.

> *Fasts and vigils, the study of Scripture, renouncing possessions and everything worldly are not in themselves perfection, as we have said; they are its tools. For perfection is not to be found in them; it is acquired through them. It is useless, therefore, to boast of our fasting, vigils, poverty, and reading of Scripture when we have not achieved the love of God and our fellow men. Whoever has achieved love has God within himself and his intellect is always with God.*
>
> -St John Cassian

Saint John Cassian also points out that all spiritual disciplines and practices are in vain unless we find love within, and all spiritual practices are only tools, aids to help us in finding that love.

> *"Love rules the court, the camp, the grove; The men below and saints above;*
> *For love is heaven and heaven is love." – Sir Walter Scott*
> *The power of love has been beautifully described by the poet in the stanza quoted above. It has been clearly demonstrated in the foregoing pages that "Love is God," not merely as the noblest sentiment of a poet but as an aphorism of eternal truth. To whatever religious creed a man may belong and*

whatever may be his position in society, if he properly cultivates this ruling principle naturally implanted in his heart, he is sure to be on the right path, to save himself from wandering in this creation of Darkness, Maya.

-Swami Sri Yukteswar

Swami Sri Yukteswar, by quoting the poet Sir Walter Scott, points out that the poet describes what love is, not only as a sentiment but as an undeniable truth. This love needs to be discovered in ourselves, for this love is our salvation, our savior. Christ and all beings are in that love supreme. Love does not revolve around our little bubble where we enclose ourselves with our satisfactions and the likes and then on rare occasions come out and spread some love but only when convenient. That is not true love at all; it is ego-love only.

He fills the cosmos, yet he transcends it. Those who know him leave all separateness, Sorrow, and death behind. Those who know him not Live but to suffer.
The Lord of Love, omnipresent, dwelling In the heart of every living creature, All mercy, turns every face to himself. He is the supreme Lord, who through his grace moves us to seek him in our own hearts. He is the light that shines forever. He is the inner Self of all, Hidden like a little flame in the heart. Only by the stilled mind can he be known. Those who realize him become immortal.

-The Shvetashvatara Upanishad

The Shvetashvatara Upanishad points to the lord supreme who lives in all hearts and, with his love, moves us into seeking him in our own hearts. He is the love of all. He is in everything and is the essence of everything, independent of anything. Those who do not find him in their own hearts, live to still suffer, but those who have found him leave suffering and death behind. The sages have told us that the treasure of infinite love lies in our hearts.

Q: Do you love the world?
M: When you are hurt, you cry. Why? Because you love yourself. Don't bottle up your love by limiting it to the body, keep it open. It will be then the love for all. When all the false self-identifications are thrown away, what remains is all-embracing love. Get rid of all ideas about yourself, even of the idea that you are God. No self-definition is valid.

-Nisargadatta Maharaj

That which you are, your true self, you love it, and whatever you do, you do for your own happiness. To find it, to know it, to cherish it is your basic urge. Since time immemorial you loved yourself, but never wisely. Use your body and mind wisely in the service of the self, that is all. Be true to your own self, love yourself absolutely. Do not pretend that you love others as yourself. Unless you have realized them as one with yourself, you cannot love them. Don't pretend to be what you are not; don't refuse to be what you are. Your love of others is the result of self-knowledge, not its cause.
Without self-realization, no virtue is genuine. Where you know beyond all doubting that the same life flows through all that is and you are that life, you will love all naturally and spontaneously. When you realize the depth and fullness of your love of yourself, you know that every living being, and the entire universe are included in your affection. But when you look at anything as separate from you, you cannot love it for you are afraid of it. Alienation causes fear and fear deepens alienation. It is a vicious circle. Only self-realization can break it. Go for it resolutely.

-Nisargadatta Maharaj

The master of non-duality, Nisargadatta Maharaj talks about the love for the self, which is a natural expressed love, but when directed in a selfish way is not true love, but rather corrupted by desires of the ego. Only when the self is realized by genuine intent will all virtues naturally express towards the self, which then is recognized in all beings and love is then directed with the same intensity for all. To talk about love and light for all, is one thing, but to realize it in everyday life is another. Love for all comes when one sees oneself in all.

Arjuna, nobody who truly
loves me will ever be lost.
All those who love me and trust me
Even the lowest of the low
Prostitutes beggars and slaves,
Will attain the ultimate goal.

-Lord Krishna

Krishna tells Arjuna that even the lowest of the low can attain the supreme reality if they have true love for God. Anyone can realize the self and therefore touch the love supreme which lies in everyone's heart. Actually, as Christ has stated, "blessed are the meek, the sick and the weak" he points out that when we undergo tribulation or suffering and when we are lost in hells of our own making, then we are more prone to come out, for in those states of mind we develop dissatisfaction with the world and are then pulled away from it, repulsed by the relative reality, therefore prone to find the true reality. In finding the real, we open to Love; in that openness, all is one.

God is Love; His plan for creation can be rooted only in
love. Does not that simple thought, rather than erudite
reasonings, offer solace to the human heart? Every saint
who has penetrated to the core of Reality has testified that
a divine universal plan exists and that it is beautiful and
full of joy.

-Swami Yogananda

Swami Yogananda points out, like many others, that God is all love and the whole of creation, as the Upanishads states, has come from his fulness of joy. We fail to see it because of our conditioning and illusions. As Christ has stated, "I will choose you one from a thousand and two from ten thousand." Here he refers to how rare we may find one who really has the intention to find reality, which in fact is love and joy. Living with this joy and peace is the benediction of grace. It cannot be explained, only lived when we have done with the world as seen from our little ego. When the ego has surrendered to the self and takes the designated place it was designed to occupy, it will remain just a tool to help us function in the three-dimensional space.

When we touch that Love, we feel a deep connection with the world and all beings. We do not become one with them in a physical sense, but the core of being feels oneness with a flower or a rock. Whatever we enter a relationship with, there are no more barriers put up by fears and judgements. In that relationship, communication is easy. We can listen to a bird and feel the unifying joy which unites the seer and the seen where union is. In that union duality is non-existent. When we have touched that love, we look at the stranger on the street and see the motherly eyes in that person and the two hearts become one. We will feel whatever the other feels and compassion is there without needing to be cultivated, for any cultivation of virtue is an illusion. Virtues are qualities of Love. If we have touched Love, we act with order which comes from the heart. It is a natural order which is whole, complete. The moment we try to mold it, we ruin it. This is what is happening in the world: we try to fix the world by not seeing the world is perfect, as it is. We need to drop all the fixing and remain with what we have always been: eternity, love absolute which words cannot touch or describe.

"Will you give me the same unconditional love?" He gazed at me with childlike trust. "I will love you eternally, Gurudeva!" "Ordinary love is selfish, darkly rooted in desires and satisfactions. Divine love is without condition, without boundary, without change. The flux of the human heart is gone forever at the transfixing touch of pure love." He added humbly, "If ever you find me falling from a state of God-realization, please promise to put my head on your lap and help to bring me back to the Cosmic Beloved we both worship."

-Swami Yogananda

In his book, Swami Yogananda describes the love his guru had for him and acknowledges the pure touch, and the transformation of heart one can have if subjected to a drop of unconditional love. This unconditional love is the love which all beings must grasp in order for us to live a life of joy, regardless of the environment, circumstances, and conditions which arise and which we need to face. One who has touched love sees the word with new eyes and in relating to other beings speaks the language of love which is understood even by the crudest of creatures.

Love is our core; it is our intrinsic nature. If we look at a newborn, we can observe this simple fact. At the same time, it is so complex. The complexity comes into being when our ego develops and veils the natural flow of love making it selfish, accompanied by personal desires and satisfactions.

Q: How do I get at it?
M: You need not get at it, for you are it. It will get at you, if you give it a chance. Let go your attachment to the unreal and the real will swiftly and smoothly step into its own. Stop imagining yourself being or doing this or that and

the realization that you are the source and heart of all will dawn upon you. With this will come great love which is not choice or predilection, nor attachment, but a power which makes all things love-worthy and lovable.

-Nisargadatta Maharaj

In the above, Nisargadatta Maharaj tells us to stop working through the ego and reality will show itself in its own time. When we are ready, we will drop from the tree of knowledge like a ripe fruit. Rare are moments of unconditional love.

Imagine being in a relationship where a betrayal of trust has occurred. How and what would the reaction of the ego be? It would be based on how the ego was conditioned and certainly the five poisons will come out like a volcano at such an experience. The awakened one will see the error in the other and the response and reaction would be love and compassion without any poisons having any effect on that being, but rare are such souls.

God is said to be the originator and begetter of love and the erotic force. For He externalized them from within Himself, that is, He brought them forth into the world of created things. This is why Scripture says that "God is love" (1 John 4:16), and elsewhere that He is "sweetness and desire" (cf. Song of Songs 5:16. LXX), which signifies the erotic force. For what is worthy of love and truly desirable is God Himself. Because loving desire is poured out from Him, He Himself, as its begetter, is said to be in movement, while because He is what is truly longed for, loved, desired and chosen, He stirs into motion the things that turn towards Him, and which possess the power of desiring each in the degree appropriate it.

-St Maximos the Confessor

In the above, Saint Maximos describes with the words from the Bible that which the saints understood and grasped: that God is

Love nevertheless and is in motion. He is all, in all, love in motion which makes life. All spiritual traditions point to the same God, to the same Love, and to the same life. Why then can't we really get it right? Why are we so lost in our own personal agenda and so much in self-love and not in love for self? It is, of course, because of our selfishness; because we work from a little center, the me, instead of being one with all centers and working from all centers in oneness putting an end to the little me and opening up to that which has no center to love and infinity.

> *Love alone among the virtues can confer dispassion on the soul, for "love is the fulfilling of the law" (Rom. 13:10). In this way our inner man is renewed day by day through the experience of love, and in the perfection of love it finds its own fulfillment.*

-St Diadochos of Photiki

Saint Diadochos recognizes that love is the key to bringing out the inner man who is full of love, renewed every day with perfect love and finding its own fulfillment in the presence of the moment in love. In that presence, we are aware of being, new every moment, always acting in the present which is the only existential time, for past and future depend always on the present moment. As we look in the memory for a remembrance of something, we look with the presence of the moment for reality and illusion can be seen only in the now. When we wake up every morning, that is now. We may say, "I wake up tomorrow," but tomorrow never comes. Only now is.

Time – like the clock – exists only in reference to something but is relative. It is like the south, west and all coordinates; they are in reference to the north pole and south pole but to someone from another planet their coordinates may differ in contrast with ours, depending on where that planet is situated. From this small example, we can see that all is relative. Nothing in existence is permanent, only the self, which does not need any references for it is the subject and the object in one. Love and the lover are one. This is why true unconditional love flows in oneness and cannot be divided by anyone and anything. This needs to be lived; it cannot be explained, for thought, as the masters have expressed, cannot describe reality which is Love.

One has to find out for oneself what it means to die; then there is no fear, therefore every day is a new day – and I really mean this, one can do this – so that your mind and your eyes see life as something totally new. That is eternity. That is the quality of the mind that has come upon this timeless state, because it has known what it means to die every day to everything it has collected during the day. Surely, in that there is love. Love is something totally new every day, but pleasure is not, pleasure has continuity. Love is always new and therefore it is its own eternity.

-Jiddu Krishnamurti

Krishnamurti talks about the timeless state where one lives in the moment and where love is and points out how pleasure has its continuity in time where love is fresh every moment anew.

"To understand anything is to find in it something which is our own, and it is the discovery of ourselves outside us which makes us glad. This relation of understanding is partial, but the relation of love is complete. In love the sense of difference is obliterated and the human soul fulfils its purpose in perfection, transcending the limits of itself and reaching across the threshold of the infinite. Therefore, love is the highest bliss that man can attain to, for through it alone he truly knows that he is more than himself, and that he is at one with the All. This principal of unity which man has in his soul is ever active, establishing relations far and wide through literature, art, and science, society, state-craft, and religion. Our great Revealers are they who make

manifest the true meaning of the soul by giving up self for the love of mankind. They face calumny and persecution, deprivation and death in their service of love. They live the life of the soul, not of the self, and thus they prove to us the ultimate truth of humanity. We call them Mahātmās, "the men of the great soul."

-Rabindranath Tagore

Rabindranath Tagore points out elegantly how love is the highest bliss, and it is only through love that we find our fulfillment in life and our true reality.

The Purusha does not love, it is love itself. It does not exist, it is existence itself. The Soul does not know, It is knowledge itself. It is a mistake to say the Soul loves, exists, or knows. Love, existence, and knowledge are not the qualities of the Purusha, but its essence.

-Swami Vivekananda

Purusha is a synonym for soul and Swami Vivekananda also points out that the soul is love itself and that is its natural state, its essence, and the one who has discovered that is blessed indeed.

There is no kind of sorrow for one who leaves off seeing through his physical senses and begins to see everything as his own Self. Further, this grief (of the loss of his wife) does not indicate real love. The love which one evinces towards external objects and forms is not the real love. Real love has always its abode in one's own Self.

-Sri Ramana Maharshi

Ramana Maharshi explains that real love is found in the soul and once found, it can be shared by just being. The love found in the external world through objects is not the real love for it comes with attachments and through the senses.

376

The Lord Buddha is Himself the essence of enlightenment. All partial manifestations of wisdom that come in the course of sādhanā culminate in supreme enlightenment. In a similar way, supreme knowledge or supreme love may be attained. As there is a state of supreme Self-knowledge, likewise, is there a state of perfection at the zenith of the path of love. There one finds the nectar of perfect love identical with supreme knowledge.

-Sri Anandamayi Mayi

Anandamayi talks about Buddha being the essence of enlightenment and that state has been found through spiritual practice. In the same way, the path of love will bring supreme love and supreme knowledge if we keep at it.

Simply giving your attention to a child is automatically experienced as an act of loving. This is what I call non-cultivated or non-associative love because it has nothing to do with your background, your race, religion, politics, or other beliefs you may hold. Quantum-Touch is about being present, which is an expression of your essence. I would call this kind of love "preconditional" and believe that your very nature and essence is made up of the fabric of love. Whether you believe it is there or not (in my opinion) is irrelevant. This love is the essential nature of your being that comes through your hands regardless of your mood. Your fundamental, instinctive, and most basic energy is that of love. You don't have to work at it — it is who you are. As a rock does not have to try to be more "rocklike" and water does not have to try to be wetter, we do not have to try to have more essence of love.

-Richard Gordon

In the above quote, Gordon states that love is our natural state, and we do not have to work at it to become more loving, we just need to be aware of our essence and allow it to manifest naturally. It is like being with a child. All the people around them try to giggle and make funny faces in order to make the child laugh, not realizing that if one acts naturally, the child will laugh anyhow and will be joyful regardless of the faces and squirting noises we make, it is the child's nature to be joyful.

> *God is love, and in every living creature He has set this faculty of love, but especially in man. It is therefore nothing but right that the Lover who has given us life and reason and love itself should receive His due tribute of love. His desire is to all He has created, and if this love be not rightly used, and if we do not with all our heart and soul and mind and strength love Him who has endowed us with love, then that love falls from its high estate and becomes selfishness. Thus, arises disaster both for ourselves and for other crea- tures of God. Every selfish man, strangely enough, becomes a self-slayer.*

> -Sadhu Sundar Singh

Sadhu Singh explains nicely that the love which God has endowed us with has to be shared with all. If we do not share, we all become selfish, and that selfishness will create suffering for ourselves and other beings.

> *As Christ said to his Disciples, and left it with them at the last, saying, Love one another, as I have loved you; for thereby Men shall know, that ye are my Disciples. If Men would as fervently seek after Love and Righteousness as they do after Opinions, there would be no Strife on Earth, and we should be as Children of One Father, and should need no Law, or Ordinance.*
> *For God is not served by any Law, but only by Obedience.*

*Laws are for the Wicked, who will not embrace Love and
Righteousness; they are, and must be, compelled and forced
by Laws.*

-Jakob Boehme

Jakob Boehme states that love does not need any laws or authority
for the laws are only needed for the wicked, and if we all give up
all opinions and judgements – which is the ego – we will find love
and there will be no strife on earth, for love comes with its own
inward order which is inherent in us, as righteousness is also, and
they are in our conscience.

*"Love [never says] it owns something, [though] it owns
[everything]. Love does not [say, "This is mine]" or "That
is mine," but rather, "[All that is mine] is yours.*

-Gospel of Philip

Philip writes that love does not have a desire to own something
for it is intrinsic in everything as God is, and has no selfishness for
all that it owns, it gives at the same time. Love is such as life, as
God and as we.

So, we could quote many beings of light on what love is but if we
do not realize Love in our own lives, then we will not be able to
overcome suffering and the like, for they will keep us bound in
illusion and in the world of senses, of judgements, and miscon-
ceptions about reality and the eternal truth. It is essential to realize
what there is that unites us, that makes us act. What it is that that
puts together the essential energies for a flower to blossom, for a
child to grow, for us to get to the moon, for the light to shine in
darkness and so on. We have to find out for ourselves for if we just
take the answer from another, we cannot fully grasp it. To grasp
reality, it needs to be unveiled by each one of us, for as we have
seen throughout the teachings which have been exposed in this
book, all point within. Not inside but within, which means the
core, the essence of all which is All. All the masters have pointed

out the same Love, the same God, the same intelligible power in action.

Is humanity at that level of consciousness wherein each of us is asking if there is another way of living, one where there is no division and conflict; where there is no authority to tell us what to do or how to love, and where we can act with the same authority which is already intrinsic in each of us? Love is our nature. When we have discovered it, we live in a state of equanimity of mind where duality exists only at the physical level of existence but at the psychological level, in our psyche, there is no duality at all. We need no followers. We need only awaken beings to change the world, and we have forgotten who we are. We need to awaken to our reality and then the world will change. In that awakening, nothing needs to be changed: the world is perfect as it is. Perfection does not come through a perfect state of society; it only comes through the inner revolution of Love – an explosion of mind in space where the mind is everything and everything is mind without any exclusion. All is inclusive. In the end, we go back to where it all started, but *how* is another question to be answered?

The masters have stated that when God withdraws its manifestation in rest, each being will rest with the state of mind they possess at the time of withdrawl and when manifestation begins again, the play starts, and all souls will join the play of life again till we find that love is life and life is love. So, this play goes on for infinity. It has no end, no beginning. It is perfect, intelligence operating. It is love in movement and love in repose as Christ has stated:

> *If they say to you: Whence have you come? say to them: We have come from the light, the place where the light came into being of itself. It [established itself], and it revealed itself in their image. If they say to you: Who are you? say:*

We are his sons, and we are the elect of the living Father. If they ask you: What is the sign of your Father in you? say to them: It is movement and rest.

-Gospel of Thomas: 50

We are also a microcosmos of a macrocosm for he made us in his image. When we unite with the absolute, we become true creators, molding love into multitudes of forms, expressing joy in the play of life. We are coming from Love and into Love we return there is not a shadow of a doubt. Love is the key to opening the human heart. All readers have this love; may you all be open to it.

May the Lord of Love Lead us from the unreal to the Real.
May the Lord of Love lead us from darkness to light.
May the Lord of Love Lead us from death to immortality
May all beings be full of Joy.
May all beings find the Lord of Love.

-Upanishads

CHAPTER 31

CONCLUSION

All our struggles and sufferings are inflicted on us by us, for in our seeking of lasting happiness we undergo lots of tribulations. So, in this search we should start with three simple things: simplicity in having only what we need; patience, in waiting for the opportunity to rise never rushing, for we create havoc in rushing; humility in being lower as the sea where all rivers end up. The sea, by lowering herself, becomes greater. If we have the intention to put an end to suffering, we must start with those three virtues and bring them up from our being and in doing so, love will show us the way further. At the right moment, a master will arrive and will guide us further.

As reality is revealed, there will be more love to share with the world and suffering will diminish then one slowly comes to an inner Peace which cannot be expressed or be induced by thought. A peace internal which will manifest also externally, and other beings will be attracted to. With that peace comes love, a love which includes even the one who has hurt us the most, for they are our greatest teachers. God works through all, in order to open our hearts to his love. Without us going through suffering, we would not question life, for when we are happy in the bubble of our own making and nothing disturbs the bubble, then we do not question much. In that state, we are stagnating spiritually, actually losing time, so to speak, and as Buddha stated, this human birth is rare to be found therefore we should make the most of it now.

We are what we think, we become what we project and in doing so we are caught in all sorts of illusions. Some are prone and still have to go through those experiences and some just have enough and are ready to peel the onion of their own conditioning. If we are ready, then the effort which is put into making our lives happy in the material aspect has to be transmuted into the spiritual aspect. In today's society, we have many divorces because everyone is focused only on material happiness where they overlook the spiritual aspect. Until we bring a balance, as Buddha mentioned, we will always live in division with one another and the ego – which is not mine or yours but is universal – will have the last laugh.

As soon as we hit struggle and suffering, we tend to run, not realizing that around the corner another form of suffering of our own creation will come and confront us until we are ready to face it. There is nowhere to hide from the ego which is always a step ahead. When we realize we cannot run and that suffering is created by our own inability to perceive with a clear mind, we have then to stop running and learn to accept what it is, with the present moment. In that acceptance, a miracle may happen, and suffering and struggle will dissipate. As we discover by ourselves, the nature of the mind – the real meditation begins – and in staying with what it is and watching it, in that watching there is awareness. As we are established in it, magic will happen whereby the ego will surrender.

We have been told by all masters that the ego – which is just an imaginary entity created by mind – is actually non-existent: where love is, ego is not. In that awareness the rust of the ego is cleaned away and the feeling of oneness sets in. Whatever spiritual practice we choose it will help us come to this realization. The more the rust is removed, the more love can flow as naturally as the rivers flow to the sea or the blood flows through our veins.

In reading any spiritual books, we come slowly to that state of mind where all reading comes to an end, all practices are redundant, all teachers can retire. We realize oneness with all; we are all existence and love. So, my dear brothers and sisters, whoever is ready to walk the path of love and righteousness, can do it if one has the intent. All beings are open to take the path. It is not only made for a few, but also open to all as our great masters have pointed out. As we walk on the path, we will experience an openness of heart and, in doing so, the door to the kingdom will be opened by love alone, which we have discovered in our path, there then is heaven, is God, is Love, is Peace and bliss supreme.

We must gather the courage and faith to walk towards it. The walk is not easy; it is as narrow as the edge of a razor. This, in the end, is the walk all beings will take, for it is rooted in our basic desire to find everlasting happiness and it can only be found within as the Lord has stated "the kingdom of heaven is within."

Love is Life & Life is Love

ABOUT THE
AUTHOR

The real authors quoted in this book are spiritual masters and their wisdom has been imparted to us from time immemorial, this book only points to the same wisdom imparted by all. The writer of this book is just the instrument who was chosen to do the task of bringing together the same wisdom coming to us from all masters and traditions.

The writer is just a normal person like any of you, the readers. I started this present life in a city called Arad in western Romania and was brought up in a loving middle-class family with Christian values. I have never written anything before, apart from essays at school; certainly nothing of this kind. I was also a less-than-average writer. Small questions have risen in my mind concerning what God is, the meaning of life, which tradition upheld the highest truth and so on.

The search for truth started after coming to Australia as a political refugee in 1988 together with my two brothers. Before arriving in Australia, I made many projections about democratic freedom and how life in the West should be, also about what feelings of happiness this would bring. From home, I brought emotions and feelings which I thought would dissipate once I arrived in Australia, but in spite of the fact that I was now free and happy to be in Australia, I realized that despite having more freedom in the physical aspect of life, the feelings and emotions and burdens of life were still there.

Material achievements in Australia did not gave me the joy which I was looking for and in little over five years after arriving I knew that anything material can only give satisfaction but does not make one really happy. I could observe this in myself and in others. I could see the suffering in me and in others. I lived in ignorance of who I was and of who we all are, but because I have undergone lots of trials and obstacles in my inner and outer life, it made me, question more and more the meaning of life. My search started and at the same time I was still drawn to desires; into having and getting, pulled into a hell of my own making on the inner level and outer level as well. With time, I was more and more attracted by knowing which spiritual tradition held the truth: Christ, Buddha and so on. It took me years to slowly, with hard work, decondition the mind, but thanks to the great masters, every time I read any of their teachings something dropped, which left an opening of the mind and heart. Buddha helped me to understand Christ's teachings and Christ made me understand Buddha's teachings and so on. I have read a lot of books and assimilated and grasped lots of teachings. I realize that in the world, everyone is my master and there is room to learn from all beings. The spiritual knowledge we grasp is found by uncovering it in our being, not by adding it from an outside source. All the teachings of our great masters sunk in slowly, one by one, and every time I read them something in me opened anew. Everything led me into writing this book after years of going through the purification of mind and heart.

If you ask me who am I, today my answer is, I am you in a different form. We cannot run from anything in the world. We have to go through it to grasp it in every experience of the now. God, Truth, Love cannot be known by the intellect but by a mind which is empty and a heart which is full of love. I have done a lot of mischief in life, made a lot of mistakes and in doing so hurt myself and others but by the grace of the Lord I was pulled back on the right path and helped to find my balance, realizing that sin is created by us and can be wiped out by us alone with the grace of love. This learning sounds very simple but at the same time, it is very complex. I hope the readers of this book drop some of the mind conditioning and look with a lighter mind to themselves and the world after grasping the energy which the masters point to. The teachings imparted should be read and contemplated on, then read again after a period of time. In that way, you will observe that every time you read, something is dropped.

I am nothing special. I am just a struggler, like most of us, on the way to unveil our true reality. Would I change if I had the power to do anything different in my life? The answer is no; it is perfect as it is, now that I know the secret – not to interfere with the flow of life. It is like someone trying to pee against the wind; we can guess the outcome. Likewise, in going against the flow of life, we create only mischief. In flowing with life, we can find peace, love and joy according to how much we are willing to surrender to the Lord of Love. In short, I am you in a different form with different agenda but still you, for we are all one with the father in oneness. My wish is that everyone one day will wake up and shake up the wine of ignorance and start loving one another as the awakened masters have loved the world. May you all be blessed by the Lord of Love.

LOVE is the only Way and there is no other Way.